MW00992970

mixing minds

mixing minds

the power
of relationship

in psychoanalysis
and buddhism

Pilar Jennings

FOREWORD BY JEREMY D. SAFRAN

Wisdom Publications • Boston

Wisdom Publications
199 Elm Street
Somerville MA 02144 USA
www.wisdompubs.org

© 2010 Pilar Jennings
All rights reserved.

No part of this book may be reproduced in any form or by any means, electronic or
mechanical, including photography, recording, or by any information storage and
retrieval system or technologies now known or later developed, without permission
in writing from the publisher.

Library of Congress Cataloging-in-Publication Data
Jennings, Pilar.
  Mixing minds : the power of relationship in psychoanalysis and Buddhism / Pilar Jennings ; foreword by Jeremy D. Safran.
     p. cm.
  Includes bibliographical references and index.
  ISBN 0-86171-616-7 (pbk. : alk. paper)
  1. Buddhism and psychoanalysis. 2. Psychotherapy—Religious aspects—Buddhism.
  3. Buddhism—Psychology. I. Title.
  BQ4570.P755J46 2010
  294.3'366168917—dc22
                                        2010043289
ISBN 978-0-86171-616-6
eBook ISBN 978-0-86171-163-5
15 14 13 12 11
5 4 3 2 1

Cover design by Gopa&Ted2. Interior design by LC. Set in Dante MT Std 11 / 14.5.

Wisdom Publications' books are printed on acid-free paper and meet the guidelines
for permanence and durability of the Production Guidelines for Book Longevity of
the Council on Library Resources.

Printed in the United States of America.

This book was produced with environmental mindfulness. We have elected to
print this title on 30% PCW recycled paper. As a result, we have saved the following
resources: 24 trees, 8 million BTUs of energy, 2,250 lbs. of greenhouse gases, 10,838
gallons of water, and 658 lbs. of solid waste. For more information, please visit our
website, www.wisdompubs.org. This paper is also FSC certified. For more information, please visit www.fscus.org.

table of contents

foreword

THE ENCOUNTER between Buddhism and Western psychotherapy has a long history. Carl Jung had an early interest in both Western and Eastern mystical traditions, and in 1954 wrote a psychological commentary for Walter Evans-Wentz's translation of *The Tibetan Book of the Dead* (first published in 1927). Other influential psychoanalysts followed suit: in the 1950s and 1960s Erich Fromm and Karen Horney took a particular interest in Zen Buddhism. While in retrospect we can see that this interest continued to percolate in the culture at large, in many respects it disappeared from the mainstream scene and went underground within psychoanalysis. In the 1990s as Buddhism became more thoroughly assimilated into Western culture, and a generation of authors who came of age in the 1960s began to emerge, the interest in Buddhism by psychoanalysts began to resurface. A series of books on Buddhism and psychoanalysis were published by authors such as Jack Engler, Mark Epstein, Jeffrey Rubin, John Suler, Anthony Molino, and Barry Magid, and isolated articles began to appear here and there in professional and popular journals.

At the same time, a certain momentum of interest began to emerge among behavioral and cognitive therapists as well. Theorists and researchers such as Marsha Linehan, Alan Marlatt, Jon Kabat-Zinn, and Steven Hayes began to incorporate principles of mindfulness into their therapeutic approaches—and these drew increasing attention. I remember attending a panel on mindfulness at the Association for the Advancement of Behavior Therapy (AABT) in the early 1990s and I remember my surprise that what seemed like esoteric fare for an ostensibly conservative organization like AABT was so packed that there was standing room only. My second surprise came when one of the panelists asked the audience how many of them meditate—and over ninety percent of the audience members raised their hands.

While the momentum of interest in the relationship between Buddhism and psychoanalysis has continued to develop at a steady pace, I think it is fair to say that Buddhism, or more specifically mindfulness practice, has taken cognitive-behavioral therapy by a storm. Since the first empirical studies came out demonstrating that mindfulness practice can reduce relapse in recovered depressives, a slew of studies have come out demonstrating the effectiveness of mindfulness practice in the treatment of a range of psychological disorders and books on what is referred to as *mindfulness-and-acceptance-based* approaches to cognitive-behavioral therapy are proliferating. Mindfulness has more than gained acceptance within mainstream therapy; indeed it has in some respects become the leading edge of the mainstream.

The assimilation of Buddhist thinking into psychoanalytic thinking, while continuing at a steady pace, has been a slower and more subtle process—and I think it is worth speculating about the reasons for this. Because of the emphasis on skills-training and self-help technology in behavioral and cognitive therapy, the process of adapting the technique of mindfulness practice and then testing it empirically is a fairly natural and straightforward one. However, I think that the popularity of mindfulness practice among cognitive-behavioral therapists is due to more than this. Traditionally the emphasis in mainstream cognitive therapy has sometimes been on changing or controlling feelings by changing one's thinking. This leads to the paradoxical situation in which the goal of self-acceptance needs to be achieved through a type of self-control. The assimilation of the principles of awareness and acceptance (embedded within mindfulness practice) has led cognitive-behavioral therapy to a subtle paradigm change that helps to negotiate or transcend this paradox.

Although psychoanalysis *does* have its techniques, it is on the whole less technologically oriented than cognitive-behavioral therapy. In some respects psychoanalysis is thus more similar in type to Buddhism as a whole, in that both are complex and comprehensive worldviews and philosophical systems, each composed of multiple schools of thought and practice. Theoretical and philosophical debate is the order of the day within both traditions, and it is only natural that any real contact between them will involve conversation at broader levels as well.

In addition, psychoanalysis from the beginning has had an interdisciplinary character to it. It both influences and is informed by areas such as cultural and historical studies, anthropology, sociology, and political science. Increasingly over time psychoanalysis has become particularly attuned to the cultural context that gives rise to various theoretical developments as well as the impact of those developments on the culture. While early forays by psychoanalysts into Buddhism to some extent had a natural tendency to emphasize and idealize certain tenets of Buddhism as antidotes to the rigidity and other shortcomings of psychoanalytic orthodoxy, a new stage in the dialogue between Buddhism and psychoanalysis is emerging that is more nuanced and sophisticated in nature.

When I edited the anthology *Psychoanalysis and Buddhism: An Unfolding Dialogue* in 2003, I was hoping that the essay and commentary structure of the book would play some role in catalyzing this new stage of dialogue. Since that time I've been gratified to see a number of important new books coming out that have contributed to this growing dialogue. Examples include: Mark Unno's *Buddhism and Psychotherapy Across Cultures*, Robert Langan's *Minding What Matters*, Barry Magid's *Ending the Pursuit of Happiness*, and Mark Epstein's *Open to Desire*. Of particular note is Harvey Aronson's *Buddhist Practice on Western Ground*, which does a superb job of embedding the exploration of the relationship between Buddhist practice and psychotherapy in a cultural context, and highlights the strengths and limitations of both approaches.

When Josh Bartok at Wisdom Publications first asked me to read a draft of *Mixing Minds*, I was somewhat hesitant because of pressing work commitments. After reading the first few pages, however, I was hooked. And after rereading it before writing this foreword, I am even more enthusiastic. With this remarkable book, the dialogue between Buddhism and psychoanalysis has finally come of age. Pilar Jennings writes from the perspective of one who has been deeply steeped in these two great wisdom traditions for many years, and who has a rich and nuanced understanding of areas of convergence, divergence, and potential synergy. By taking into account both cultural differences in the origins of these two practices as well as differences in emphasis (spiritual / universalistic vs. psychological / personal), Jennings is able to highlight the strengths and limitations of both traditions, as well as potential stumbling blocks along the path of practice for Western Buddhists. In this way she deepens our understanding and appreciation of both traditions, and clarifies the way in which they can complement one another. In a voice that is personal, humorous, yet at the same time wise and sophisticated, Jennings takes us on a fascinating and deeply rewarding voyage of discovery. Sit back, relax, and enjoy.

Jeremy D. Safran

preface

A FEW YEARS AGO my Buddhist teacher asked me if I would be the personal driver for a senior teacher in our Tibetan lineage during his upcoming visit to New York City. I was flattered but also concerned about taking so much time from my various professional responsibilities. After having agreed, I spent the first day driving the *rinpoche* (an honorific meaning "precious one") and his entourage of monks throughout the city. Passing by the many New York landmarks, I found myself pointing out historic buildings he might have heard of, the parks and famous avenues. We passed by the hospital where I was born, which I indicated with a childlike enthusiasm.

My lama, who had been sitting quietly in the back, leaned forward. "Is that Bellevue?" he asked. I looked at him in the rear-view mirror, a sly smile overtaking his face. I laughed and tried to explain to the rinpoche why this was funny. If I had been with my analytic friends, I might have blurted out, "Projection!" milking the joke for more laughs. So too, I might have—in the spirit of fun—divulged that my lama had called me the week prior to find out if there is a diagnosis for people who will not eat a bowl of noodle soup if the noodles are stuck together. After I suggested that this could indicate obsessive-compulsive disorder, or perhaps anxiety and thus repressed hostility, he wanted to know if this "was right."

"Is this for *your friend*?" I quipped. I took the high road and processed this humorous exchange and the many memorable moments that transpired during this week with my psychoanalyst, who was forever curious about my relationship to a Tibetan lama and Buddhist practice. With my analyst, I worked through the fear of having "fallen behind" in my secular life during this time with the rinpoche, and consciously integrated the precious experience of immersion in my spiritual community and the riotous moments of cross-cultural communication I had experienced as a Westerner pursuing traditional Asian Buddhism.

I come to this world of "mixing and matching" healing traditions through a lifetime in which the boundaries between East and West have been constantly blurred. As a child I slept on traditional Japanese bedding in a macrobiotic study house where I lived with my mother, after years of wolfing down Lucky Charms swimming in whole milk. Periods of quiet pervaded my early childhood household, when my mother may have been reading Krishnamurti or D.T. Suzuki, but such moments could be followed by a blaring Beatles record that my older brother played along with on his sparkly red drum set. My upbringing with a Peruvian psychoanalyst mother and a Scottish, New York City–born ad man father was an ongoing study in contrasts. After their separation when I was eight years old, I was raised on either side of the country, where the values and goals of each seemed as different from the other as those of any two countries. Not surprisingly, it was during my time on the West Coast that I was introduced to meditation and Eastern religions.

As an adolescent and young adult, I continued my interest in both Eastern and Western perspectives as they manifest in the divergent realms of spiritual and psychological healing. I read the literature of great Zen masters and Tibetan lamas alongside Freud and D.W. Winnicott. In this exploration, I found a balance between these disparate healing methods. The Eastern approach to well-being struck me as being a more primary process—a truly experiential mode of coming to know oneself (and eventually *no-self*, as one discovers in Buddhist terrain) and one's world with greater depth and clarity—that was perhaps more heart-centered and less diluted or defended against by cognitive processes. Western psychological healing efforts, in contrast, seemed to me more rooted in discursive thought, despite the intention to honor emotionality, and a stronger emphasis placed on our capacity to make meaning through analyzing our own history and character.

In the former I learned of the interplay between perception, reality, and universal markers of humanity. In the latter I explored my personal history, the nuances of my family of origin, and how my unconscious and conscious psychic halves intertwine. Between the two, I envisioned and began to experience a more encompassing net in which to catch the complexities of the human mind as it intersects with the turbulent and challenging experience of relating to others. And most relevant to this work, I learned through my comparative experience with Buddhist teachers and psychoanalysts how to enter into and sustain the formidable experience of interpersonal relationship amid this ongoing turbulence.

Over the years ideas have taken root, offering me a roomier way to see and understand our complex world. Through these many compelling ideas of healing and my own pursuits of spiritual and psychological well-being, I have entered into relationships with Buddhist teachers and Western psychoanalysts, and have in recent years been working with my own clients as a therapist and psychoanalyst. As I have deepened my practice through the experience of these interpersonal relationships, I have learned about each tradition through the other. And perhaps most importantly, the unique experience and perspective I have gained in each interpersonal relationship has given me necessary tools for remaining in relationship when the work involved has been difficult or unsettling.

It is for this reason that I now write about the many radical differences and areas of synergy between Buddhism and psychoanalysis, with a focus on the primary relationships within each system. In the following pages, I will explore how each tradition helps us enter into and sustain relationship. I will propose that the core teachings of each tradition come to life by examining how Buddhist teachers relate to their students and how psychoanalysts relate to their analysands.

I take up this exploration of Buddhist and psychoanalytic healing dyads—the teacher/student and analyst/analysand pairs—at a time when interest in the convergence of Eastern and Western healing paths is flourishing. Nevertheless, I find myself writing amid a growing community of American Buddhists and psychotherapists interested in Buddhist practice who approach this exploration with radically divergent perspectives and goals. People such as Jeffrey Rubin, Mark Epstein, Jack Engler,

Polly Young-Eisendrath, and Mark Finn, who are both psychoanalysts and Buddhist practitioners, have explored the far-reaching compatibility between these two healing traditions, as well as the many blind spots that have hindered conversation between spiritual teachers and psychologists. These contemporary theorists carry the torch for those seminal psychoanalytic theorists whose interest in Eastern religious practice pioneered this now-burgeoning field.

Psychoanalyst Joseph Thompson, working under the pseudonym Joe Tom Sun, published the earliest exploration of the parallels between psychoanalysis and Buddhism in 1924. Carl Jung followed suit, bringing forth passionate caveats for Western practitioners of Buddhism alongside a genuine respect for the ego-softening tools he discovered in his ventures east. Franz Alexander, an eminent Hungarian psychoanalyst and colleague of Freud, continued this exploration in a 1931 essay on Buddhism from a psychoanalytic perspective in which he noted the relevance of concentration practice in Buddhist meditation to the Freudian notion of regression.

Erich Fromm and Karen Horney carried on this nascent tradition of investigating Eastern spiritual practice as it interfaces with Western psychology through their shared interest in how culture influences our psychological experience. For Fromm, waking up to reality and enlightenment were universal categories of human experience, suggesting that Buddhist practice was in no way restricted to Asians or those born in Buddhist countries (Fromm, 1960). In her theories of self, which became increasingly fluid throughout her career, Horney discovered a meaningful resonance with a Zen Buddhist approach to reality as unfixed and forever reconstructed. British psychoanalyst Nina Coltart picked up the torch, offering insights into what she found to be an easy compatibility between Theravada Buddhism and psychoanalysis. She discovered that her practice of mindfulness brought a new understanding of her capacity to listen to her patients with deepened analytic attunement (Coltart, 1996).

Through the application of what some Buddhists call "friendly curiosity" and what Freud called "evenly hovering attention" to contrasting approaches of psychological healing, many more theorists joined in with their particular insights, concerns, and wishes for the next generation of theorists interested in the dance between the Western psyche and the Eastern spiritual path. Within this expanding group of authors there are clear differences in methodology and mission. Some theorists express an interest in finding ready parallels between Buddhism and psychotherapy. While all of the writers I've mentioned reveal a depth of appreciation for the potential compatibility between these two systems, some are more inclined to focus on what Jeffrey Rubin has called "a pseudo-complementary/token egalitarian model" (Rubin, 1996). In this approach, the young Western theory of psychoanalysis and the ancient Eastern tradition of Buddhism are perhaps too easily conflated, rendering neither realm clear enough for the rigorous investigation that both Freud and the Buddha were committed to pursuing (Molino, 1998, p. 235).

Others present an equal personal investment in both realms while being tethered to neither (Epstein, 2007). On the spiritual side of this discussion there are those who are wary of the growing tendency to psychologize Buddhism. In this camp important red flags are raised about the dubious assertion that psychoanalytic processes can produce the same results as in-depth Buddhist practice (Batchelor, 1997; Kornfield et al., 1998, p. 99). So too, there are those who propose that Buddhist practitioners might be well served in their efforts to reduce suffering by investigating personal psychological experience, which is typically minimized in spiritual practice (Rubin, 1996; see also Engler, 2006; Unno, 2006, p. 29). Yet others recognize the potential pitfall in expecting either of these two contrasting realms to provide ready answers to all of life's struggles (Eigen, 1998a; Rubin, 1996). From their perspective, human experience is too vast and complex to be fully and adequately addressed by any one teaching or teacher.

Where do I find myself in this growing web of theoretical exploration? Having grown through my commitment to both traditions, I feel strongly that the human quest for happiness and wellness begs for conscious exploration of our psyche *and* our spirit. To embark on one path of learning and healing without the other, I believe, limits our true potential for transformation. Throughout my life I have used psychoanalytic tools in my spiritual practice and Buddhist tools in my psychoanalytic process. This capacity to bring a spiritual perspective to psychological experience, and a psychological perspective to spiritual endeavors, has been helpful to me. With this dual perspective I have felt better equipped to work with and honor what each tradition provides, and less tempted to give up when the wellness promised felt illusory and intangible.

While I am aware of the clear differences in the history, cultural contexts, and goals of these divergent approaches to human wellness, I have written this book in the spirit of encouraging a committed curiosity from both camps, and particularly from Buddhist teachers and psychoanalysts, about the tools and methods found in the contrasting tradition. Through comparison, I hope to clarify what is unique to each tradition and healing relationship as they stand in contrast with the other. This, I believe, is the primary benefit of comparison: it can offer increased understanding of what any one category or system can be. To compare a rose to a Star Gazer lily expands exponentially our sense of what a flower can be. To compare a green apple to a scone helps us understand and relate to nourishment (Paden, 1994, p. 5). The same is true with healing systems. Through a comparative study of religion and psychology we may begin to imagine new ways of addressing vexing personal struggles and the wish to live fully and joyfully.

Throughout this exploration of Buddhist teachers and students, alongside the analysts and analysands, I will propose that the process of awakening to reality, which in Buddhism is often called enlightenment, happens *within the context of relationship*. I have discovered that in both enterprises it is through relationship to healers that the teachings and methods begin to mix with one's mind. Perhaps most importantly, I have found over many years in divergent Buddhist lineages that the relative health and resonance of the student/teacher relationship has a profound impact on a student's willingness and ability to incorporate Buddhist teachings into their lived experience. The student's ability to engage with reality—their own and that of others—is shaped through the many subtle psychological dynamics that take place within the teacher/student relationship. In my experience, these complex dynamics are not easily worked through—particularly for Western students—without another healing system designed to address how the psyche responds to the labyrinth of interpersonal relationship.

In offering a glimpse into my own history with Buddhism and psychoanalysis, I will explore the particular traditions I have practiced and the influence of each tradition on my evolving interest in primary healing relationships within Buddhism. Out of this subjective exploration, I hope to clarify why this topic may be useful for Western students of Buddhism, for Buddhist teachers (both Eastern- and Western-born), and for clinicians working with Western Buddhist clients who need or want to explore their particular convergence of psyche and spirit.

I offer this book particularly to Buddhist students and to analysands (and their analysts) for whom healing and the wish to be happy and free from suffering are the driving forces toward wellness. It is with an abiding respect for the courage and fortitude necessary for any authentic effort at healing that I enter into the topic of relationship to religious mentors and psychoanalysts. I know well the risks we take in sharing our most vulnerable and tender places with people we hope will prove trustworthy and capable of ushering in the wellness we seek. So too, I bring to this project my deep appreciation for the healers in both traditions, whose care and kindness I have gratefully received.

While I have not attempted to provide absolute answers to how healing happens in these divergent realms, I hope that this exploration will offer a mirror for the journey of Western Buddhist students and people in psychoanalysis who come to these contrasting paths to experience fuller and more authentic relationships—with themselves, with others, and with the world they inhabit.

a personal journey through buddhism and psychoanalysis   1

A FTER THE YOUNG PRINCE Siddhartha Gautama experienced enlightenment under the Bodhi tree some 2,500 years ago, he made no initial effort to translate his psychospiritual awakening into language. Having moved beyond the realm of discursive thought, he felt strongly that its very depth and complexity could not be adequately articulated. One could argue that his first challenge as an awakened being, a buddha, was to bring his altered consciousness back into relationship with those still awaiting enlightenment. Others wanted to know about this purported awakening, which was so dramatic as to change the very nature of his lived experience until his passing some forty-five years later.

After six days of silent meditation following six years of asceticism that had left him so malnourished as to be nearly dead, he had turned the swords of Mara, the embodiment of evil and delusion, into flowers. With unfettered composure, he had tolerated the seductive dance of Mara's beautiful daughters, responding with neither aversion nor grasping. He had seen into the nature of the mind, with its profound struggle to find solid ground in which to cultivate a lasting identity.

Perhaps most importantly, the Buddha realized that relief from suffering is not a miraculous achievement unique to him, but our common birthright. What we most need is readily available to all by virtue of our very being. Contrary to his earlier views, turning our backs on the secular world in order to forsake all earthly pleasures misses the mark. Nor are we doomed to give in to the pull of desire, losing our awakened birthright—our purest state of mind untouched by negative emotion—to the undertow that is perpetual grasping. There is a *Middle Way*, and he had experienced this for himself after a lifetime of living in both extremes. When asked if he might explicate this experience so that others could benefit from his insight, he was at first disinclined. It seemed to Siddhartha Gautama, the historical Buddha Shakyamuni, so named for being a sage (*muni*) of the Sakya clan to which his family belonged, that his internal explorations and ensuing realizations defied language. The transformation he had undergone was experiential, not theoretical. But after forty-nine days had passed and he was asked again by Brahma, the mythical chief of the three thousand worlds, if he might try for the sake of those with a readiness to hear his life-altering insight, he agreed. Thus began the transmission of Buddhist teaching, the giving of the Buddha's wisdom from one awakened being to another.

As we fast-forward to the early twenty-first century urban milieu in which I write, transmission from teacher to student remains a primary vehicle through which students learn the Buddha's spiritual, psychological, and philosophical teachings. Over the course of many years as a Buddhist practitioner, I have come to know that the relationship between Eastern and Western teachers and their primarily lay Western students can either facilitate or impede the successful transmission of the Buddha's teachings.

I have discovered both from personal experience and from the Buddha's example that this particular spiritual path does not typically progress toward the psychospiritual liberation that it promises outside the context of intimate, one-to-one, human relationship. The intimacy between teachers and their students acts as a kind of gestational container for the many challenges and gifts an authentic and committed Buddhist path ensures. It is potentially a place of dyadic creativity—a relationship that sparks discovery—where sacred spiritual lessons may pass between two people with living psyches through which the Dharma is processed and integrated.

The Buddha modeled this relational path for the many who would seek his transformed relationship to reality. Before he began his first teaching, known as the first turning of the wheel of Dharma, which would spawn a new religious paradigm throughout the East and the West, he first sought his primary Hindu ascetic teachers in order to share with them the nature of his experience (Dalai Lama, 1995, pp. 9–14; Ray, 1994). After having done so, it was time to seek his original spiritual companions. These five ascetics had joined the twenty-nine-year-old Siddhartha Gautama after his initial departure from his childhood palace and from his wife and young son. They were his devoted students until he called into question the asceticism that had endangered his life through chronic starvation. When he began to move toward the Middle Way of spiritual practice, they lost faith in his mentorship and left. The separation, however, would be short-lived. After the Buddha's awakening under the Bodhi tree and his ensuing decision to share this experience with others, he sought their company in preparation for his very first teaching. Legend has it that they were so struck by his transformation, the joyful and steadfastly placid presence that was readily apparent, that they prepared his seat, lovingly washed his feet, and listened to what was the first of over 84,000 teachings that would follow. These companions became the first members of the *Sangha*, or community committed to following the Buddha's path.

Two centuries would pass before the Buddhadharma was recorded. During this time it was established as a religious tradition transmitted (offered and received) within the teacher/student pair. Eventually the Buddha's teachings were passed on through two main streams, one oral tradition and one written, referred to as the *dharmadhara*, or "holders of teaching" (Cleary, 1994, p. 5). In the Western, postmodern setting in which I have come to practice Buddhism, both streams continue to be practiced. But despite the abundance of incisive literature available to those who wish to study Buddhist teachings, most committed practitioners of Buddhism eventually find themselves in relationships with teachers who transmit their own particular understanding and experience of the original Dharma. For this reason, the interpersonal dynamics of the teacher/student relationship drive my wish to discern what is most helpful to contemporary lay Westerners in their efforts to integrate the Buddhadharma into increasingly complex lives. If the student's (*and* the teacher's) life experience and understanding of self and identity have changed over the past 2,500 years, I wonder how contemporary teachers are adapting the Dharma and transmitting it to students so that it can be received and woven into our lives.

My curiosity about how the student's psychic anatomy and spiritual needs may change depending upon their particular life circumstance has been shared by others since the very inception of Buddhist teaching. Historians have suggested that as the Buddha lay dying in his eightieth year, he told his faithful attendant Ananda that his followers could alter the Vinaya, a system of 250 rules governing monastic life, changing or dispensing with the less foundational rules to meet their changing needs (Fields, 1992, p. 9). The ripple effect of this instruction would have a powerful impact on the evolution of the Buddha's path.

During the First Council (ca. 480 BCE), held to clarify doctrine and discipline after the Buddha's passing, Ananda relayed this instruction to the five hundred monks gathered. There was disagreement over which of these rules could rightly be considered less foundational, which resulted in a decision to simply leave the teachings untouched. But during the Second Council (ca. 386 BCE), a group of monks felt that the monastic rules should indeed be altered to fit the specific circumstances of their sociocultural milieu. These monks, now numbering ten thousand or more, were eventually expelled from the initial order and formed their own order, which evolved into the various schools of Mahayana Buddhism (the vehicle of universal salvation). The monks who opted not to alter the Buddha's original teachings formed the vehicle of individual liberation, only one school of which, the Theravada school, or school of the Elders, survives.

Like so many of my fellow Western Buddhists, I have been influenced by both the Theravada and the Mahayana traditions. Divergent in practice and approach, each tradition has offered me a particular path into the Buddhadharma. In my early adulthood I was drawn to the practice of *vipassana*, or Insight Meditation, which is a Theravadan tradition. Historically, the Theravada path has emphasized the individual obtaining of wisdom, and it is exemplified by the Buddhist arhat—an enlightened being who achieves liberation through his or her own spiritual efforts (Fields, 1992, p. 10). In contrast, the Mahayana traditions, including Sakya Buddhism (one of four Tibetan lineages), which in more recent years has been my primary practice, emphasize compassion as exemplified by the bodhisattva, a being who chooses to take cyclic rebirth until all sentient beings are together free from suffering (Smith & Novak, 2003).

These two major families of Buddhism—Theravada and Mahayana—when considered in tandem offer important insight into one's personal relationship to the Buddhist spiritual path. The Theravada tradition is based upon the Pali canon, a vast array of spiritual teachings recorded by the monks of Ceylon several hundred years after the Buddha's passing (Boucher, 1988, p. 18). Noted Insight Meditation teacher Joseph Goldstein suggests that a central motivation for those historical disciples of the Theravada path was the wish first to tend to their own minds and hearts as a necessary precondition for the ability to live the Buddha's teachings of compassion toward all beings (Goldstein, 2003, p. 116).

In contrast, the Mahayana tradition, which developed in northern India during the first and second centuries CE and is based on Sanskrit texts—especially the Lotus Sutra—identifies the key to one's own freedom and enlightenment as the very process of helping others. The bodhisattva's way puts relationship at the heart of spiritual practice. For in the Mahayana teachings it is said that the bodhisattva is as endowed with wisdom as the arhat but chooses to delay his or her entry into nirvana—that supreme state of mind where all afflictive emotions are cooled—in order to assist all sentient beings in their efforts at happiness and freedom from suffering (Boucher, 1988, p. 19).

The differences between these two traditions are extensive, giving rise to contrasting communities, teaching styles, and spiritual processes. The vipassana tradition in the West has in large part been carried by lay Westerners and thus lends itself to an approach that is in many ways secular in nature. Vipassana Buddhist centers are typically spare in decor, with a calming simplicity that is friendly to people of any religious tradition. The teachers are usually Western-born, educated, and professional (Coleman, 2001, p. 8). Often they are schooled in Western psychology and sensitive to the particular psychological experience of Westerners pursuing a Buddhist practice. Vipassana teachers in the West are also likely to be married or in romantic partnership. In this way their priorities and life experience may closely match those of their students who also work to balance and integrate their secular and spiritual lives.

In my experience each tradition has posed both gifts and potential pitfalls. The tradition of Insight Meditation provides what is in certain ways a more culturally neutral approach to the Dharma. Students may spend decades in vipassana centers, attending retreats, speaking with senior Western teachers, and cultivating a deep and abiding practice while remaining relatively unmoored to much of the history and/or cultural context out of which the Theravada tradition evolved. On the one hand, depending upon a given student's relationship to this neutrality, they may find themselves more easily integrating the basic and foundational Buddhist teachings because they are unobscured by some of the arcane traditions more commonly found in Mahayana practice. Or they may utilize this empty cultural space as a screen upon which to project their own particular spiritual and psychological needs (Coleman, 2001, p. 125; see also chapter 5). For this reason, I think it is not uncommon for Western Insight Meditation practitioners to imagine and erroneously anticipate that their spiritual practice will also effectively address their psychological condition and needs (ibid.).

The world of Tibetan Buddhism, often referred to affectionately as the "smells and bells" tradition by Western adherents, is both more overtly "religious" in nature (see chapter 2) and more clearly influenced by traditional Asian cultures. The teachers are frequently monastic and Tibetan- or Indian-born, and they may have left their families of origin in early childhood for entry into a Buddhist monastery. As a result, their priorities and overarching life experience tends to be dramatically different from those of their Western students. So too, the practice is composed of ornate rituals in foreign tongues that serve as a constant reminder to Western practitioners that they have embarked on a spiritual journey that did not originate within their own sociocultural milieu.

As in the world of Insight Meditation, there are clear riches and potential difficulties for Americans practicing Tibetan Buddhism. Abstruse teachings, made more challenging by language barriers and rituals that are often never fully explicated, may leave students with a murky understanding of the Buddhadharma. At the same time, these obvious challenges can inspire students to recognize the parameters of their Buddhist practice—what it can and cannot address—and to wrestle with teachings that may feel quite complex due to arcane ritual and the teacher's decidedly non-Western communication style.

Throughout many years in the Insight Meditation tradition, I enjoyed a comfortable identification with fellow sangha members and teachers alike. I regularly attended vipassana retreats, and I practiced sitting meditation daily. The benefits were clear to me. An increased and deepened ability to listen with mindfulness and compassion seemed to elicit a depth of gratitude and trust from friends and family members that was both touching and meaningful.

That said, during these many fruitful years I rarely experienced a visceral sense of personal communion with a vipassana sangha or with my teachers. While I recognize that this may have much to do with my lack of readiness for intimacy with a group and/or teacher, I also suspect that this more tepid emotional relationship was partially a response to the nature of the practice itself. The spiritual process, for me, was both an essentially private one and one that stayed within a particular range of emotional experience. In retrospect, I am inclined to attribute this more affectively contained experience to the relative absence of the teacher/student model in Western Insight Meditation sanghas.

Practicing vipassana outside the context of intimate relationship with a teacher made the Dharma feel easy on the psyche and spiritually malleable. There were no masters to defer to or to challenge my sense of spiritual identity or understanding of the teachings. (This, however, was not the case for people immersed in the Asian tradition from which Insight Meditation sprung—e.g., Sharon Salzburg, Joseph Goldstein, and Jack Kornfield—who studied in Thailand and Burma with the great masters.) Within this secular approach to Buddhism, my sense of privacy and anonymity remained firmly intact. The extent to which I might engage a particular teaching or method was entirely up to me.

During this time I was not uninterested in the more ritualized approach to the Dharma that I had encountered within Tibetan Buddhism. As someone with an essentially secular upbringing, I was intrigued by any religious gathering where "deities" were invoked, prayers were recited, or prostrations and bows were performed. I had no religious baggage to unload, no bitter or conflicted memory of prior religious training to avoid. Nonetheless, I sensed from my observation of numerous American devotees within this tradition that settling on a particular sangha was a decision that could not be made lightly. From the literature I had read throughout my earlier adulthood, and from my cursory anthropological assessments, I understood that commitment to a Tibetan Buddhist community was at its heart commitment to a teacher who would become my spiritual guide.

As I reflect on my previous relationship to Buddhism, it is clear to me that my spiritual interests and needs changed over the years. Like many

Western Buddhists, I was initially attracted to the experience of meditation and the life-altering insight that one could choose to relate to one's
own mind, including the stormy realm of affect, consciously and with a
sense of loving discipline. This primary interest in meditation is one of
the central attractions—if not *the* central attraction—for Western Buddhists. It is also the common ground between many of the Buddhist traditions, including Japanese and Korean Zen, Pure Land, Tibetan, and
Insight Meditation. How meditation is taught, however, and whether it
is linked to strictly personal transformation or included as a requisite
part of a more inclusive path toward freedom, demarcates these divergent traditions.

Sociologist Daniel Capper, in his compelling exploration of a Tibetan
Buddhist community in upstate New York, has found that in addition to
meditation, American Buddhists are interested in moral systems, cognitive frameworks, mystical experience, and most importantly, relationships with teachers that are ameliorative and life-giving (Capper, 2002, p.
8). Given this broad spectrum of interests, it is understandable that American Buddhists (we currently total more than one million) would find
themselves attracted to contrasting traditions that typically emphasize
one particular method and spiritual approach to the Dharma; or, as was
true in my experience, that we would seek out different traditions at different stages in our lives.

In a recent conversation with my Buddhist teacher, the Venerable
Lama Pema Wangdak, a senior lama of the Sakya school of Tibetan Buddhism, we discussed the driving motivation behind the Western exploration of meditation and Buddhist teaching. With his characteristic
combination of single-pointed attention and casual demeanor, he waved
his hand and said that his American students "mostly just want to relax,
not feel too stressed." Initially this sounded right to me—we Westerners
are notoriously pain-averse and disinclined to sit with discomfort of any
kind (Rubin, 1996, p. 91). We are also frequently overstimulated, living in
environments that encourage a frenzied pace and a generalized fear of
missing information or personal and professional opportunities.

On further reflection, I found myself considering the pervasive addiction, anxiety, and depression that permeate the urban setting that is my
home. Despite our culture's great material wealth and educational and
professional opportunity (albeit unevenly distributed based on race and

social location), I have witnessed and experienced remarkable levels of basic unhappiness and distress. This sense of unsatisfactoriness—which the Buddha called *dukkha*, a word that evokes the experience of being out of sync, like a wheel out of alignment or an arm out of its socket—strikes me as being something altogether more serious than the high stress levels that are commonly acknowledged by physicians and sociologists. What I have come to discern, both within my Buddhist community and among secular friends and family members, is a near desperation for some systemic manner of relief from a life that can so easily feel devoid of value and meaning. Carl Jung suggested, and I agree, that it is ultimately lack of meaning that leads to mental illness (1965, p. 340). He argued that the riches of the material world, including romantic relationship and professional achievement, are insufficient to provide the meaning we are instinctually bound to seek.

In the environment in which I have practiced the Dharma, Western students are indeed relentlessly burdened with a cultural credo of materialism and consumerism that can have spiritually and psychologically deadening results. While the history and myriad cultural factors that have created this particular fever pitch of consumerism—the addictive need to have and be more than we realistically can at a given moment—are beyond the scope of this work, I hope to underscore my sense that Western seekers of Eastern spiritual traditions bring with them something more than the general desire to successfully manage their stress levels.

For many American Buddhists there have been multiple efforts at healing that predate their forays into Eastern spirituality. This suggests to me a conscious readiness and a potent desire to absorb and make tangible use of our spiritual teachings, so that life may begin to feel like something more than an occasion for frayed nerves. What I have observed within my current spiritual community is the wish to have meaning in life with roots that can be relied upon in times of loss, struggle, and confusion.

While Siddhartha Gautama came to his enlightened mind in cultural circumstances that stand in marked contrast to the cultures we live in now, his world was suffering from a comparable level of turmoil and instability. Buddhism has been compared to a protestant movement in its direct response to the perceived power abuses and dogmatism of the Hindu tradition (Smith & Novak, 2003, pp. 21–30). Gautama was well aware that too many people were suffering in a system that protected the

Brahmin class while ignoring the suffering of people who lacked for their basic needs during a time of social and political upheaval. He saw the evils of greed played out on a macro scale, and it pushed him to locate a more authentic and reliable source of well-being and happiness. Out of this concerted reflection he developed insight into the human mind that brought him into the relational realm, where he saw the dangerous pitfalls of attachment, ill-will, and ignorance. He saw that a skewed understanding of our true nature would manifest in feelings of aversion toward ourselves and others, in desirous grasping, or in a flat-line neutrality that lacked the necessary human warmth of any relationship with another sentient being.

The Buddha's way was not a path of hiding, although his teachings of no-self and emptiness can be appropriated for those with the wish to hide (see chapter 8). Instead, he encouraged his followers to carefully consider the subtle but profoundly healing Middle Way, which could fundamentally alter our human tendency to react with clinging, neutrality, or aversion to all people, circumstances, and experiences. He recognized within his particular historical context that the accumulation of material riches for some might present the illusion of happiness, and by extension, a sense of being inherently more worthy than those with less. So too, he saw that in a highly stratified society, where one's socioeconomic standing could offer a false sense of protection and confirmation of inherent value, a simple life in which only one's basic material needs were met might evoke pervasive feelings of unhappiness and deprivation.

It was in response to this grasping at external circumstance for a sense of inherent worth or protection from pain and loss that the Buddha's most fundamental teachings arose. He would question the logic in grasping at any circumstance, or person, given the impermanence that is the nature of all phenomena. Perhaps most importantly he would underscore our basic interdependence—that there is no fixed and unchanging nature that defines and therefore separates us. Rather, humanity is like the "Jewel Net of Indra," in which the jewel found at every intersection of the net completely reflects all the others. Human beings are jewels that reflect back to each other and in turn are made up of the reflections they receive (Bobrow, 1998, p. 309; Smith & Novak, 2003, p. 61). Similarly, we are all empty of inherent meaning, but rather depend upon all others for our changing qualities and circumstance.

While contemporary theorists (e.g., Stephen Batchelor, Robert Thurman, and Joan Borysenko) are right to affirm the call to individual consciousness that Buddhism requires—the Buddha explicitly instructed us to check our own experience to determine whether or not his teachings meet with reality—ultimately his path was one of treasured interpersonal relationship.

Beginning with the historical Buddha's own community of followers, the importance of forming relationship with spiritual guides was exemplified in his instruction to seek out a *kalayamitra*, or "spiritual friend" (Klinger, 1980, p. 10). The spiritual friend would have been witness to the Buddha and could therefore affirm the truth and impact of his awakening. Such a friend could pass this experience along to the disciple, creating a human chain in the process of enlightenment (Capper, 2002, p. 75). In this way a joining of spiritual hands would facilitate the transmission of awakening, as it connects the disciple with the living experience of the Buddha (Podgorski, 1986).

The emphasis on a spiritual guide or teacher was as emphatic in the Pali canon as in the Mahayana sutras. In the Theravada tradition, finding a teacher who knew the circuitous ways of the Buddhist path was critical for any serious disciple. So too, the intensity of one's meditation practice was understood as an act of devotion to the spiritual teacher (Ray, 1994; see also Capper, 2002, p. 76). In the Mahayana tradition, the importance of the spiritual friend was equally affirmed, but the role changed to that of one who inspires the disciple to move along the bodhisattva's path. In contemporary Tibetan Buddhist centers, teachers actively encourage their students to cultivate awakened minds and hearts that more naturally respond with compassion to the suffering of others. This *bodhichitta*, or "awakened heart," is understood as the necessary state of being that allows for the life of a bodhisattva.

The Pali canon and Mahayana sutras are filled with detailed guidance for seeking a spiritual friend. These literary blueprints make for reading that is both captivating and at times quite funny, given the simultaneously specific and circuitous nature of the advice.

As stated in the *Bodhisattvabhumi*, a fourth-century Mahayana work, the spiritual friend should, among other things, possess a bodhisattva's discipline in ethics and manners, fully comprehend the ultimate real, be full of compassion and love, have patience, have an indefatigable mind, and use the right words (Capper, 2002, p. 78). The spiritual friend is depicted as a person of great compassion, with clear and discerning intelligence and an unshakable faith in the Buddhadharma. Lest we envision such a being as having a physical presence comparable to that of the Buddha, the literature goes on to remind eager disciples that spiritual friends can take many forms. Children, elderly women, merchants, and mendicants can all be endowed with this special capacity to inspire bodhichitta. In the *Gandhavyuha Sutra*, the process of finding a spiritual friend is delineated in a conversation in which the bodhisattva Sudhana seeks advice from the great bodhisattva of wisdom, Manjushri. After embarking on his own journey to find such a spiritual friend, he comes back to tell us that "spiritual benefactors are hard to get to see, hard to encounter, hard to visit, hard to attend, hard to approach, hard to stay with, hard to be perfected by, hard to associate with" (Cleary, 1987, pp. 68–69).

Sogyal Rinpoche, in the *Tibetan Book of Living and Dying*, spends considerable time both clarifying the attributes of a "true teacher" and underscoring the necessary preconditions for embarking on a relationship with such a teacher. He describes such authentic spiritual guides as "compassionate [and] tireless in their desire to share whatever wisdom they have acquired from their masters." They "never abuse or manipulate their students under any circumstances, never under any circumstances abandon them, serve not their own ends but the greatness of the teachings, and always remain humble" (1993, p. 130).

While he is less inclined to drill down into the difficulties of being in relationship with such a spiritual friend, Sogyal Rinpoche nonetheless quickly moves this evocative portrait into a reminder that it is *not* the personality of the teacher one must rely upon, but the truth of the Buddha's teachings. He cites the *Four Reliances Sutra*, in which disciples are encouraged to

> Rely on the message of the teacher, not on his personality;
> Rely on the meaning, not just on the words;
> Rely on the real meaning, not on the provisional one;
> Rely on [the] wisdom mind, not on [the] ordinary, judgmental mind.

Alongside these critical reliances, disciples are reminded that indestructible devotion is also needed. For it is through devotion (*mö gü* in

Tibetan) that we are able to access and reveal "our innermost heart" to the spiritual guide. In this way teachings are imparted not to our judging, ordinary minds but to our wisdom mind (*rigpa* in Tibetan). Once a spiritual teacher is found, "patience and endurance, wisdom, courage, and humility" are all necessary attributes for the maintenance of such a revelatory and heart-opening relationship (ibid., pp. 132 and 136).

When traversing the literary lore of Tibetan teachers and their disciples, it quickly becomes apparent why devotion is repeatedly emphasized as a necessary ingredient in the teacher/student relationship. The story of Naropa, the great Indian scholar of Buddhism, and his efforts to find a teacher exemplify the patience and psychological fortitude necessary for this arduous, potentially crazy-making task.

Naropa hailed from an illustrious family. As a child, he displayed a keen intellectual curiosity, and he later became renowned for his erudition and Buddhist scholarship. While teaching at Nalanda, the prestigious Buddhist university, he revealed a remarkably trenchant mind as a formidable opponent in philosophical debate (Finn, 1998, p. 164). The story goes that during this time he had a rather distressing vision of an elderly woman who was disfigured in thirty-seven horrifying ways. She asked him if he understood the Dharma, to which he replied in the affirmative. With waves of derisive laughter, she challenged his ready confidence. Bemused by her reaction, Naropa asked her if there was anyone else who better understood the Dharma. "Oh yes," she said. And in a moment of tepid courage, he took up the challenge to meet this true teacher of the Dharma, whom he was instructed to find. This set in motion a series of events that would eventually lead to the advent of Tibetan Buddhism (ibid.; see also Capper, 2002, p. 90).

Through a string of encounters with various thieves, lepers, and other apparent tricksters, Naropa continued on an exasperating search for the person who was said to understand the Dharma authentically. He found that in the person of Tilopa, who turned out to be the brother of the disfigured elderly woman who had visited Naropa in his vision (Finn, 1998, p. 164). In each unsavory encounter Naropa was inclined to reject the lowly figure before him, but he came to realize that these were in reality manifestations of the teacher he sought. His journey demanded a new capacity to see beyond the illusory nature of identity—to recognize that carriers of wisdom transcend the trappings of social position, gender, and intellectual prowess.

When Tilopa finally appeared in physical form, he continued to test Naropa's readiness for an authentic journey into the realm of awakening. Naropa was asked to hurl himself into a blazing fire, to assault royalty, and to endure a beating with Tilopa's shoe that would ultimately precipitate his enlightenment (ibid., p. 166; see also Capper, 2002, p. 89). The years in which he was repeatedly challenged to cultivate an unshakable devotion to Tilopa's wisdom, and the patience necessary for this wisdom to be imparted, opened Naropa's heart and mind to the transmission of his teacher's awakening.

This tale of enlightenment via exasperating relationship underscores the Tibetan Buddhist tradition of minds mixing and becoming one. It is a story of interdependence, where the disciple's consciousness and independent ego position is powerfully challenged over time, and every foreseeable defense against her own inherent wisdom is shattered. Naropa's original and illusory insight into the Buddha's teachings based upon his scholarly endeavors serves as a critical reminder that without a true teacher—someone who has undergone the painful and necessary confrontation with her own delusive self-concepts—we easily miss the heart of the Buddha's way. What we perceive to be wisdom may in reality be little more than our very defense against wisdom.

The teacher has the rather unpleasant task of pointing out and correcting this primary misunderstanding. A teacher's method must be pure in intention but may include challenges that feel abrasive and powerfully unsettling. The Tibetan Buddhist teacher and writer Pema Chödrön characterizes this essential process in the following way:

> The job of the teacher is to help the student experience that their mind and the mind of the teacher are the same. The teacher realizes that the student doesn't understand that, doesn't believe it, and doesn't trust…Sometimes someone needs love and sometimes harshness. But whatever the teacher does is always about helping you to see layer after layer of defense mechanisms and self-deceptions that block your innate wisdom. You have tremendous devotion because without your

teacher you would never have discovered this confidence in your own wisdom. (Gross, 1999, p. 47)

This tradition of awakening through the mixing of minds is perhaps the very foundation of Tibetan Buddhism. After Naropa experienced enlightenment, he passed the sacred teachings on to Marpa, who is noted for having then trekked across the Himalayas to Tibet, where he passed them on to Milarepa. The legendary teacher/student probationary ordeals that Milarepa underwent with Marpa solidified this internalization of the teacher's wisdom mind as the basis for a continued Tibetan Buddhist tradition (Chang, 1989).

The history of these foundational teacher/student relationships strikes a resonant chord for many contemporary Tibetan Buddhist practitioners. We recognize in these stories the colorful personalities of our own teachers, the depth of devotion that has been necessary to sustain relationships across significant cultural divides, and the process of softening a Western ego that from its very inception has been reinforced in its capacity to defend against such reliance upon another. From a psychoanalytic perspective, we might describe this experience with our teachers as a conscious state of merger, where any sense of discrete identity is dissolved into a common experience of "interbeing."

As Westerners, with our contrasting notions of self and ego, we bring to the historical interpersonal difficulties posed by the teacher/student relationship an additional layer of culturally informed complication that our Buddhist teachers will challenge with both the sensitivity and harshness characteristic of them. It is understandable, given the depth of complexity and strife inherent in the teacher/student relationship even without these additional opportunities for miscommunication, that the Dalai Lama would offer caveats to Westerners interested in pursuing a Buddhist path. In various public teachings, he has been known to gently and subtly discourage Westerners from embarking on a cross-cultural interpersonal journey that might ensure yet more suffering for people who presumably hope to assuage rather than augment their personal difficulties and dis-ease. Rather, he proposes that we learn from the Dharma and make every effort to live the Buddha's teaching of nonviolence and compassion for all beings as we practice within our own religious traditions. Implicit in these avuncular suggestions is his sage insight that there may be a more direct, less problematic way for Westerners to pursue spiritual integration and wellness.

Despite his genuine respect for and interest in Buddhist practice, Carl Jung was also disinclined to recommend this path for Westerners. He recognized the pervasive Western tendency to avoid our own psyches, thereby co-opting any new and exotic spiritual practice as yet more distraction from the unconscious (Jung, 1971, p. 490). He encouraged Westerners not to grasp at a novel spiritual belief system and instead to face the stronger religious imprints that were likely within their own psyches by virtue of their cultural inheritance, with methods more readily available to them.

Having embarked on a long-term Buddhist practice myself, I appreciate the intention behind these efforts at dissuasion. We Westerners do indeed typically have an ego-driven grasping impulse that is so lightning-quick as to be almost imperceptible—especially to ourselves. There is an ever-present temptation to cultivate a Buddhist identity that may in reality serve to defend against our own enlightenment or freedom from suffering. We may bring the notorious "supermarket mentality" to our explorations of Buddhism with only the conscious awareness of having attempted a good and worthy challenge. This sense of spiritual savvy may easily give way to the spiritual elitism that is commonplace in many American Buddhist centers, particularly among younger practitioners who have yet to engage in the trying experience of entering into and sustaining relationship with a teacher. The ego can so easily swell with the first sense of having gleaned real insight that transcends conventional and mundane reality.

Was this true for me, too? Probably. As I've mentioned before, my initial relationship to Buddhist practice remained within a certain range of emotional experience. I had neither the readiness nor the internal resources to engage in a spiritual process that would identify my most entrenched ego defenses. Instead, the first several years were a time of building self-esteem through cultivating insight and quieting the mind. Coupled with my intellectual curiosity about the psychology of the Buddhadharma, this initial boon could easily have stopped with a bolstered sense of personal agency and philosophical insight.

This is not to suggest that if insight into the ability to generate one's own sense of well-being were the only byproduct of spiritual practice, it would have been without great personal value. Recognizing that it is possible to experience a sense of rest that resides within our own minds and hearts can be a terrifically helpful insight, particularly in this highly medicalized climate, where prescriptions for all manner of emotional or psychological distress have reached record numbers. I would be delighted if more young people struggling to become viable in a culture that is so fiercely individualistic felt equipped both to tolerate the immense anxiety that this culture can so easily induce and to self-soothe in ways that are nonharming. The practice of meditation could serve as a real cultural boon, addressing the addiction, anxiety, and depression that are almost rites of passage in the contemporary urban setting where I have practiced.

It is for this reason, among others, that senior Tibetan teachers continue their efforts in the United States. Beyond their appreciation for the culturally enforced challenges that Western Buddhists face, the teachers I have come to know seem to have an intuitive appreciation for the highly subjective nature of learning and practicing the Dharma. They strike me as being, at bottom, most interested in the possibility of a meaningful connection with students who for reasons of personal circumstance, karma, and sensitivity are primed to explore a tradition that challenges basic Western values, cultural mores, and priorities.

Such teachers exhibit a remarkable patience. They believe that despite the cultural divide—the many differences in language, moral codes, and personal values they encounter among their students—there is nonetheless a universal need to find others from whom one can learn the essential nature of our being. They have found over the past several decades of teaching Western students who are often highly accomplished in their particular fields—well-known authors, physicians, and educators—that this need to be guided by others seems to be a defining human attribute. Even in the spiritual domain, where conclusive answers cannot be found, we are forever in search of someone who can provide a sense of direction and, perhaps more importantly, inspire an enduring trust in where we may ultimately arrive.

In his instructive study of gurus, including spiritual and psychoanalytic figures, psychoanalyst Anthony Storr suggests that our adaptation to the world is largely predicated upon our capacity to learn (1996, p. 215). He found, through an extensive exploration of spiritual disciples across traditions, that people are largely disinclined to make up their own minds about matters that cannot be scientifically verified. In our efforts to learn more about our own relationship to the extramundane, we seek those who we trust can teach us something of value. With this operative capacity to learn, which continues throughout our lives, we are perpetually on the look-out for teachers.

The Tibetan Buddhist teachers I have known seem to continue in their mentoring endeavors with this basic understanding. While they are aware of the difficulties posed in crossing a cultural divide, they also recognize that the overarching desire to seek spiritual guidance from another presents a real and eminently valuable opportunity to meet the Dalai Lama's call for a nonharming way of life, regardless of whether a student is ready to embark on a full-blown Buddhist path.

———

I trace my initial interest in Buddhist practice back to a meditation course I attended with my spiritually curious mother. We were living in Los Angeles in the mid-1970s—a time when transcendental meditation, EST seminars, macrobiotics, and all things Eastern were on the rise. We made frequent trips to the Bodhi Tree, a Hollywood bookstore lined with texts on every facet of Buddhism, mindfulness training, and alternative healthcare. It was through this neighborhood bookstore that my mother learned of a local meditation course. Together we drove in our rust-colored Pinto down a winding Sunset Boulevard to our first meditation class.

I recall sitting in a small circle of ten or so students. The instructor guided us through a brief meditation in which we relaxed our shoulders and visualized the color orange filling us with vibrant, healing energy. I wasn't that fond of the color orange—I would have preferred baby blue or even a soft, feminine yellow—but I was soothed by the quiet in the room and the instructor's kindly voice. So too, I was happy to feel safely surrendered to another person who on first meeting seemed gentle and well-meaning. Encouraged by her mellifluous voice guiding us in meditation, I allowed this lively sense of color to connect with the idea of restorative energy that somehow made its way inside of me.

Later that summer my mother and I took a canoe trip down the Colorado River. I was ten at the time, and very much an urban kid. Stories of scorpions crawling over sleeping campers in the dead of night made me feel less than delighted at the prospect of four days unbathed and besieged by nature. That said, when I found myself alone in a slender kayak gliding down the shimmering green Colorado River with warm sun on my back, I suddenly became conscious of the wonder of nature. In the days following, I relaxed into our adventure, anticipating each morning ride in the water, free from the growl of recycling trucks and the ubiquitous croon of the Bee Gees.

But then the weather changed and the warm sun turned brutally hot. Together we suffered an unrelenting heat that made it hard to breathe, or to enjoy a midday canoe ride where our pale skin would surely fry. On the last day we took shelter in our bus, having decided that it was time to return to the comfort of our city lives. As we waited for the driver to arrive, our group of twenty or so fellow campers sat on the sweltering bus bemoaning the insufferable heat. I remember sticking to the seat, rivulets of sweat pouring down my arms and legs.

My mind flashed on the meditation course and the memory of quietude and comfort I'd felt while listening to the meditation instructor. "We could imagine that it's actually very cold," I said. A few people laughed. I continued, egged on by their good humor. "We could imagine that there's a cool breeze that we feel in our hair and on our faces. The breeze is so pleasant and cooling, because the sun is safely hidden behind soft clouds."

I noticed the woman sitting across from me. Her eyes were closed; she seemed to be listening. So I continued, instructing my fellow campers to imagine this sense of coolness throughout their whole bodies, noting that the sky had turned a striking whitish gray. The temperature was dropping, turning us from cool to cold. With my ten-year-old's logic at hand, this imagined cold warranted putting on an imaginary parka, which I carefully instructed the willing meditators to do. With this grand gesture, my visualization ended.

A woman from the back of the bus said the meditation had helped.

My mother looked at me, eyes wide with disbelief. "They were really listening to you." I nodded. My little-girl ego took note—it was striking to consider a group of adults with the willingness and humility to follow the instructions of a child. I had, after all, suggested they mentally don a parka in scorching desert heat! But even in the midst of feeling proud, I intuited that in times of great discomfort, people get desperate. They may be moved to try something new when there is no other discernable option. And when there is nothing left to do but alter the nature of their perception, they will do so—and it might help.

Years later, as a college student, I would read Victor Frankl's searing account of the Holocaust. In his writing I was reminded of this initial semiconscious awakening to the potential of our own minds to shape our perception of and engagement with external reality. Frankl proposed that when no action could be taken to alter or improve one's environment or circumstance, we must change our perspective. He called this one's *attitudinal value*, which he also described as "a person's attitude toward an unalterable fate" (Frankl, 1955, p. 44). Frankl suggests, and I wholeheartedly agree, that it is how one moves through periods of great suffering that creates meaning in life. It was through this insight and, I would propose, his ability to share this insight with others that Frankl took refuge and ultimately survived a harrowing period in our history. In hellish circumstances, where his very survival hung in the balance for years on end, he discovered an internal capacity for making meaning through altering one's perception with painstaking effort and commitment. In such a circumstance, where suffering was dominant, nothing else worked.

Reading Frankl's gripping story of total reliance upon his internal state reinforced what I had learned through my initial exposure to meditation. While my childhood forays into meditation can in no way be compared to the brutality and devastation of Frankl's experience in the Holocaust, I believe that his insights landed squarely within my psyche due to personal losses and struggles that had readied me for appreciating the importance of one's relationship to one's own mind.

In my early adulthood I would discover a deepening interest in the relationship between perception and human suffering. By this time the fact of suffering was dreadfully clear to me. Pictures of ethnic cleansing in Bosnia were plastered across every newspaper. Grizzly tribal warfare raged in Rwanda, and Haitian refugees perished by the thousands in their desperate efforts to reach relative safety from brutal regimes. Closer to home, racial strife had erupted on the heels of yet more police brutality, recession threatened the working and middle classes, and earthquakes had sent my neighbor's home sliding down a small Los Angeles mountainside.

After I moved back to the East Coast, the terrorist attacks of 9/11 and the subsequent invasion of Iraq reinforced my growing awareness that the Buddha had emphasized an unavoidable reality in the first of his four noble truths: Life is suffering. Like many New Yorkers, I found myself relying heavily upon spiritual beliefs and practice during a time of collective depression and grieving. I found to be true Carl Jung's sage insight that we cannot hold our own darkness alone (1932). The help we needed from others, which I found in my Buddhist practice, reinforced our shared capacity to enter into periods of great strife, loss, and devastation with a radically altered perspective. In this way, painful external circumstances did not lead to a loss of meaning but were mined for an increased awareness of our courage, our compassion for others suffering a similar fate, and our willingness to grapple with the reality of our basic vulnerability.

In retrospect, I suspect that this experience of global crisis served as a critical reminder to me and to many American Buddhists that the temptation to forget the Buddha's three additional noble truths (the cause of suffering, the end of suffering, and the way out of suffering) was a constant personal pitfall. To imagine that life was *nothing but* suffering only seemed to engender more suffering. This reminder lent itself to something other than mere denial, for it seemed nearly impossible to deny that life was a process that involved great suffering for most people across the globe. From the more overt forms of violence suffered by so many throughout the Middle East, to the chronic anticipation of yet more loss suffered by those who had survived the various acts of terrorism raging throughout the world, where personal trauma mixed with the collective in ways that were psychologically unmanageable, pain was a clear marker of human existence.

To stop with this constant awareness, however, felt like a sure-fire method for madness. What of Frankl's ability to keep himself psychically alive and intact during a time when his basic human value was called into question by those in power? What inspired the Buddha to propose three additional noble truths beyond the stark reality of dreadful, shattering, and soul-wrecking human suffering?

For me, a New York City resident, a person of Buddhist faith, and a psychoanalytic trainee, those initial years following the World Trade Center attacks were a time of ongoing reflection. How to make meaning out of suffering seemed a vitally important question to contemplate. An intensive consideration of this potential conundrum seemed the only way in to a life that included something more than depression and martyrdom. It was also the common thread between my personal experience, my deepening spiritual practice, and my continued experience as an analysand and psychoanalyst in training. In all facets of my spiritual, academic, and professional life, the need to understand suffering as a catalyst for living that transcended mere survival seemed critically important.

At the time I was in the midst of my graduate school course work, taking a seminar on Freud and Jung. I had recently given a presentation on the relationship between these founding figures of Western psychoanalysis and depth psychology, suggesting that these joint founders had met on the first noble truth, with their shared interest in the reality of human pain and suffering. Together they moved solidly into the second noble truth, where they dove into the many causes of this pain, endeavoring to shed light on the unconscious as a potential source of both the cause and alleviation of pain. It seemed to me that when Jung felt pulled toward the third noble truth, with its emphasis on the potential for life beyond perpetual suffering, their friendship and professional relationship was destined to shatter. Jung, very much in line with the Buddha's proposition, offered a radical prospect—that with an altered perspective and awakening to the true nature of our psychic apparatus, life could be something more than Freud's "common unhappiness" achieved via sublimation. Transformation was possible.

After my presentation, one of my colleagues took issue with the concept of a life beyond suffering. As a Christian, he was troubled by a proposition that challenged his understanding that such transformation is to be had only at the end of time. We live life *in* suffering and must adjust accordingly. At the time, I found myself listening to his quiet umbrage at my interpretation of the great masters of the psyche—Freud, Jung, and the Buddha—with a curiosity that was unmoored to a theoretically backed response. I was struck by a certain resigned sadness in his eyes, and so remained quiet.

Later that week I attended a question-and-answer session with a Tibetan lama of the Sakya tradition, the Venerable Lama Pema Wangdak. Sitting cross-legged on a thin maroon cushion, I asked the lama how I might explicate the fourth noble truth to a Christian colleague who seemed curious about the Dharma. I wasn't sure if he fully understood my question—his face was a veritable kaleidoscope of emotion.

"Don't worry about teaching anyone the Dharma," he said. "Just be a good friend; be compassionate and a good listener and a nice person who is patient, and then if they like you they will pursue the Dharma when and if it's right for them."

I nodded respectfully and thanked him. He had understood more than I thought possible.

In the days that followed it occurred to me that what he recommended was precisely what I found hardest to do. To be a good friend to someone who was unreceptive to the very ideas I found most inspiring was an unpleasant notion. I preferred to offer arcane teachings that underscored the powerfully substantive and inherently analytical spiritual path that was Buddhism as I understood it—or to simply avoid him. The lama, instead, encouraged me to be in relationship with others, to forsake the tendency to offer up ideas in lieu of simple and warm human connectedness. Implicit in his advice was the bodhisattva's way, a path that is ever mindful of providing for others what *they* most need.

In the weeks that followed, I enrolled in a class that the lama was teaching on the practice of Tibetan Buddhist mind training (*lojong*). The class took place during an oppressively hot New York City summer. The small group of students sat together, looking a bit wilted from long workdays and commutes. The room was too small for my usual comfort zone—I was too noticeable, and it was too easy for the lama to ask my name and ask me if what he was saying "was right." He clearly liked television and pop culture, and he tended to reference recent *Law and Order* episodes in his Dharma talks. The Mafia and their purported interest in world peace were also fairly common themes. Who wasn't interested in world peace? he often asked, with his eager smile and clear wit. Even guys with guns want peace within their families, their communities. So let's probe a little deeper, he seemed to be saying.

I kept coming back, and when my advisor recommended that I study Tibetan language for my doctoral studies, I called the lama and asked him if he might be available to help.

"Who are you?" he wanted to know. I described my basic physical characteristics. After a moment of silence, he said, "Oh yes. You're the one who's always smiling!" I laughed with guarded discomfort—I was indeed too visible in his tiny sangha. And in the years that followed, I grew to know this tiny lama from Tibet as my teacher and dear friend.

Out of fairness to my Christian colleague who inspired me to make that trek downtown to my initial meeting with the lama, I must confess that there have been many times when I wished dearly to have my privacy back again, to be spared the responsibility of friendship—even with a great lama—which is so much harder than a mere exchange of ideas among colleagues or even a meditation practice. Over the years, studying with and developing a friendship with this wise, kindly, eminently human Tibetan lama has been no easier than my paltry efforts at friendship with my graduate school colleague. Our differences have seemed just as stark, just as troubling, as the differences between my Christian colleague and myself.

As a long-term analysand and psychoanalytic trainee, I brought to this relationship my ongoing interest and studies in the psyche. In combination with the years of mindfulness training, I took note when the relationship left me feeling happy to be alive, buoyed in spirit, and even grateful for the many personal losses that had in part kept me tethered to my spiritual path. These feelings of direct contact with joy were fodder for analytic sessions, where the wish to understand what contributes to a sense of aliveness and gives meaning and nourishment is ongoing.

Like many other Americans involved in the Tibetan tradition, I was deeply touched by the feeling of being warmly received simply by virtue of having a "precious human life." My lama displayed an unconditionally compassionate attitude toward me and toward all others I witnessed him interact with. Initially, this experience of receiving such compassion was both a balm to the soul and a poignant contrast to the interpersonal dynamics I had known intermittently within my family of origin and in the culture in which I was raised.

While it would be entirely inaccurate to suggest that I had never known such gentle receptivity, I nonetheless could discern the clear difference between having conditions placed upon the love I was fortunate to receive and the free and unquestioned compassion that was simply the lama's way. This offering of genuine interest and good feeling was not personal in nature, although it in no way felt contrived or rote. Instead, I experienced him as modeling a tolerance for our shared human tendency to be flawed and relationally inadequate by receiving his students' respective idiosyncrasies with affection and good humor.

His patience with himself and with others stood in stark contrast to the taut sense of entitlement and consequent frustration that New Yorkers are notorious for displaying. In general (and for the record let me state that I love my fellow New Yorkers dearly), we have a rather unsavory inability to tolerate frustration, to allow for the humanness that manages to seep into most encounters throughout a given day. I think it fair to suggest that we tend to greet human limitations—our own and those of others—with a sense of anger and frustration (see Young-Eisendrath, 1998, for a helpful analysis of these limitations in the context of the Buddhist/psychoanalytic conversation). In contrast, the lama's tempo, personal style, and ability to take things as they come, and not a moment sooner, were all distinctly outside the realm of the urban culture and upbringing I had known. And yet, at the same time, I felt a clear resonance with this altered approach to relationship and to the greater lived experience. There was a gentleness in the lama's attitude toward life that felt natural. So too, the psychic weariness and spiritual fallout of the more frenzied pace and approach to life I had known was in my mind, without question.

These responses to the larger environment in which I practiced Buddhism were key elements in my own analytic process. A feeling of being out of sync with the culture from which I emerged was an ongoing theme in my own psychoanalytic treatment. Lacking interest in all things technological, including cell phones and iPods, and feeling alarm regarding the bizarre infiltration of Valley Girl–isms into the English language, increasingly I had grown to feel like Margaret Mead amid a foreign people. But psychoanalysis is not a conceptual process. Psychoanalysts of all schools typically construe the wish to discuss overarching theoretical issues or markers of identity as resistance to conscious awareness of prior losses and personal psychological struggles. (My analyst did this, too, whether or not he made this explicit.)

The psychoanalytic process, in both its historical and current incarnations, was designed to address the particularities of individual and personal experience. While one's relationship to culture might emerge within the analytic process (see Karen Horney, 1937, and Harry Stack Sullivan, 1953), an analyst would seek to underscore the personal meaning in an analysand's relationship to this broad category of human experience. (For Horney, a compromise between the typical psychoanalytic focus on the individual psyche and her sensitivity to the larger context from which an individual developed intrapsychic difficulty involved the analysand's readiness to withdraw the psychic energy invested in whatever cultural nuance or norm was experienced as problematic and reinvest this energy into the analysand's real and authentic self [1950].)

Most psychoanalysts have tended to bring this narrow focus to bear when examining the range of experiences analysands bring to their analytic endeavors. Buddhist psychoanalyst Jeffrey Rubin writes of the farsighted psychoanalytic approach that typically seeks to decontextualize the individual from larger systems of meaning that include morality, ethics, or culture (Rubin, 1996, p. 77). The emphasis is squarely on individual experience. In this context, the nature of my relationship to Buddhism and to a Tibetan lama was explored in connection to my particular life circumstances, family of origin, and interpersonal tendencies.

In contrast, Buddhist training had brought my attention to the universal psychic tendencies that are influential in one's psychospiritual life (Young-Eisendrath, 2003, p. 303). This more expansive and inclusive approach to lived experience seemed to affirm that the sense of dissonance I had known in a culture fixated on bolstering the individual, without paying attention to how the individual affects others, was understandable and important to consider.

Each enterprise brought me closer to different realities that I experienced in personal ways. Within my psychoanalytic process there was ample room for the early childhood experiences that would in part lay the psychic groundwork for future interpersonal behavior. The parenting I had received and the specificities of experience that resulted from these particular caretakers with their particular histories were all visited and revisited as centrally important to the analytic endeavor. For a relatively private person like me, the analytic space was a unique realm where I felt sanctioned and encouraged to divulge personal content and process. I felt my analyst's genuine interest in details of my daily life of a kind that many would save for the sole benefit of diaries and dreams. In this way psychoanalysis created a space where moments of great depth and personal meaning that might otherwise remain in a private, nonverbal, and thus only semiconscious sphere could come forth and be received with the friendly curiosity I associated with my lama.

A capacity to listen with a nonjudgmental attitude has been a cornerstone of both healing traditions. In Buddhism it is often called *bare attention*, whereby we bring the spirit of mindfulness to all that is heard, seen, and experienced through our full sensory capacity for perception. The idea is to practice engaging with the reality of whatever is presented without lapsing into a habitual response of aversion, attachment, or disinterested neutrality. With regard to what he called "evenly hovering attention," Freud recognized early on that the most effective way to encourage an honesty and disclosure from his analysands, and to receive the psychic information that was communicated, was through an analytic stance that tabled the analyst's personal biases and moral judgments (1912).

In relationship with my lama, I experience this bare attention as a kind of affection for my very being. With my analyst, this evenly hovering attention feels less affectively charged (although it can become more so as an analysis progresses) and more focused on the specific issues or experiences I seek to bring forth in our work together. In both relationships I have felt licensed to move into a place of rest, a sense of being received for who I am in a given moment. And yet I have been simultaneously aware that each tradition, and each practitioner in these contrasting traditions, is primed to catch specific facets of my lived experienced with highly divergent tools and methods.

By way of example I will share a recent experience that reinforced my increasing respect for the marked differences in these two healing traditions and interpersonal relationships.

After several years of sharing colorful stories with my family of origin regarding my participation in a Tibetan Buddhist sangha, I introduced my lama to my parents. He came over for Thanksgiving dinner, where we ate arugula salad and lamb. I prayed that they might all be moderate in behavior for one meal of their lives. They engaged one another in conversation with their respective personalities and interests, and thankfully all was pleasant. Yet when on the way home my lama referred to my parents as "normal," I semiconsciously sensed difficulties on the horizon.

Several months later I received a call from my mother asking if I'd like to join her for dinner. I was busy with a writing project and suggested that we meet another time soon. A few minutes later it occurred to me that my lama was teaching a class on the bodhisattva's way later that evening. I called her back and suggested that she attend. She sounded delighted at the prospect.

Soon enough I was living with the fallout of this hasty suggestion. When greeting me, my Peruvian-born mother would bring her hands together at her heart and bow. Our conversations were littered with various inquiries into my continued interest in Buddhism, as in "Are you still studying with the lama?" The insidious vestiges of maternal envy were making themselves known to me in an arena that had remained protected from this aspect of my life. A few weeks later I would find myself in the lama's small room with a group of students sitting demurely on the floor, with my mother sitting prominently in the middle of the room on a chair, parallel to the lama.

As a person given to impulsive and at times highly amusing off-the-cuff banter, she raised her hand throughout his talk to ask about the differences between ghosts and spirits, what we could do as a people to combat the recent conflicts between Tibet and China, and the parallels between the Dharma and psychoanalytic theory (my mother is a psychoanalyst).

I died a mini-death that early spring night. The operative word, however, is *mini*. Nothing catastrophic happened; this much I understood. She managed to bypass the impulse to crack wildly inappropriate jokes, and there were not any obvious bodily noises produced for humorous effect. But a lifetime of experience with this iconoclastic personality had me bracing myself for the worst. I knew in my bones that it had been a bad idea to include my mother in my spiritual community, despite the Buddha's directive to pass along the Dharma in the service of helping all sentient beings.

The lama drove us home that night. As we pulled up in front of my mother's building she began pointing to the young doorman who would soon greet us. "I'll tell him you're the Dalai Lama! They'll start bowing and I'll be famous!" She laughed with childlike excitement. The lama didn't laugh, which was unusual. I have since recognized in my own analytic work that he shares some startling similarities to my mother's rather "wacky" personality, which is to say that her behavior hardly registered on his psychic radar screen. After we dropped her off, I apologized on her behalf. He seemed conspicuously serious.

"You're too hard on her," he said. I felt my shoulders stiffen, my temperature rise. "If you only knew," I longed to say. Instead, I laughed and said matter-of-factly, "She was on her best behavior," before changing the subject to his recent travels.

When I recounted this evening for my analyst a few days later, the evenly hovering attention I have come to rely on was nowhere to be found. He shook his head from side to side, looking dismayed and annoyed. What was I thinking, he wanted to know, when I extended this invitation to my mother in the first place? Implicit in his question was my history of vigilant caretaking, which was perhaps a more significant source of psychic depletion than my various culturally informed challenges.

Feeling defensive of my wish to share what has been healing and meaningful in my own life with others, I sparred: "It was an honest gesture! And one I admittedly didn't think through. But it was just a nice thing to share." He was unmoved, no longer shaking his head, but radiating a resigned incredulity in his steel-gray eyes.

Already we begin to see some of the clear relational differences between the psychoanalytic dyad and the Buddhist teacher/student one—the more direct expression of anger, the parsing of personal reasoning with particular players. But there was more, much more, to come. After defending my innocence and good intentions, I was quickly engulfed in an unpleasant feeling of guilt. What was I to do—uninvite my mother to an opportunity for life-changing spiritual healing? This struck me as being decidedly un-Buddhist, almost satanic in nature. As I put my head in my hands and surrendered to the dreadful realization that once again the need to "save" others would come at my own expense, I settled into the feeling that there was no way out of this current jam. It was of my own creation, and I would simply have to find another lama and another spiritual community.

I expressed feelings of genuine remorse for having acted on impulse without bringing the spirit of mindfulness to the initial decision to include my mother in my spiritual life. Sitting with this latest wave of discontent, I tried once again to convince my analyst that there was another way to approach this scenario. In a direct challenge to his entire profession, I suggested that the lama would bring a larger, more encompassing perspective to this ostensible dilemma.

Before I summarize my analyst's efforts to minimize what he imagined the lama would have to say, I want to emphasize the overarching respect my analyst clearly feels for the healing impact of religious practice. Throughout our work together, he has been quick to reference religious and spiritual ideas in his own interpretive communication. From the very beginning of my analysis he struck me as being an analyst for whom religion and spirituality are held in high regard (see chapter 8 for discussion of the religiously attuned analyst). Alongside this reverence for spiritual practice and belief, he has expressed a clear awareness of the psychological complexities of spiritual practice, and he is attuned to the many ways it can offer healing and, conversely, be co-opted to reinforce places of psychic hiding and repression.

With this as a compensatory backdrop, he took me up on my offer to imagine a Dharmic approach to this latest relational complication. "If I were your lama, this is what I'd have to say: 'Your mother has precious human life. She too wants to be happy and free from suffering. Just be compassionate with her, and oh so patient. And remember—she is empty of inherent existence, neither fixed in her colorful behavioral tendencies nor tethered to driving you to the brink of insanity again and again.'" Then he sat back, looking annoyingly smug and self-satisfied.

Perhaps still determined to find a way out that bypassed any difficult feeling, or to avoid impugning my analyst for being too narrow in scope, a psychoanalytic simpleton with only a surface understanding of the Dharma, I told him that I liked the way this sounded. I felt relieved of the burden of self-obsession and hyperconsciousness. The anger, guilt, and feelings of entrapment were immediately assuaged.

"Must we always reduce my various life experiences to the particularities of my mother and father," I asked, revisiting a complaint I had expressed countless times in the past.

We sat together in silence, these two contrasting perspectives intersecting in my psyche. I felt both truths converge, knowing that the compassion I preferred to feel for my loveable and well-meaning but highly provocative mother could not be used to disown the reality of our rich and complex personal history. The latter needed to be suffered through consciously before the former could take hold with authentic roots in my own psyche and spirit. I needed both a personal and a transpersonal perspective to come to a place where my personal truths could be consciously felt and known within the larger container of universal truths I looked to as a reference point whenever a personal struggle arose. I felt pushed to consider what was left out of each tradition—my early childhood experience and development in Buddhism, and a non–self-centric perspective that made room for questions of ethics and morality in psychoanalysis (for further discussion see Rubin, 1996, p. 77).

Sitting with both perspectives, I began to consider how I might explore an authentic expression of compassion that included my own flawed self. How might I struggle through this recent interpersonal snafu in a way that did justice to the bodhisattva's way without dismissing the psychoanalytic point of view that I could not simply use the magic wand of mindfulness to run from my unconscious behaviors, beliefs, and relational tendencies? I needed a "double vision," an ability to stay with my self in all its intrapsychic glory as I simultaneously honored the much larger realities that were underscored in my spiritual practice (see Ulanov, 2007, for discussion of double vision from a Jungian perspective). The Buddhist teaching of impermanence, which is ultimately a call to cherish all beings, met up against the reality of the psyche, with its wily capacity to appropriate even the most sacred of spiritual teachings as an easy psychological exit point. Conversely, the psychoanalytic efforts to bring into consciousness the trap doors in my ego formation ran into the temptation to see all of reality through the narrow lens of this small but personally meaningful psychological tendency.

As has typically been the case, in these psychoanalytic forays I found myself wrestling with my relationship to spiritual processes with greater clarity. Here was a space in which I could examine whether or not I was able to truly bring mindfulness into the realm of interpersonal relationship. Could I tolerate sustaining consciousness of the reality of who I was at a given moment as I interacted with another flawed, eminently human being? On the other side of the healing equation, in my religious life I was coming to know my own psychic processes. Endless opportunities arose in which I might observe my own emotional and psychological reactivity to the lama's call to move beyond my own ego perspective.

Throughout these past two decades of traversing the divergent worlds of Buddhism and psychoanalysis, increasingly I have come to note my proclivity for identifying what these traditions respectively are not, rather than what I can rightly state they are. Perhaps this has something to do with a deepening respect for the basic unknowability that is the defining attribute of the psyche and the spirit realms. This expanding sense of surrender to not knowing what is in the unconscious, and what a personal awakening may entail, has lent itself to a playful relationship to both enterprises.

In his exploration of the psychology of religion, Paul Pruyser notes the playfulness involved in tinkering with the malleable concepts of psyche and soul, and in the "as if" games of all religious inquiry (1968, p. 330). In the spiritual and religious domain, the imagination is our playground. While religion has historically been a "serious" endeavor focused on such weighty matters as the nature of reality and how this reality came into being, so too it exists in a whimsical space between an individual's psychology and the world beyond. Contemporary practitioners of Buddhism cannot know the particular and historical truth of the Buddha's awakening. We can only imagine, and continually play with the rich and vast array of ideas that have been sent forth from his generation onward.

I broach the issue of humor and play in the spirit of honoring the levity that has been a saving grace and a constant through-line in my forays into both healing paradigms. As Nina Coltart has written, Buddhist centers are for the most part places of great mirth (Molino, 1998, p. 174). We are forever laughing at how seriously we take ourselves and our many losses and triumphs, despite the impermanence, suffering, and emptiness of self that are the nature of all things, including ourselves. In a Buddhist context even our most devastating losses have real levity in their midst. They too are empty of inherent meaning, which is to say they will give way to something else that is contingent upon the forever-changing conditions of our shared reality.

When the deliriously happy Indian saint Neem Karoli Baba, affectionately known as Maharaj-ji, was told by a grieving student that his life was filled with suffering, he smiled and said, "So is mine. But I don't mind the suffering so much" (Lemle, 2002). Here, after all, was an elderly man nearing death wrapped in a paltry blanket, shoeless, toothless, and impoverished. He wasn't forever smiling because he had somehow been spared the great suffering that is so pervasive to the human condition. His enlightenment spoke to an altered relationship to suffering, and not its extinction (Unno, 2006, p. 19). So too, when I began to learn more of my

Tibetan lama, who was forever breaking into convulsive belly laughs over just about anything, seemingly without having suffered loss that would give way to chronic despair, I was humbled to learn of his many early childhood losses and a traumatic flight from the Chinese invasion of Tibet in 1959.

In the psychoanalytic realm, both as an analysand and clinician, I have had countless experiences where tears turned into guffaws in an almost imperceptible shift from psychic overload to an ameliorative surrender to a sense of shared human reality. What began as my private turmoil, the loss, devastation, or mortification suffered, became a way into the human family, with its history of pain and suffering that was not mine alone to inherit. Laughter came when I realized that I was on a Job treadmill, with a million little Job-sters behind me, all suffering boils, death, judging "friends," and fist-shaking ire with the divine. These moments of playfulness have served as a needed reminder that making meaning, and moving toward spiritual and psychological wellness, need not be purely lugubrious endeavors. In that playful and creative space that D.W. Winnicott wrote of, between the "me" and the "not me" world, were whole systems for relating, composed of religious imagery, artistic vision, and richly arcane psychospiritual insight. Playfulness with others was the way in and out of pain.

Both Western psychology and Buddhist philosophy recognize that we are by our very nature relational beings. A playful spirit of good humor can help ease us into our efforts to live more consciously, to skillfully accept that we need another to push up against in order to know where we end and another begins. This is how our very ego formation comes into being, and how our evolving capacity for adult interpersonal relationship is sustained. If the historical Buddha had opted not to seek his small sangha of five after his awakening, the evolution of Buddhism into its current global incarnation would never have come about. Without the reality of Ananda, the Buddha's faithful servant, and the various monks who received the Buddha's teachings in contrasting ways, there would not be the richness of diversity that exists within the many divergent Buddhist traditions.

For Western psychologists of every school of thought, the human relationship is central both as a pathway for healing and as the source of primary wounds that prevent us from living happily and with a sense of meaning. It is for this reason that I have come to see comparison of the Buddhist teacher/student dyad with the analytic dyad as a potentially illuminating focus for those with the wish to explore how contemporary Western Buddhists are coming to know and integrate an ancient, psychologically demanding, and culturally challenging spiritual tradition.

It is through the eyes of teachers and students, and psychoanalysts and analysands for whom the Dharma is a significant influence, that a brighter light may be shed on how Western psyches are interfacing with this Eastern religious tradition, and how the contrasting endeavors of Buddhism and psychoanalysis continue to receive and shape each other in ways that may be surprisingly creative, lively, and generative.

is buddhism a religion? is psychoanalysis a scientific system?

2

EFFORTS TO DEFINE and ascertain the value of religion and religious experience have been with us since before the inception of the written word. The sense that there is "something more" than our discrete, incarnate personhood permeates almost every demographic in every part of the globe. It precedes even the separation of races that happened some 80,000 years ago (Horrobin, 2001). Yet as members of a human family who have coexisted for thousands of years with those who practice divergent religious traditions or no discernable religious tradition, we seem no closer to agreeing upon what constitutes authentic religious belief or tolerating those whose beliefs, or lack thereof, contradict our own.

Broadly defined, religion is a system for making meaning organized around symbols, ideas, and behaviors that are deemed sacred (Paden, 1994, pp. 10–11). What the sacred referent is may or may not include a supreme being, but it will in all faith traditions manifest in communities that invest great power and value in the shared sacred beliefs and behaviors. Religion, in my experience, is a way of orienting one's life toward discernable sources of meaning and constantly challenging the consciousness one brings to experience in the secular world.

The difficulties inherent in the process of discerning religious experience, and either condoning or seeking to eradicate it through whatever methods are *de rigueur*, are as operative in Buddhism and psychoanalysis today as they are in Christianity, Islam, and Judaism. Within the larger world of Buddhist thought, perspectives vary widely on whether or not Buddhism even qualifies as a religion, as opposed to a philosophical system or individual contemplative method. Particularly within the realm of American Buddhism, where the practice is at times almost entirely culturally decontextualized, it is not hard to find committed, long-term Buddhist practitioners who self-define as atheists, agnostics, and/or people generally disinterested in religion.

On the flip side of this contingent are the thousands of Asian monastic Buddhists living and teaching in the West. They have taken vows of chastity, poverty, and religious devotion, often sacrificing contact with their family of origin and their own spiritual mentors in order to teach and support Westerners interested in the Buddhadharma. The students of these monastics cover a broad spectrum of beliefs as to whether or not Buddhism is a religion, and they may or may not be people of religious faith. And yet, if pressed, they would likely all agree that the Buddha, Dharma, and Sangha—the Triple Gem—are sacred referents that organize our behavior and beliefs.

In the history of psychoanalysis, the answer to whether or not religious belief and practice has any ameliorative value individually or for society at large has tended to be a resounding no. Freud was instrumental in encouraging this attitude toward all things religious, despite the religious inquiry and theoretical musing that would pervade his literary opus. Yet Freud displayed a clear reverence for the impact of religion, having endeavored to address its inception by linking it with his ultimate theoretical legacy—the Oedipus complex. For Freud it was not possible to understand the formation of family units, society and culture, or our most primary experience with early childhood caretakers without also addressing the evolution of religious fantasy and practice.

Many contemporary psychoanalytic theorists believe that had Freud lived on, he would have come to recognize that inherent in religious experience was psychic content as rich and valuable as anything housed in his prized unconscious (Finn, 1998, p. 168; Loewald, 1978). These theorists speculate that in time, simply through continued clinical experience, he would have discerned that these two timeless containers of human experience—religion and the unconscious—are intimately connected and worthy of comparable levels of analytic attention and respect. Having spent considerable time in recent years with Freud's wealth of insight and theoretical blueprints, I tend to agree. Throughout his career, he was forever pointing to the relevance of religion as a necessary arena in which to explore human experience (see Freud's marvelous piece "On Transience" for a reverie with a particularly Buddhist tone). He was simultaneously, however, in the business of legitimizing psychoanalysis as a scientific endeavor through which behavior could be quantified and examined with precise and unerring methods. In his efforts to sanitize the psychic domain through identifying clear and well-defined causes for psychic disturbance, his approach to the psyche was almost surgical in nature.

I broach the topic of religion as it pertains to Buddhism and psychoanalysis for several reasons. As a Buddhist practitioner, I have been witness to a remarkable spectrum of fellow Buddhists whose feelings for and beliefs about religion are striking for their divergence. Over the years I have come to take note of the stark aversion toward religion on one end of the spectrum and the profound devotion to religious ritual and Buddhist deities on the other end. Having pursued psychoanalysis and psychoanalytic training alongside my continued Buddhist practice, I have been exposed to a comparable discrepancy in perspectives toward religion within the clinical realm. To this day there are clinicians who remain in strict adherence to Freud's original perspective on religion as a grand illusion, in contrast with those who actively integrate their reverence for religious practice and belief in their own clinical endeavors.

The fact of these potent feelings in response to the very idea of religion within Buddhism and psychoanalysis calls for the attention of practitioners and clinicians interested in the relationship between the psyche and spiritual or religious practice. In entering into this vast and challenging topic, perhaps we may find a greater clarity about the relationship American Buddhists are building both to their practice and to their teachers. We may also discover the particular ways in which psychoanalysis transcends or creatively works with the traditional boundaries of the analytic process. The alternative of bypassing altogether the questions of whether or not Buddhism is in fact a religion and whether or not psychoanalysis is something more than pure science seems to me to set the stage for a less conscious approach to our efforts at healing in either enterprise.

I propose that negotiating the question of religion will push us up against the reality of our beliefs, consciously or unconsciously harbored. In taking up the challenge to consciously explore our feelings and attitudes toward religion, we will look into our capacity for and understanding of what constitutes trust, devotion, and most importantly, dependence.

Spanning the many traditions within Buddhism and psychoanalysis, one finds a common history of addressing human suffering through a vigilant examination of the mind with special attention paid to issues of trust and dependency. With divergent tools, they have a shared wish to bring a spirit of open-minded inquiry to these central issues, with psychoanalysis tending to emphasize the mind's content and Buddhism its processes. Yet they have both struggled to bring this spirit of analytic inquiry and bare attention to the discussion of religion, where dependency plays a central role. It is my hypothesis that this murky, largely unconscious terrain has tended to infuse both healing dyads, where strong feelings about religion among teachers, students, analysts, and analysands alike have caused them to miss the quality of attention that both the Buddha and Freud encouraged.

The history of Buddhism involves a complex evolution from the Buddha's personal awakening to a global movement that is both religious and secular in nature. Despite the absence of a creator God in any of the various Buddhist traditions, striking contrasts have emerged between those that cultivate ornate religious systems with spirit and hell realms, and a clear hierarchy of people ordained to translate the Buddha's message, and those that are exclusively secular in practice and belief. As a starting point for this examination, I begin with the historical period of the Buddha, for wrestling with the question of Buddhism as a religion versus an individual process of awakening requires a look back at its inception, to a time in which religious faith was narrowly defined.

Scholars of Buddhism have depicted the religious climate out of which Siddhartha Gautama developed his spiritual teachings as one of pervasive religious dogma. The Brahmin caste espoused a Hinduism that was categorically favorable to some and altogether unkind to others. It was a tradition that emphasized the unquestioned importance of authority and deference to deities, religious leaders, and, not surprisingly, the Brahmin caste.

In response to this emphasis on religious authority, the Buddha proposed a method for engaging with ultimate reality that was heavily reliant upon individual experience. Despite the teachings of interdependence that would lay the foundation for Buddhist philosophy and psychology, the capacity to rely on oneself for affirmation of the value in Buddhist practice was a constant theme in his pedagogical efforts:

> Be lamps unto yourselves. Those who, either now or after I am dead, shall rely upon themselves only and not look for assistance to anyone besides themselves, it is they who shall reach the topmost height. (Burtt, 1955, pp. 49–50)

The Buddha discovered a radically new approach to religion and religious experience that relinquished the need for a God or gods, or for specially ordained interpreters of divine wisdom. Instead, he implored his disciples to do the hard work of turning inward and finding out for themselves whether or not his teachings on suffering and the end of suffering brought about the transformation they sought. The reverence he felt and expressed was for the true nature of the mind; discovering this internal truth was up to the individual practitioner.

In close connection with this teaching on self-reliance was a rejection of the Hindu emphasis on metaphysical speculation (Smith & Novak, 2003, p. 22). This reorientation from theorizing to personal transformation seemed to frame the practice of Buddhism as a vigilantly personal process that moved beyond the realm of religion, with its traditional emphasis on a divine referent. Deference to what is outside the scope of suffering within lived, incarnate experience was posited as a great and costly distraction. Thus Buddha told the parable of a poisonous arrow in his efforts to affirm the need to take necessary action that is freed from the "thickets of theorizing" (ibid., p. 25):

> It is as if a man had been wounded by an arrow thickly smeared with poison, and his friends and kinsmen were to get a surgeon to heal him, and he were to say, I will not have this arrow pulled out until I know by what man I was wounded, whether he is of

the warrior caste, or a Brahmin, or of the agricultural or the lowest caste. Or if he were to say, I will not have this arrow pulled out until I know of what name of family the man is; or whether he is tall, or short, or of middle height; or whether he is black, or dark, or yellowish; or whether he comes from such and such a village, or town, or city; or until I know whether the bow with which I was wounded was a chapa or a kodanda, or until I know whether the bow-string was of swallow-wort, or bamboo fiber, or sinew, or hemp, or of milk-sap tree, or until I know whether the shaft was from a wild or cultivated plant; or whether it was feathered from a vulture's wing or a heron's or a hawk's, or a peacock's; or whether it was wrapped round with the sinew of an ox, or of a buffalo, or of a ruru-deer, or of a monkey; or until I know whether it was an ordinary arrow, or a razor-arrow, or an iron arrow, or of a calf-tooth arrow. Before knowing all this, verily, that man would have died.

Similarly, it is not on the view that the world is eternal, that it is finite, that body and soul are distinct, or that the Buddha exists after death, that a religious life depends. Whether these views or their opposites are held, there is still rebirth, there is old age, there is death, and grief, lamentation, suffering, sorrow, and despair…And what have I explained? Suffering have I explained, the cause of suffering, the destruction of suffering, and the path that leads to the destruction of suffering have I explained. For this is useful. (ibid. p. 27, from Majjhima Nikaya, Sutra 63)

In this parable the Buddha simultaneously rejected an adherence to dogma that was endemic to his religious and cultural milieu and pointed to the very essence of religion across faith traditions. In his call for a vigilant attention in combination with action that is life-preserving, he underscored the process of assessing our place in the natural world through seeking a remedy to our basic fragility (Pruyser, 1968, p. 330). His call to bypass the sea of metaphysical musing associated with the religion of his time was not to suggest that questions of what lies beyond our earth-bound suffering were without merit (his teachings on after-life and cyclic rebirth are central to his path of enlightenment), but rather to bring a sense of urgency to understanding the causes of human suffering and their impact on *this* life.

The Buddha's process was one of precise problem solving, not unlike Freud's method of causation and determinism. He sought to address our pervasive sense of lack, to resolve the feeling of deprivation and fundamental separation from the people, circumstances, and skills we need in order to live fully and joyfully.

Noted Buddhist practitioner and writer Stephen Batchelor has addressed the provocative question of the Buddha's primary intention in sharing his teachings of personal transformation. For Batchelor, Buddhism as we know it today was founded upon an "authentic vision born from experience" (Batchelor, 1997, p. 9). Through direct experience, Siddhartha Gautama had discovered a process that included *understanding* anguish, *letting go* of craving, *realizing* its cessation, and *cultivating* the path (ibid., p. 11). His intention in presenting the four noble truths about the nature of suffering and its end was not to espouse a set of beliefs that must be adhered to with blind faith. On the contrary, from Batchelor's perspective, the historical Buddha proposed a courageous "confrontation with reality," not the easy default to consolation in beliefs (ibid.).

Batchelor takes issue with the institutionalization of Buddhism, which he suggests served to eclipse the Buddha's orientation toward practice. Instead, as the immensely personal process of internal investigation was appropriated by larger governing institutions, beliefs were laid down that camouflaged a highly experiential, action-oriented spiritual path. The fallout of this "religious Buddhism," for Batchelor, was that enlightenment was progressively presented as less accessible as it became inextricably linked to complex teachings and arcane ritual.

A proponent of "agnostic Buddhism," Batchelor emphasizes confrontation versus consolation. He equates a deep and abiding agnosticism with an ongoing mindful awareness that cannot rest upon consoling beliefs or fidelity to tradition. He eschews religious ritual and belief in rebirth as dependency on mollification and consolation, a failure to courageously engage with the reality of human existence.

Along the same lines, Buddhist scholar Robert Thurman has approached the issue of religion and Buddhism with a strong tendency toward secularism (although he is also a long-term practitioner of Tibetan Buddhism and displays a deep reverence for this more explicitly "religious" Buddhist tradition). In his extensive writing he has characterized religion as a belief-based system for making meaning that demands certain behaviors, ethical conduct, and participation in prescribed ritualized devotion (Thurman, 1998, p. 59). Thurman does not square Buddhism as a religion with the Buddha's teachings on avoiding theorizing so that we may cultivate a capacity for critical thinking (ibid.). Instead, he defines this ancient tradition as an "educational movement" that begins with the individual and works its way outward from there.

Thurman places a supreme value on individual responsibility for attaining freedom and enlightenment (ibid., p. 119). His analysis of the history of Buddhism, even as he describes its progression under King Ashoka—the third century emperor who actively sought to integrate the Buddha's teachings into government and society—focuses on individual consciousness as the catalyst for worldwide healing and change. In this way Buddhism is characterized as a decidedly nonreligious endeavor.

Batchelor and Thurman speak for a wide swath of Western, lay Buddhists. They find at their ready numerous examples of this secularized perspective in the Buddhist canon and in the personal biography of Siddhartha Gautama. Indeed, after his enlightenment, the Buddha used the local vernacular when teaching in an effort to reach people of all educational and socioeconomic levels (Cleary, 1994, p. 4). He was a pragmatist who professed by way of example a strong disinterest in any religious trappings that would dissuade humans being from recognizing their own buddha nature. There was no revealed scripture or divine personality in this examination of the mind. His path was a "way of life and thought…a religion of accumulated wisdom" (Boucher, 1988, 17).

As I consider these theorists of agnostic and/or secular Buddhism, who have contributed greatly to the oeuvre of contemporary Buddhist philosophy, I find myself wishing for the application of certain core Buddhist teachings to this question of Buddhism and its relationship to religion. In these discussions—in which I believe there is at bottom a noble intention to preserve the Dharma for people on both sides of the religious/secular divide—I detect an investment of inherent meaning in religion as a category of human belief and behavior that renders it a fixed phenomenon and not a product of ever-changing perspectives and personal engagement. Where is the Buddhist teaching of emptiness, or *shunyata*, I wonder, as it relates to the meaning, experience, and value of religion?

The doctrine of emptiness is complex and can leave students feeling easily befuddled. But at its bare bones, it expresses the Buddha's realization that because of our very impermanence we do not and indeed cannot have an inherent and unchanging essence. The Buddha posited that all phenomena, including people, concepts, institutions, and relationships, are empty of inherent, fixed attributes and absolute, defining qualities insofar as they are all affected by the changing conditions of all other phenomena. Thus he invited a certain spirit of play to our various investigations into lived experience and categories of meaning. When we understand that nothing has an essence impervious to change, then we may approach our wish for unchanging good fortune or absolute protection from suffering with a hint of good humor. From this perspective, no person or circumstance is without a dynamic capacity to evolve—for better or for worse.

When I apply this teaching to religion, there is a lively sense of possibility very much in line with the Buddha's description of emptiness as a "pregnant void." By its very nature, it is no longer a system of blind faith, thoughtless devotion, or childlike denial of human vulnerability. Instead, it becomes a way of relating to our shared human experience that is as fluid, imaginative, and potentially transformative as the consciousness we bring to our religious practice. In much the same way that marriage as an institution may, depending on the consciousness of the participants, facilitate remarkable depths of human kindness, responsibility, and emotional honesty *or* stunning acts of brutality, negligence, and psychological regression, religion too is a process that reflects the consciousness and maturity of its practitioners.

To suggest that it is defined by an uncritical deference to belief is to posit an inherent and fixed attribute that seems at odds with the Buddha's teachings on our basic interdependence and the emptiness of all form and phenomena—including religious traditions and our relationship to them. I propose that the effort to define Buddhism as a secular movement takes it outside the web of relationship that is the very nucleus of the Dharma. While the tension between individualism and relationship with others dates back to the original Theravada/Mahayana divide, it has important ramifications for contemporary practitioners in their efforts to integrate the Buddha's teachings into their everyday interpersonal lives. If Buddhist practice is examined outside the larger religious and historical context from which it emerged, it does indeed appear to be a profoundly solitary process (Finn & Gartner, 1992, p. 110). Although it is clear that the Buddha hoped to impart to his disciples the strong wish to transform *their own* minds and hearts, he did so with the belief that this transformation would usher in the steadfast compassion for others and ethical conduct necessary for generating both individual and collective life beyond suffering.

Buddhism, like all faith traditions, is a practice that is relational at its core. It demands of its practitioners a capacity to hold in tension one's own highly personal experience with loyalty and faith to established tradition, teachers, and ritual (Knitter, 2009). This process of discerning our own authentic experience within a given tradition becomes a necessary fuel for sustaining relationship to a tradition that bears fruit in our personal lives (ibid.). Religious practice, in this way, can become a remarkably edifying process of distinguishing the *me* from the *not me* world, of owning what is ours by virtue of projection (both helpful and limiting), our own ego consciousness, and what comes to us from the religious traditions already set in place (see Winnicott, 1971).

Theorists in the secular camp may ask why religious tradition is in any way necessary for contemporary practice. If the historical Buddha clearly modeled reliance upon one's own mind and heart for transformation, why tether this to prescribed prostrations, prayers, robes, and the hierarchy of relationships that compose much of the world of Mahayana Buddhism? Yet I believe we find significant psychological ramifications when meditation is lifted from its larger history of spiritual community and relationship to teachers. Buddhism has always been a process of imparting wisdom from one incarnate being to another; this outward form of "religious" Buddhism is how the Dharma has been transmitted and kept alive. We learn in this spiritual process through our belief (in combination with our critical thinking skills) that particular teachers who have shown themselves to be willing and able to impart their own wisdom may help us discover our own forgotten and camouflaged wisdom within.

The secularists may ask again why we need another to help us discover the true nature of mind, which is free from the delusional perspective of our conventional consciousness. They might point out that in his final stretch toward enlightenment Siddhartha Gautama sat himself under a tree, alone.

In response to this question, I turn briefly to Carl Jung, who repeatedly emphasized the psychological implications of cultivating a conscious relationship to religious tradition. Jung was among the very first depth psychologists to write of belief in religion and the divine as an indisputable part of human consciousness. In his efforts to clarify this inquiry into the nature of religious belief, he emphasized that his interest was in the psyche—he was not a theologian and therefore not in the business of determining whether or not God exists. Rather, he was interested in the psychic fact of religious experience and belief, and his empirical findings were based on clinical work with patients for whom belief was either dormant or conscious and operative.

In his clinical explorations, Jung discovered a striking corollary between psychological wellness and the capacity to make meaning through religious beliefs. It was not freedom from neurotic symptoms that his clients sought, but a connection to meaning (Jung, 1965). So too, he discovered that his clients could not hold their own pain and suffering alone. Something more was needed in order to bring value to the experience of loss, trauma, and psychological struggle. Ultimately, Jung posited a religious instinct that sought a conscious relationship with the divine (Jung, 1938, CW 12, para. 11; Ulanov, 2005, p. 149). To ignore this instinct was to render us vulnerable to all manner of addictive behavior and dysfunction. He likened this disavowal to the process of denying or repressing our sexual instincts and our physical need for nourishment.

Jung argued that human beings are equipped with a balance of psychic energy that instinctually directs itself into relationship with the extramundane. When this does not happen, the energy goes toward substitutes in the material realm, including food, sex, drugs—all the addictive substances and behaviors well known to clinicians worldwide. Worse yet, it will go, says Jung, toward our own egos, setting the stage for the various interpersonally destructive manifestations of egomania (Jung 1929, para. 55; Ulanov, 2005, p. 149). There is no ridding ourselves of this need to tap into our instinctual impulse that calls for a conscious relationship with religion and religious symbols.

Like the Buddha, Jung prized the impact of direct experience with "the ultimate" (Ulanov, 2005, p. 147). He sought to explore how individuals flesh out their relationship to the timelessness of archetypal inheritance, those influential patterns of behavior that we inherit—including the God archetype. In this way his theories also posed a critical relationship between the personal and the collective. One could not be substituted for the other. As it pertained to religion, personal experience was essential, and so too were the collective rituals and creeds of religious tradition. For Jung, the presence of tradition served as needed protection from the overpowering impact of the *numinous*. It was a veil through which one might sustain contact with the divine that could also serve as a screen that receives our projection and the personal content of our particular God imagery (Pruyser, 1968, p. 337).

It could be argued that since Buddhism is a no-God tradition, there is no *numinous force* from which one needs protection. I would respond to such arguments with the suggestion that the experience of emptiness, and by extension, the emptiness of self (no-self, or *anatman*), that is, the nondualism that lies at the heart of Buddhist doctrine, can be powerfully destabilizing in ways that may not be manageable when one's practice is exclusively or mostly a solitary experience. Emptiness and the "groundlessness" that practitioners are encouraged to enter into indeed constitute a *spiritual impact* that will invariably affect the student's psyche. As I will address in my discussion of Buddhist psychoanalysts (see chapter 8), the impact of this spiritual practice—both healing and potentially destructive—is well known to clinicians and senior Buddhist teachers alike.

Add to the influence of groundlessness the cultural hurdles that Westerners face in practicing Buddhism and we have yet more potential for overwhelming or confusing psychic impacts. American Buddhists especially come to this spiritual tradition out of a culture and history that is predicated upon individualism (see chapter 3). We prove our very worth through what we alone accomplish and sustain professionally and personally. In this way ours is an ego-based culture in which we pay homage to our own egos and those of others as the pinnacle of human development. The individual is held up as a kind of demigod who depends upon success in navigating the material world. To engage in Buddhist practice, however, is to constantly challenge our notions of individuality and ego, and of where and how meaning is ultimately made.

In the past several years, I have received numerous letters in response to my research on the psychological pitfalls of Buddhist practice from people who have embarked on a Buddhist path, largely in isolation. The vast majority have written to tell me of their meditation practice and the unexpected difficulties faced. Primarily, they write of overwhelming feelings of anger and distress that have arisen through this solitary practice. They wonder if this spiritual path is simply not for them. While I am not suggesting that all people who do not cultivate a relationship to spiritual teachers and community will have such experiences, I believe that it is reasonable to propose that Buddhism as a spiritual practice, like all theistic traditions, can cause us to confront disquieting and destabilizing truths, both internal and external, that we are typically unconscious of and poorly equipped to manage alone.

In the case of the solitary practitioners I have been in correspondence with, these truths often point to the reality of their emotional and psychological condition. And while these conditions would not be the sole responsibility of a Buddhist teacher or community, when practicing with these support systems in place, there would be far greater opportunity to talk about difficult or overwhelming experience with more seasoned practitioners who might offer insight into how to manage the force of increased consciousness that results from any serious effort at Buddhist practice. So too, they may have the good fortune to speak with a teacher or practitioner who consciously appreciates the limitations of the Dharma as a psychological healing system and may therefore recommend a spiritually attuned therapist or analyst.

The practice of religion across traditions speaks to the ultimate psychic *tremendum*—dependency. For Buddhist practitioners within an established community and in relationship to a teacher whose experience, insight, and commitment we defer to, there is a necessary reliance on others that may not come easily to those of us raised in Western, individualistic cultures. Senior Buddhist teachers throughout the Mahayana tradition speak openly of this Western struggle with devotion and dependency (Coleman, 2001, pp. 11–16; Sogyal Rinpoche, 1993, pp. 133–39). Through their experience as teachers in Western cultures, they have come to understand that American Buddhists, for the most part, have been inculcated with a strong suspicion toward any hierarchical structure that encourages relinquishing one's basic autonomy.

Within the Tibetan tradition, many lamas I have spoken with suggest that American Buddhists prefer to "take the Dharma on their own terms," sustaining a tenuous commitment to the traditional rituals of Dharma study and practice. They are, generally speaking, uncomfortable with dependency upon another person who may prove to be merely after an "ego boost." These teachers imagine that many of their students struggle with the cultural hurdle involved in this kind of dependency, where hierarchy is easily associated with abuse of power and efforts to demean another in order to bolster the self. In these conversations I have discerned an occasional sadness that the real gifts of the Dharma may remain unopened by Western practitioners whose conflictual relationship to devotion and dependency upon a spiritual guide (two processes that mutually inform the teacher/student relationship) prevent the critical process of internalizing the enlivening wisdom of another. In this way the Dharma can be mistranslated into something altogether different and more reductive than it is, becoming a "way of managing stress" that does little to soften or challenge a dominant ego position.

This push-pull dynamic that I have observed within my own spiritual relationship, and within my Buddhist community, is perhaps the very heart of the difficulty in embarking on this cross-cultural religious path. For those of us attracted to the Buddhadharma, this basic conflict between depending on self or ego and deference to another (in this case, one's teacher) may not surface for some time. Initially, if the attraction to the teachings and one's teacher is strong, it may lead to active participation in a community or in relationship with a particular teacher that is unquestioned in its value. In this way the early stages of this spiritual process have some of the romantic overtones of a new love affair. One sees only the good in coming to recognize the ability to generate happiness, one's own and others—a skill that is often wonderfully modeled by the teacher one has come to love and respect. These initial stages are often powerfully grounded in joyful feelings of freedom from long-term suffering and potentially life-changing discovery.

In response to this immensely influential experience, some Western Buddhists may go on to take monastic vows, a path that is clearly differentiated from a secular Buddhist practice and identity. The donning of robes, an act that (depending on the tradition) may include relinquishing future sexual relationship and accumulation of material wealth, is a process that lifts practitioners out of a prior secular identity and into a conspicuously religious role. I can imagine no other act that would bring into starker relief any discrepancy between our conscious and unconscious beliefs about who we are and who we wish to become. I have a genuine respect for Westerners who embark on such a path, given the lack of support, both financial and emotional, for monasticism in the West. So too, I can appreciate the unforeseen shift in life circumstances, or the influence of troubling experience within monastic community, that may cause some to ultimately take off their robes and return to secular life.

It is tempting to globalize from personal experience, particularly in Western cultures where the personal ego is held up as a kind of sacred entity. In my discussion of Western monastics who choose later to disrobe, and/or lay practitioners who opt for a more solitary practice, I am humbly proposing that our personal struggles with dependency may obscure its potentially healing nature, particularly in the realm of Buddhist practice. When Buddhism is presented as a fiercely individualistic process, I wonder if the baby of interdependence gets thrown out with the bathwater of rigid institutional hierarchy and disillusioning experience with teachers.

Is there a *tremendum* in the analytic space, one may ask? If so, does it too demand our conscious recognition? To answer this question, I return to Freud and the inception of his psychoanalytic movement.

Freud was a renowned determinist, interested in the cause and effect of psychic experience (1933). His approach involved tracing back in time the history of a current symptom, using the psychoanalytic process of "working through" to determine the psychic source for a given neurotic or psychotic condition. He brought a certain fervor to this method in a cultural milieu that paid great respect to the realm of scientific discovery. Freud sought to buoy the psychoanalytic process by protecting it from any association with personal revelation, faith, or systems of morality. He worked with great and unbridled devotion to create a system for investigating the human mind that was free of personal biases, emotionality, and value judgment—all categories of human behavior intimately connected to the religious domain.

The vestiges of this Freudian perspective remain in many psychoanalytic schools of thought. Yet despite Freud's wish to link psychoanalysis with science, few analysts would deny the personal revelation that is a dominant aspect of clinical work. There are relatively few psychoanalytic theories that can be proved or disproved through scientific methods (Storr, 1996, p. 110). The proof of wellness is almost exclusively in the subjective experience of the analysand. For no clinician is actually without personal biases that inform their observations of subjective experience (ibid.). There is not now, nor has there ever been, a way to consecrate the psychoanalytic endeavor as a scientific process.

So if it isn't science, what is it? The answer to this elusive question depends almost entirely on one's own experience within the analytic space. There is an unfortunate history in psychoanalytic communities of vitriolic debate about the nature of the analytic relationship, the end goals of clinical process, and how each party of the analytic dyad should engage this process. But ultimately, despite this widespread theoretical sectarianism, the process is defined by the consciousness and perspective of the two parties involved. My interest is in exploring whether or not spiritual and religious experience is relevant to the analytic dyad. Why should the spiritual realm matter if the point is to effectively address the psychic domain?

Today, spiritually inclined psychoanalysts such as Ann Ulanov, Jeffrey Rubin, Mark Finn, and Nina Coltart all write of the far-reaching reluctance to broach the issue of religion, let alone God, in the psychoanalytic world. Rubin speaks of the "conspiracy of silence" regarding religion in psychoanalytic training institutes and conferences (1996, p. 35). Mark Finn writes of the "religious phobia" still prevalent in psychoanalytic circles, as if it were in some way dangerous even to entertain a curiosity about the impact of religious experience on the secular world. Nina Coltart has written of the continued taboo on openly addressing any religious topic in analytic communities, despite the interest in "spiritual" endeavors such as meditation and yoga (Molino, 1998, p. 178).

In her marvelous compilation of essays on the relationship between religion and psychoanalysis, Ann Ulanov writes that within psychoanalytic circles, "religion has been seen as augmenting psychotic processes, as tempting the ego to fall into identification with archetypal energies, as offering an eternal mother's lap with instant gratification for pregenital strivings, or as offering ammunition for a punitive superego" (Ulanov, 2004, p. 40). This evocative summary of the traditional psychoanalytic perspective on religion offers insight into the nature of this historically unfriendly approach to the religious domain.

Ulanov goes on to point out that the chilly relationship between psychoanalysis and religion is not solely the product of psychoanalytic theorists. In years past she has also written of the "Christian fear of the psyche" (1986), tackling the edgy topic of aversion to the mere concept of psychic reality in many religious circles. The religiously observant have often seen the analytic endeavor as a process that eschews ethics and morality, and that is solipsistic in nature, encouraging entrenched self-obsession and naval-gazing. In many contemporary Buddhist communities it is not uncommon to hear teachers poke fun at how Westerners are forever "running off to see therapists," seeking consolation for their poor, beleaguered egos. Similarly, practitioners are often proud of their spiritual practice as an antidote to this unseemly psychoanalytic trend, particularly in urban settings where psychoanalysts are as commonplace as hungry pigeons. I have sensed a quiet shame in some Buddhist communities about the need for additional healing support, as if this need belied a tepid spiritual practice that had not been adequately prioritized and/or nurtured.

I propose that somewhere between these two places of aversion there is perhaps a middle way, where the value and/or impact of both healing endeavors might be approached with the friendly curiosity and evenly hovering attention posited in each respective tradition. But I would like to go a step further and suggest that when conscious relationship to religion and/or spiritual processes is absent in the clinical realm, the potential for psychological transformation is made more tenuous. Again, I feel the call to tread lightly, having worked with psychotherapists whose basic kindness, capacity for emotional generosity, and insight into the complexities of interpersonal relationship was immensely helpful and received with much gratitude. I cannot know whether or not some of these therapists were themselves people of religious faith; I can only know that our work together was valuable and generative.

I write now, however, as a practicing psychotherapist and analyst, as well as an older analysand, who has weathered more psychic terrain and has brought an increased spectrum of experience into the analytic space. My sense of what is possible between the analytic dyad, and what healing may look like and evolve into, has changed and expanded over the years. While I will address in greater detail the impact of spiritually oriented psychoanalysts in chapter 8, here I wish to suggest that when the psychoanalyst relies on something other than psychoanalytic theory or their own ego-based capacity for trenchant insight, the possibilities for what psychoanalysis might offer to the individual and relational experience are both augmented and deepened.

Ann Ulanov characterizes the clinical imprints of this more inclusive perspective as follows:

> Large implications arise for clinical work if this religious perspective is real to either, or both, analyst and analysand...The process of clinical work is set in a larger bowl, so to speak. We cherish the theories that guide our work, perhaps more so because we also see through them. They are not ultimate; they may be wrong, or opposing theories may be just as good. Theories are not the point; living experience is. We see our theories as symbols, as our own subjective-objective ways of trying to relate to ultimate mystery...In Winnicott's terms, we enjoy more elbow room. The discovery of truth, of what heals, of what works with this particular client, can come in from any direction, not from the analyst or analysand alone but addressed to both persons, surprising them, coming from between them, around them, through them, though they know it did not originate from themselves. (Ulanov, 2001, p. 142)

Ulanov is not suggesting that psychoanalysis and religious perspectives are the same. They are not, as she notes throughout her extensive writing on the subject of psychoanalysis and religion. Yet these divergent processes and perspectives may act to support both members of the analytic dyad in moving toward our own creative ability to make meaning, to be more receptive to what can help us heal, and to tolerate the mystery of when and how healing will manifest. With such an augmented perspective, the analyst ceases to be perceived as the sole catalyst for wellness and positive change. As proposed by Wilfred Bion in his analytic explorations into the ultimate nature of being, the analyst in the best-case scenario is not the *knower*, but rather the one pointing to what is unknown (Eigen, 1998b, p. 76). Such an analyst would have a steady stream of humility running through his analytic relationships, having relinquished the limiting tendency to insert theory in lieu of an open-minded curiosity about what has not yet been revealed to either analyst or analysand, and even about what cannot and will not be revealed during the course of an entire analysis.

I have come to understand this willingness to tolerate the unknown, and to be curious about what surprising element may promote healing in psychoanalytic work, as something more than merely *waiting* for an accurate interpretation or insight to arise. For when the analyst is consciously fueled and informed by psychoanalytic theory alone, by the need to link up human experience with interpretation, the analysand will often feel it. No amount of ostensible patience or absence of overt reactivity on the part of the analyst will negate the analysand's intuitive sense of the theoretical filter through which the analyst receives everything shared in the analytic space. This experience can feel like a psychological tightrope: the analyst seems to be offering nothing but time, space, and interest, but in reality, unless the analysand is in accord with the analyst's perspective, she may experience a psychic freefall, a sense of being dropped with no discernable safety net below.

Freud's esteemed colleague Sandor Ferenczi noted this process in his discovery of *professional hypocrisy* (1949). Ferenczi discerned an "exceedingly refined sensitivity" in the analysand, whereby schisms between what the analyst said and felt were traumatizing to the analysand in ways reminiscent of trauma suffered within dysfunctional family systems. If the analyst presents herself as polite, cool, even, and receptive while secretly she feels averse to the patient or some aspect of the patient's experience or personality, the dissonance will not go unnoticed by the analysand. Ferenczi proposed an open discussion of the analyst's genuine feelings so that an authentic trust and confidence in the analyst could be nurtured. This would help the analyst establish a clear distinction between the present psychoanalytic treatment and the original traumatic circumstance.

Years later, Gregory Bateson and fellow researchers Jay Haley and John Weakland introduced something similar with the *double-bind* concept (Bateson et al., 1956; Goldenberg, 1991, p. 63). In their study of schizophrenia and family systems, these theorists discerned the presence of maddening communication patterns in which a family member continuously receives contradictory messages from a person who cannot tolerate any direct commentary on or recognition of these contradictions. For example, a young child who receives verbal confirmation of parental affection that is not backed by psychological holding and authentic expressions of love will be left with a dissonance that can have disastrous intrapsychic and interpersonal ramifications. So too, the analysand can detect a comparable dissonance in analytic experience with clinicians who seem to patiently contain their wish to diagnose and make the lived experience line up with psychoanalytic concepts. But when analysts lack a conscious reliance upon something other than their own capacity to be in the know and skillfully traverse the psyche, the unspoken presence of analytic ego can be a real hindrance and has the potential to retraumatize analysands already ensnared in a history of tacit and covert feelings, expectations, and parental attitudes.

Conversely, when analysts work with a conscious sense of mystery and weave into their clinical endeavors an abiding awareness that they are in reliance upon something more than their analytic training, their colleagues and mentors, and their own psychological insight, I believe analysands learn of dependency in a way that is far-reaching and may ultimately allow them to continue life without the ongoing support of the analyst. Carl Jung wrote of his efforts to help analysands cultivate a reliance on their own internal connection with the Self archetype—that organizing agent of wholeness that is inherited from time immemorial—reaffirming that what both members of the analytic dyad rely upon is a shared and equal-opportunity phenomenon (Ulanov, 2004, p. 37).

In the Tibetan Buddhist teacher/student pair, the "working through" process is designed to awaken students to their own wisdom mind. The intention is not to cultivate a lifelong dependency on the person whose wisdom the student seeks and admires, but to point the student toward the source of this wisdom. This kind of dependency is practiced within the teacher/student relationship so that ultimately the reliance may shift from the teacher to the mind of clear seeing within.

The parallels to the analytic dyad are interesting to consider; there the experience of dependence upon the analyst must also be offered in the spirit of helping the analysand bring this capacity for trusting reliance out into life beyond the analytic domain. How this happens, and what allows for this increased ability to rely on something and someone other than the analyst, is open to speculation.

In my own analytic work I have experienced moments when I felt received through my analyst's open-hearted and open-minded state of consciousness. In such moments, words came later, after an affective *taking in* and *being with* that seemed to provide a kind of psychic fuel necessary for carrying on with whatever challenges life had offered up. Analytic encounters of this nature have typically been highly charged with a sense of unfiltered reality breaking into a worn-out ego perspective, where I have sensed my analyst's own well-tested capacity to be pummeled by life only to be restored by a shift in feeling and sensing that comes through immense courage, humility, and patience with the healing he trusts will come. These are decidedly primary-process moments that call to mind Loewald's characterization of the mystery and timelessness of a nonverbal and nondiscursive state of consciousness (Finn, 2003, p. 125).

While these are elusive analytic capacities I speak of, I believe that such moments transpire via an analyst's ability to surrender fully to a place of not knowing in combination with a deep faith that no suffering is beyond potential for transformation and healing. Such analysts are in steadfast reliance upon what in Buddhist circles we refer to as a *don't know mind*, where one's conventional perspective is in constant deference to a well-camouflaged but thriving wisdom that resides underneath the limited discursive mind of theories, comparisons, and expectations. What I found in my own analytic process, in which this deference was operative, was my analyst's ongoing faith in my own deeply buried wisdom mind, which he trusted would eventually emerge with the support of a more encompassing wisdom that held us both.

I think again of Bion, who wrote of this more contemplative engagement with the psychoanalytic space from which any worthy verbal communication must emerge (1970). I think too of Michael Eigen, who has written with great candor and poetry about the mystical and prayer-like experiences he has had in his ongoing clinical work (1998b, p. 11). Both theorists pay homage to an ultimate reality that transcends the limits of interpretive thought. They point to an analytic experience where dependency on theory and attachment to a given course of treatment, which Bion calls markers of a deadening use of memory and desire, are forsaken in deference to ultimate truths we must go within to find. For me, such experiences in treatment have been times of healing surrender for both myself and my analyst, where together we have moved beyond the temptation to reduce our respective humanness to what is readily understandable and easily articulated. I think of moments of great creativity, of seeing things with the fresh eyes that Winnicott speaks of in his psychoanalytic journey, where the feeling of having jointly entered into new territory is relished like a gift that was sorely needed but not expected (Winnicott, 1971).

What I have experienced in such moments as an analysand is the profoundly moving experience of feeling genuinely valued and accepted for the reality of who I am at a given moment. Anthony Storr writes of analysands who discover in their experiences with an analyst that another person is prepared to listen, to learn about them in all their grizzly humanness and still embrace their personhood. This comes as a true revelation (Storr, 1996, p. 123). What he is describing is something that transcends the psychological realm; it is heart-centered, potentially shattering work that speaks to our deepest capacity for trust and faith that we will not be destroyed by the person with whom we have shared so much. These are moments when the truth of one's suffering breaks out into the space between the analyst and the analysand and is held with reverence, and with no effort to transform it into something else. It can simply be, and by extension, the analysand too may be who they are more fully, more openly, and without the camouflage of shame or protective pride that may leave people feeling wholly unknown to themselves or others.

While I speak of the depth and mystery that is part of the analytic process, I do so with a respect for the parameters of the clinical realm. Analysts are not gods, nor are they necessarily particularly enlightened people. Sometimes they are downright limited by unconscious blinders and biases that can set the stage for all manner of abuse and acting out (Gabbard & Lester, 1995). In my own training I have been encouraged to forsake the temptation to imagine that I am necessarily any better than my analysand's parents or primary caretakers. For all I know, I might be worse! It is in part for this reason that I think it necessary to consider carefully the nature of this healing system, and what it can and cannot provide.

As a process involving two human beings equally vulnerable to the vagaries of environment, illness, and old age, psychoanalysis does not offer to the analysand the false hope of bypassing difficulties of our shared human vulnerability. It cannot protect people from future pain or loss. Rather, it can at best help us relate to the human condition, to the limits of our ability to stave off pain and suffering with increased equanimity and peace of mind, and with an increased trust that we are not alone in our suffering. In this way an effective analysis can orient an analysand toward a more abiding sense of gratitude for what is good and life-giving, and toward compassion for self and others when the pain we must all suffer comes to pass (Young-Eisendrath, 1998). I believe that such an analytic outcome depends upon the meeting of wisdom and compassion, for both analyst and analysand. This is no small achievement, but it is often quite different from what people expect when they begin analytic treatment, particularly if it is unconsciously imputed with magical or religious properties.

Psychoanalysis is not a religion, although it is often revered in the secular world, where religion itself is disavowed. There is a danger in expecting too much from this healing endeavor, only to be stunned back into the realization that we are all, healers and those seeking healing, prone to moments of delusion, where psychological projections loom large and the need to feel all-powerful reigns supreme. I think of friends and colleagues who in their own analysis are working through various losses and traumas, trying to weave together a psychic fabric that has enough give to withstand any future loss. But the tendency, I notice, particularly when there is no other healing endeavor where dependency is practiced, is to deify analysts, to make them larger, more all-knowing and powerful than they can humanly be.

There is an irony in this process of deifying the analyst and the psychoanalytic endeavor that may have something to do with Freud's heartfelt wish to be the "father" of a new tradition that would rival Darwinism in its impact on our understanding of the human condition (1917). His demand for allegiance is legendary; he sought a kind of religious devotion from his followers that was conspicuous for its absence of neutrality, an attribute that he otherwise prized in the clinical realm. In this way psychoanalysis became a substitute religion whose leader sought to implement an analytic credo that could not be questioned without severe consequence (see Gay, 1998, for extensive exploration of Freud's relationship to his adherents and naysayers within the original Viennese circle). In reference to the growing and increasingly rancorous theoretical debate over Jung's redefinition of libido as inclusive of sexuality but also a larger mental energy, and his treatment of religious phenomena as psychologically relevant, Freud responded (in a later conversation with Ferenczi), "We [not Jung] are in possession of the truth!" (Gay, 1998, p. 237).

Psychoanalyst and psychoanalytic biographer Charles Strozier has suggested that psychoanalysis has been burdened by this Freudian legacy of dogmatic hubris and disavowal of the religious domain; in psychoanalysis, needs that might be met in a religious practice are displaced onto a process and a person that are not equipped to tend to such needs (1997, p. 167). Strozier evokes Heinz Kohut, who also expressed a deep respect for religion as something wholly other than psychoanalysis. In his writings on psychoanalysis (as a system under the umbrella of science) and religion, Kohut wrote, "Science deals with cognitive issues, with explanations. Art deals with beauty, creating beautiful things. And religion is neither one nor the other. Its unique function is to shore up, to hold together, sustain, to make harmonious, to strengthen man's self" (Mason, 1980). He believed that Freud had erred in applying psychological systems to religion, which from his perspective was an altogether different domain.

I would not go that far. I suspect that Kohut was reluctant to trespass further on the sacred ground of psychoanalysis and risk further attack (he was pilloried by the Freudians for his ground-breaking theories on empathy as a psychological tool of investigation, an experience that was personally devastating). Yet I appreciate his efforts to protect both systems, to keep their meaning alive, and humbly to suggest that neither enterprise is equipped to meet the full spectrum of our human needs.

While I have intimated that my own analytic experience on both sides of the dyad has at times clearly transcended the finite realm of discursive thought, I suspect that this has been possible *because* I have a religious practice outside this endeavor that both allows me to tap into the potentially generative realm of primary-process states, while sustaining consciousness of having done so, and provides tools for tolerating the frustrations and limitation of the psychoanalytic process.

When my analyst seems not to understand a critical point I have made, or when he gives in to the temptation to offer theory in lieu of a deeper, wholehearted analytic attunement (see chapter 6 for Karen Horney's theory of wholehearted listening), or when he simply strikes me as being a dud who lacks the intellectual pizzazz of some sparkly analyst I know of, my Buddhist training can be particularly useful. I cannot give sway to these projections for long without remembering that my analyst, too, is empty of inherent meaning or a fixed nature. And just as spiritual training may protect the longevity of a given treatment, so too if misappropriated it can act as a defense against both feeling and expressing strong affect toward the analyst. It is in such cases that the analyst's own insight into and experience with spiritual practice and concepts is enormously helpful to the spiritually attuned analysand who may unconsciously utilize their spiritual practice as a defense against the emotional healing they consciously seek (see chapter 8 also for further discussion of spiritual processes co-opted as defense mechanisms in psychoanalysis).

Psychoanalytic theory also addresses the process of withdrawing one's projections within the analytic space, of working through the transference of early childhood experience with one's primary caretakers onto the analyst, where indeed the analyst may take on a beastly hue that rivals the grotesquely deformed woman of Naropa's fantasy. However, when it is not set in the larger bowl that Ulanov refers to, this process can easily be disrupted by the difficulty the analysand may have in sorting out her projections from the reality of the analyst who sits before her. Analysts are well aware of this analytic crucible, where the analysand has successfully brought into the analytic relationship her particular interpersonal experience and history and must either begin the difficult and fruitful work of exploring these projections, or defensively terminate treatment in reaction to the projections that are mistakenly perceived to be a current and external reality from which she must protect herself.

Recognizing the reality of emptiness as expressed in relationships has been, in my experience, a real analytic boon; the temptation to run from an analyst or analytic process that presents itself as having inherently problematic attributes, and/or built-in limitations for healing, has been tempered by an awareness (dare I say, belief) that no person, situation, or relationship is fixed in its meaning or content. Emptiness is a call to stay in relationship and watch it change, as it will invariably do. It is not a call to be passive, or to relinquish one's critical thinking skills; it is a reminder to bring one's attention to the perceiver and not the perceived. Analysands trained in this teaching, and who honor it as a core part of their religious practice, may indeed find that an analysis has reached its healing potential and opt to terminate, but ideally they would also find a depth of internal resources that allows them to stay until this healing potential has come to fruition.

This is but one example of how a conscious religious practice can support the analytic process. It is a way of keeping the analyst and the analytic relationship right-sized. Potentially, it may also be a way of letting the analyst off the proverbial hook when there is an ongoing temptation to blame him or her for a perpetual inability to wave a magic wand and eradicate the analysand's life struggles and suffering. This setup for finger-pointing may be tempered by the Buddha's toe-pointing, in which he indicated during a teaching by placing his big toe on the ground before him that we are living in a place in *this* life and on *this* planet, which is perfectly suited for the evolution of happiness and freedom from suffering (Thurman, 1998, p. 25).

My intention in sharing this small example of how a larger framework may support the analytic endeavor is not to use the language of one system to explain the other. My understanding and appreciation for the complexities of the psychological processes of projection and transference do not stem from my Buddhist studies and practice. I am indebted to the history of analytic theorists who have addressed these critical facets of interpersonal relationship and their impact on the analytic dyad. My intention is to suggest that I am better able to make use of each tradition due to my experience in both. For it is not just my analyst who can suddenly appear to be terribly deficient and altogether troubled. My lama has been just as vulnerable to the transference and projection that transpires in any intimate relationship. Understanding this human tendency to see others through the filter of prior life experience has also given me the insight and fortitude necessary to sustain a spiritual relationship that is challenging in every conceivable way. I bring my training in early childhood development, in psychological trauma, and in the complexities of the unconscious to my spiritual relationship, just as I bring the teaching of emptiness to my analytic work.

In recognizing what a particular healing enterprise does not address and the tools that it does not offer, I find myself better able to cultivate gratitude for what *is* addressed and offered. In my experience, this gratitude has been an effective antidote to the potentially corrosive feelings of frustration and deprivation that can arise in any worthwhile healing endeavor in which the needs we attempt to meet simply transcend the parameters of the system we are in.

The Buddha had much to say about this bottomless sense of lack, which can easily translate into a pervasive feeling of unmet needs that we long to fulfill (Loy, 2003, p. 27). In his second noble truth, he spoke of the craving or thirst (*tanha*) for something that will fill the reality of our basic emptiness. We look for ways to cultivate an unchanging identity that will spare us the confrontation with the truth of our impermanence. According to the Buddha, we have groundlessness at the core of our being, and the anxiety that ensues from this groundlessness sets us on a wild goose chase for a person, a substance, a job—some way to find ourselves on solid ground that will temper this root anxiety.

Is it too much to suggest that this thirst has been operative in psychoanalysis, and even in the evolution of Buddhism? I will go out on an analytic and dharmic limb, for I see this basic human fear that there may be no solution to the problem of suffering in the fervor of Freud's psychoanalytic theories and methods. He was, after all, a terribly vulnerable person who came up against the brutality of war, racism, chronic sickness, and the devastating loss of his own child and grandchild (see Gay, 1998). Freud was no stranger to suffering, and the remarkable fortitude and insight with which he addressed it left a legacy of invaluable analytic tools. But he did not consciously engage with the reality that our shared suffering has no solution, except to be endured with awareness that it connects us to all other beings and is a basic mark of human existence (the Buddha's three marks of existence are suffering, impermanence, and noself); hence he invested psychoanalysis with a power to address the totality of human experience that it does not have.

We cannot always prevent the loss of a child, for example, or a terminal illness that comes far too early in life. And most relevant to the Dharma, we cannot bypass the anxious search for a fixed identity and alleviate our fears of groundlessness through analysis of our personal histories. These experiences call for reliance upon something other than the consciousness that Freud identified as a cure-all.

As Buddhism has evolved into its current incarnations, it too has fallen prey to our human desire to be complete entities that lack for nothing. The irony here is clear: Buddhism as a path of awakening to reality is predicated on relinquishing the universal wish to hold on to anything that seems to offer absolute protection from our impermanence and lack of inherent, unchanging identity. Yet, as a collective byproduct of the many people who share this struggle, it too has sometimes been presented as an absolute answer to the full spectrum of human experience. Despite its historical disinterest in creeds, Buddhism has been just as disinclined as psychoanalysis to emphasize what it doesn't adequately address within human experience.

It is the rare Buddhist teacher (particularly within the Mahayana traditions) who will reference early childhood development, trauma, sexual abuse, or the impact of drug-addicted or severely narcissistic parents ill-equipped to care for their young children. For the most part they do not recognize these highly personal experiences as germane to the many ways in which we suffer or find freedom from suffering. When pushed by their contemporary American students, some will acknowledge that Buddhism is not in sole possession of all necessary healing tools. But in my experience, this is rare.

To suggest that Buddhism is a religion is to bring it squarely into the realm of mystery. Religions are systems that allow us to explore what cannot be known—the meaning of life, of death, and what comes after death. It is for this reason that I think it worthwhile to consider Buddhism as a religious practice that provides a method for tolerating and skillfully working with our unanswerable questions. Like psychoanalysis, it is not a system that can lift us above the confusion that is a pervasive aspect of the human condition. Life and death are indeed confusing, shocking, dumbfounding processes, and I propose that no capacity for compassion or equanimity can abolish this reality. Instead, I'm inclined to think that true enlightenment is the ongoing acute consciousness that we will forever be dumbfounded by lived experience, and that no system can offer a categorical truth that will spare us the perpetual funhouse that is living and dying.

With this heightened sensitivity to what each healing system most effectively addresses in lived experience, practitioners of one tradition may be encouraged to augment their approach to human suffering and wellness. Buddhist practitioners might more readily explore their early childhood experience, their emotional and psychological responses to their families of origin, and the important intersection of psyche and religious practice with therapists and analysts trained to recognize the nuances of the psyche. And conversely, analysands and people exploring healing work with therapists might more readily bring spiritual inquiry and practice to their efforts at wellness, learning to quiet the mind and to practice renunciation of the endlessly addictive substances of the secular world, and reminding themselves that even the most personal experience can be used as raw material for connection with and compassion for others.

Personally, I would like to see both traditions, mediated by the primary healing dyads, work more skillfully with the recognition that the human desire for wellness and healing covers a vast territory of psychological and spiritual experience that transcends the parameters of either system. It is for this reason, perhaps more than any other, that I think a conscious relationship to religion is critical to both dyads and traditions: it keeps us tethered to the reality of the unknown, ever mindful that while our efforts at healing are crucial, they are neither final nor perfect answers to the human condition.

asian monastic teachers and the western psyche

3

THE RELATIONSHIPS between Asian monastic teachers and their Western lay students are as rich and varied as any other kind of interpersonal relationship: differences in personality, tempo, age, or ethnicity may combine for a terrifically unique confluence of relational dynamics. Opportunities for outrageously funny and somehow surreal encounters abound. While students are sharing tales of a controlling boss, or the stress of some financial calamity, teachers will be hearing a radically different story of inflated ego railing against our basic nature, or a childlike expectation that somehow this student should be spared the suffering we must all encounter. And neither teacher nor student are likely to relinquish their position.

At the same time, another well-known reality serves as a tacit backdrop to these cross-cultural relationships: it is simply easier to communicate with people who share our dominant identity markers. People are generally wary of difference, intuiting the built-in challenge of communicating the nature of our differences in ways that can be understood or appreciated. The vast majority of Americans marry within their own ethnicity and socioeconomic stratum, and live in communities that are relatively homogenous, even in cities noted for their diversity such as New York, Chicago, or Philadelphia. There are many reasons for segregation, not the least of which is the basic human need to be understood in order to live one's life without undue complication.

The interpersonal experience between two people with divergent backgrounds is, indeed, a complex and potentially exasperating process. Its success necessarily involves the conscious wish to understand better and more fully the perspective of someone who is informed by a different history, perhaps another language and use of verbal communication, and even an altogether different view on the meaning and expression of human emotions. These differences and complexities are built in to the relational dynamics of the Asian monastic/Western student dyad, and opportunities for miscommunication are ever present.

The focus of my exploration is the content of these cross-cultural communications between Buddhists working as spiritual guides and their Western lay students. What happens when Westerners bring their personal experience, both spiritual and psychological, to teachers who come from radically different cultures? What is the nature of their communication, and how does each member of the dyad navigate a way through this relational maze? In order to answer these questions, I will begin with a look back at the evolution of the Western psyche.

Western students of Buddhism, whether we are conscious of it or not, bring to our spiritual endeavors a history deeply oriented toward the individual as the ultimate agent in learning, forming relationships, and the many potential manifestations of personal success or failure. The shift toward individualism as a cultural ideal began in the religious arena during the Reformation (Roland, 1996). This change brought a new reverence for the individual's capacity to build an intimate relationship with the divine. During the seventeenth and eighteenth centuries, Western philosophy fastened onto the idea of the discrete individual through the compelling theories of Locke, Hobbes, and Rousseau. The Enlightenment period fleshed out this reverence for the individual with Descartes' theories of dualism, which further separated one individual from another, mind from body, subject from object, and opinion from fact.

This bedrock of dualism, with its clear delineation between self and other, set the stage for the creation and development of psychoanalysis. Psychoanalyst and writer Alan Roland proposes that this history has given rise to the idea, ubiquitous in psychoanalytic thought, that one person's mental content can be clearly differentiated from another's. He posits that in this way the psychoanalytic process is the pinnacle of modern Western individualism. The analyst seeks to help the analysand live skillfully as a discrete being and to assume total responsibility for his own wellness or struggles. In this way psychoanalysis has endeavored to bolster the Western psyche, to enrich the sense of individual agency that is necessary in order to thrive within the culture of individualism.

Whether or not Western Buddhists have pursued psychoanalysis, it is the psychological self that they will invariably bring to their spiritual endeavors. This is the self that is the focus of traditional psychoanalytic theories, but it is also, after the previous four hundred years of Western philosophy, religious reorientation, and economic theory, the self of Western consciousness. In the words of Buddhist psychoanalyst Jack Engler, this psychological self is experienced as "an autonomous individual with a sense of differentiated selfhood having its own nuclear ambitions, goals, design, and destiny" (Engler, 2003, p. 50).

This Western experience of selfhood stands in stark contrast to the self as it is experienced in most non-Western, and certainly Asian, cultures (Geertz, 1979). In the Asian cultures from which most monastic teachers emerge, the "I" is not experienced as something discrete but instead as part of an interlocking relational system, a *"we-go,"* rather than an ego. Alan Roland has written that in most Asian cultures, this sense of "we-ness" as a defining attribute of selfhood results from communal upbringing, with extended ties to the mother figure and with emotional investment in the family (1996, p. 103). Jack Engler suggests that this non-Western sense of we-ness extends even beyond the relationship between two or more people to the relationship between the self and nature, or to the cosmos at large (Engler, 2003, p. 51). The fundamentally autonomous Western self is an altogether different animal than this Asian self, where one's very self-experience is inextricably linked to a larger body of consciousness.

Out of this we-go experience, communal cultures reinforce a remarkable capacity for empathic attunement, a sense of needing and wanting to preserve others as one seeks to preserve one's own self that is neither encouraged nor particularly valued in Western society. According to Roland, the extended Asian family depends upon this ability to develop immense interpersonal sensitivity, to attune oneself to the needs of others in deference to the stability of the collective we-go (1996, p. 103). Even with this cursory summation of the basic differences in Asian and Western concepts of selfhood, the complexities of the Asian Buddhist teacher/Western student relationship begin to appear unsurprising. Add to these differences in self-concept the contrasting concepts of psychological versus ontological self that are utilized in psychoanalysis and Buddhism, respectively, and we have a veritable dyadic tornado in the making.

Consciously or not, Buddhist teachers are in the business of helping others understand the nature of what Harvey Aronson refers to as the *ontological self* (Aronson, 1998; Engler, 2003, p. 52). This is the self conceived of as having an inherent and abiding nature. It is the object of Buddhist discourse and psychology, and the self Buddhist teachers address in their pedagogical and spiritual lessons. In the Buddhist view, such a self (*atman*) can never be found.

Tibetan teachers of all traditions are fond of using the "chariot" parable from the Buddhist sutras to explicate their teachings on self. In the parable, the chariot as a whole and enduring entity is *unfindable*. Instead, one finds a combination of materials, including wood, nails, and paint, that will eventually rust, fade, and disintegrate. Together, these variable and changing parts make up the concept of "chariot." It is a notion that serves our engagement with conventional reality. For if we were in the market for a chariot, we would need a symbol that denotes a single object rather than the reality of its many interlocking parts in order to communicate our interest and needs. But such a symbol does not address the nature of ultimate reality, which speaks to the unfindability of a single, unchanging, and defining essence.

In his teachings on no-self, one of my first Tibetan Buddhist teachers referred often to this parable when describing the body as similarly a combination of many systems, attributes, and substances—blood, water, oxygen, cells—that collectively compose the concept of "body" as one whole and enduring organism. This particular teacher was fast approaching middle age and seemed to relish in a rather macabre fashion the forever aging, failing, miserably decaying body as a terrific example of the fantastical falsehood of the idea of self as fixed and impervious to the many variables that provide life and ensure death. I found these teachings to be quite depressing, but sadly convincing.

The idea, I understood, was to liberate us from wayward notions of an ontological self, which is not findable, in order to engender a far deeper and more gratifying appreciation for what *is* real and thus truly findable— human kindness, compassion, the positive impact of saying what is true and helpful to others, and ways of conducting one's life with reverence and gratitude for beauty and goodness, which are impermanent and therefore precious gifts. Teachings on no-self were presented in the spirit of helping students unburden themselves and others of a false notion of self that one may be tempted to defend or protect in ways that are harmful and potentially destructive. If no innate self can be found, if the "self," like the proverbial chariot, is rather just an ephemeral collection of parts—family, culture, gender—why do we grasp at it so mightily? Why grasp at something as ephemeral as a rainbow?

These teachings were resonant and brought to mind the dreamlike traces of another form of consciousness and mode of living that might be more conducive to the happiness and sense of ease I wished for. Yet it was not always easy or possible for me to keep in mind that an ontological self can never be found, given the ever-present ego looming large in my psyche. There was another part of me—we might call it the psychological self—that longed for importance, for a sense of inherent meaning that could not be altered with the passage of time.

I brought this psychological self to my own analysis, where at times I talked about the confusion of wanting to let go of one kind of self while bolstering another. Was this whole Eastern spiritual endeavor a set-up for psychological splitting, where I consciously took pride in my ability to integrate no-self teachings into my waking life, while unconsciously I longed to be loved, to make a professional contribution that is meaningful and of some import, and to be wholly, completely, and inherently *me* without apology?

I am fortunate to have studied and participated in psychoanalysis during a time in which theoretical notions of self have grown more nuanced and compatible with non-Western notions of self. It seems probable that this increasingly augmented perspective of self and self-experience made it possible for me to work through the differences between the unfindable ontological self addressed in my Buddhist study and the psychological self that yearned for more "me-ness." Working with analysts who were at least conversant in Buddhist doctrine was also a significant asset, as I tried to reap the benefits of no-self teaching while simultaneously recognizing another self that perhaps rightly yearned for strength.

The self of Freud's era, which was largely intrapsychic in nature, a discrete organism of drives and body-based urges of sexuality and aggression, gave way to Melanie Klein's object relations theory. Here the child was thought to take in, or introject, her parental objects only to then project or hurl her introjections back upon the caretakers; finally, the psychological products of this process are reintrojected (1975b, chapter 1). In this way interpersonal experience is mixed with the intrapsychic tendencies of a Freudian self.

D.W. Winnicott advanced the notion of self as a more complex interpersonal organism in his famous assertion that "there is no such thing as a baby" (1952, p. 99). Instead, one sees only a "nursing couple." Through his several decades of work with mothers and their children, he developed a deep appreciation for the psychic impact and necessity of early psychological care and emotional holding that sustained the baby's sense of well-being. Experience showed him that without the mother's (or a committed caretaker's) unfettered attunement from the first days of its birth, the baby was not a viable being. There was we-ness built into the baby's very capacity for ego formation and development.

Many additional theorists would critique the discreteness of a Freudian self model. This development was reinforced with the advent of the intersubjective theorists, who turned their attention to the dynamics that evolve out of the space between the analyst and analysand (see Stolorow et al., 1995). These theorists formulated a model in which the self was found to be multiple rather than discrete and abiding, as in the Freudian model. As Philip Bromberg has written, we have as many selves as we have relationships (1991/1993).

I am not suggesting that the self I focused on in analysis, even given these increasingly fluid notions of self, was the same as the unfindable ontological self of my Buddhist studies. Rather, this fluidity around the self of analysis offered a more inclusive lens through which I could explore and appreciate the empty nature of the ontological self. This process was helpful in my efforts to tease out the difference between the self of Buddhist doctrine and the many selves of my waking, conscious life. The very notion of multiplicity seemed a psychoanalytic middle way, where my wish for subjectivity that could withstand the impact of others could co-exist with the groundlessness of no-self doctrine. I could be a me and a not-me in ways that were mutually supportive.

But what of Western Buddhists who have not had the good fortune to find support from wise analysts conversant in both languages of self? Even for those of us who have, what of the Western psychological self, writ large, and its efforts to sneak back into any conversation? Can it ever really be tabled? Can any dominant part of our being ever be truly absent, or is it like an animal constantly awaiting a time to safely reemerge from hiding?

Buddhist scholar Harvey Aronson offers insight into the complexity of Westerners practicing Buddhism with teachers who come from Buddhist countries (Aronson, 2006, pp. 61–85). Citing cultural psychologist Richard Shweder, he speaks of the "narratives" that infiltrate our interpersonal communication across cultures. According to Shweder, all human beings are confronted with intrapsychic experiences that bemuse us and elude our capacity for understanding. We may find ourselves beset with feelings of dread or discomfort that we cannot rationally link to a given experience. In such moments, we attempt to make sense of these bewildering feeling states through "explanatory motifs" that vary in dependence upon one's cultural milieu.

Buddhist literature and traditional Buddhist society present a "karmic narrative," whereby the difficulty of a current moment would be understood as the result of some prior intention or action that was destructive, unhelpful, or lacking in moral grounding. With this teaching of karma, which means cause and effect (not predestiny or cosmic retribution, as commonly thought), one would make sense of befuddling and distressing moments by understanding that prior actions lacked the right intention, or "wholesome karma." This understanding would then help to eradicate the current mental disturbance.

In contrast, Westerners are more inclined to default either to a "psychological narrative" or to a "somatic narrative." In the psychological narrative, difficult moments would be explored in light of some previous interpersonal experience that may have touched upon one's struggles to be understood or respected. Making sense of distressing and elusive internal states would necessarily involve one's own individual psyche rather than issues of morality and ethics. The somatic narrative would seek to find links between feeling states and physiological conditions such as food allergies, recent illness, or exercise.

Both narratives, the psychological and somatic, speak to the evolution of the Western notion of self as a wholly separate and autonomous agent for change that must tap into its own internal resources for mastery, pragmatic achievement, and acquisition. This notion of self, the collective inheritance from our Enlightenment forefathers, paved the way for an emphasis on self-help, the wish to bolster and reify this independent master of existence (ibid., 97).

These contrasting narratives and concepts of self come together for an alternately grand and subtle stand-off in the relationship between Asian monastic teachers and their Western students. In my experience, it is the Western self viewed through a psychological narrative that Western students of Buddhism tend to bring to their spiritual practice and relationship with teachers. We seek answers to our wish to have sturdy identities that can withstand the pressure of our secular lives. My sense is that while we're intellectually curious about the Dharma and the philosophy of no-self and emptiness, we do not (as a general cultural tendency) experience these teachings as personally relevant or applicable. It is for this reason, I imagine, that so many Tibetan lamas speak of their students' wish to take the Dharma on their own terms.

In general, I suspect that we Westerners, consciously or not, seek to reify rather than soften our discrete I, or self. We look to our religious teachers for guidance on living within Buddhist parameters of ethical and moral conduct, where compassion is freely expressed, but in such a way that our basic autonomy remains untouched. Solidly within a dualistic framework of self versus other, we struggle to integrate a spiritual system that has nondualism at its very heart. I propose that our attachment to self belies a culturally embedded fear: If we were to realize no-self, who or what would carry on our Western self journey? We have not yet found a way to reconcile the need to be self-sufficient in this individualistic culture with a we-go that has no perceived system of support.

Buddhist psychoanalyst Mark Epstein has discerned a marked tendency among Western practitioners, and certainly among psychoanalysts, to overemphasize the psychological aspects of Buddhist meditation practice (2007, p. 78). While he is referring to the psychological lens through which Western practitioners view the concentration practice of the Insight Meditation tradition, I think the observation is equally applicable to Western practitioners of Tibetan Buddhism. Epstein writes of the wish to utilize this practice to generate a greater sense of ease with all variety of emotional states, a process which can be greatly enhanced with the vipassana meditation technique of *noting*, whereby the meditator is instructed to simply note the many passing feelings and thoughts that arise in meditation without engaging the storyline that is built around a given feeling or thought.

In my Tibetan training I was encouraged to be mindful of the "proliferating mind" that endlessly seeks to escalate feelings and thoughts into stories and melodramas. This process of bringing mindful attention to the fleeting nature of all mental content, in both traditions, can support practitioners in softening their identification with feeling states and "dropping the storylines" around which whole identities can be reinforced, an experience that can also be a real and significant psychological boon.

However, when the Western practitioner unconsciously utilizes meditation practice to stave off feelings of coming unglued, of being an unruly bundle of disjointed feelings and thoughts—an experience that is common and commonly fought against—the real gold of a Buddhist practice is rendered intangible. There is a fierce temptation in Buddhist practice to cultivate a steadfast calm and peace of mind that somehow sits loftily above this chaos—the "monkey mind" as it is known among practitioners. In this way, reified identity as a *Buddhist*, or as a *serious and committed meditator*, may eclipse the far more demanding and spiritually nourishing experience of entering into fragmentation, of consciously being just the moments of disparate thoughts, desires, fantasies, rages, longings, and passion that collectively compose our waking lives.

The end goal of this practice, says Epstein, is not a sense of personhood less prone to fragmentation, but rather an altered relationship to the fragmentation that will likely ensue throughout our lifetime (2007). When Western Buddhists bring to their practice the culturally reinforced wish to shore our*selves* up, our spiritual growth as it is presented in the Buddhadharma is potentially stymied. We lose out on the possibility of viewing our self-construct through another lens, a process that may feel destabilizing but ensures insight into the nature of the psychological and ontological selves we bring to our spiritual path (Unno, 2006, p. 65). Consciously observing one's hard-won identities come apart at the seams tends not to elicit halcyon mental states, but it will proffer insight that can be forever life-altering.

How a Tibetan lama or any Asian monastic Buddhist teacher will respond and relate to Western students with their culturally reinforced relationship to the Dharma is determined by their particular philosophical orientation and personality (Fields, 1992, p. 279). In my experience Tibetan Buddhists are generally warm-hearted, feet-on-the-ground people with a pragmatic approach to life. With my lama and the many Tibetan monks I have met and spoken with over the years, I have been struck by their gentle sense of humor, their genuine gratitude for others, and a basic (albeit inconsistent) humility in their interpersonal manner.

The lamas and rinpoches I have studied with tend to bring this humility to their teaching style, which is not self-effacing, but rather expresses an attitude of willingness mixed with a small dash of resignation. One could almost call it a psychospiritual place of neutrality that the student may fill with his or her particular needs, struggles, and relational style. This too, I find, is very much determined by the personality and dominant pedagogical orientation of the teacher.

Mark Finn has compared four defining attributes of an "analytic attitude" to the approach and interpersonal dynamics that the legendary Buddhist teacher Tilopa used with his famous student, Naropa (Finn, 1998, pp. 163–67). These attributes are an attitude of neutrality, avoidance of either/or binary thinking, a focus on analysis of psychic material, and an attitude that is affirming and respectful. According to Finn, Tilopa's teaching displays these attributes. In this way Finn has discerned a history of "ethno-psychoanalysis" in which the relationship between Buddhist teachers and their students is another valuable source of psychic data (1992, p. 110).

While I agree wholeheartedly that the teacher/student relationship is a treasure trove of psychic information for both the teacher and student (and certainly for the analyst privy to such spiritual relationships), I struggle to equate the interpersonal dynamics within this relationship with those of the analytic dyad. Of course, my perception is informed by my particular experience, and I do think it is possible to work with teachers whose capacity for interpersonal neutrality, containment of emotional reactivity, deliberate and conscious expression of feeling, and a steadfast attitude of curiosity may feel deeply resonant with one's analytic experience. What I have found, however, is that the challenges of the cross-cultural nature of the relationship between Asian monastic teachers and their Western lay students quickly moves into and dominates the space of neutrality that Tilopa was perhaps more readily able to provide.

Naropa, after all, was not in pursuit of advice for his marital difficulties, nor was it his intention to study with Tilopa on conveniently scheduled Thursday evenings before leaving town with his family for the weekend. I jest, of course, but I do so to underscore the essential point that from Naropa's perspective, Tilopa was the most important person in his life, without exception.

He had no rival relationship or community; he brought his fullest efforts at being, and being with, to his teacher. In his many legendary trials—his willingness to jump into fire, to defame his character, and to lose everything associated with secular life—he was moving steadily toward a nondualistic merger, toward becoming one with the wisdom mind of his teacher. He was, in a sense, burning off the membrane of a discrete self in order to realize the interbeing that was his true nature. Through devotion to his teacher, Naropa was finding himself beyond the realm of conventional reality, where one's sense of "I-ness" is vigilantly protected. In this process one relinquishes the subjectivity with which one has formerly identified (a process I will examine in chapter 4 in reference to transmission), but in its place a greatly augmented sense of clarity and wisdom emerges.

In the urban and contemporary Western setting in which I have practiced, teachers are not typically prioritized, and certainly not as they were in Buddhist lore. They are respected and deeply appreciated, but they are understandably peripheral to a student's life in comparison to a romantic partner, child, or boss. While the teacher's humility (obviously not in all cases, but in most) may temper and assuage the dissonance they will necessarily feel with students who simply do not understand and have not typically been exposed to a devotional approach to relationship that enhances self-esteem and is psychologically safe, there is nevertheless another affective presence that I believe is the result of the basic cross-purpose within the Asian monastic/Western lay relationship.

Teachers, in my experience, will show immense patience with their Western students, and a deep curiosity about their interest in the Dharma. Any interest in Buddhism or meditation, no matter how ephemeral, will typically be greeted by teachers with genuine delight. But there is also a quiet and (at times) amused awareness that Western students, generally speaking, cannot and will not challenge their overarching psychological-self–based perspective. They are looking, *à la* Jung's caveat, to take what they like from the Dharma, to consume what is experienced as self-enhancing and leave the rest. This process of decontextualizing certain aspects of Buddhist practice, for example meditation or philosophical ideas, chronically infiltrates the teacher/student dyad.

It is not uncommon for Western students to bring a pervasive psychological narrative to their Buddhist teachers, who will in turn respond through a karmic narrative, as Aronson suggests, or with an emphasis on morally based choices specific to the more communal cultures from which they come. For example, a Western student may speak with a Buddhist teacher about a parent or child whose struggles with addiction have rendered the relationship untenable. The student, unknowingly, will tend to emphasize the psychological aspects of this experience, the anger and anguish of being a perpetual caretaker, and/or feeling chronically neglected or unacknowledged for the care he provides. The student may feel enmeshed and long for a "healthy separation." Also, he may express feelings of terror that he will ultimately lose his beloved family member in a way that is tragic and traumatizing.

Most Asian teachers are likely to interpret such experiences through both Dharmic and cultural lenses. Which is to say, they may respond to the separation and individuation Western students seek in a culture that is structured around clearly defined markers of self and other with reminders that all our present difficulties have prior roots in our own actions and misperceptions, or that there is a moral imperative to honor our family even in the midst of crisis or relational turmoil. The we-go nature of the teacher, his sense of self as intimately related to others, will tend to loom large, making it difficult to fully grasp the challenge a Western student faces when enmeshment with her nuclear family prevents her from the separation that in Western culture produces self-esteem.

Such a student would be well served in seeking psychological support from therapists or analysts rather than attempting to address these psychological difficulties with spiritual teachers. This is particularly important, as no Buddhist teacher who is genuinely committed to his students' well-being and growth will prevent them from expressing these psychological challenges. The lamas and rinpoches I have known will listen to any personal, spiritual, or intellectual conundrum a student presents and attempt to address it to the best of their ability. The Dalai Lama has spoken openly and with much humor about his students' wish to discuss even their sexual difficulties with him—a man who has been under monastic vows since he was a toddler. He does not discourage his students from addressing these matters, although he openly acknowledges the limits of his personal experience. Indeed, he may have a perspective that is uniquely helpful as it pertains to the spiritual aspects of working through trauma. That said, the psychological issues would largely remain unaddressed.

It is therefore up to students to recognize the nature and parameters of their spiritual endeavors, and to understand what aspects of self-experience may be more specifically addressed with a healing modality designed to address highly personal matters. For this reason, a student's frame of reference and knowledge base become important for discerning which issues and/or experiences are psychological in nature and not specific to spiritual and/or religious systems.

I would argue that Westerners cannot simply shelve the culturally informed need to be a viable unit of skillful agency and independence, or the wish to be gratified and successful professionally, romantically, and socially. Nor can our Asian monastic Buddhist teachers simply table their upbringing in communal cultures where dependence upon others is self-esteem–enhancing and the softening of identification with a discrete sense of I, or ego, is a monumental spiritual, ethical, and intellectual achievement that suggests a real maturity and engagement with reality.

Am I suggesting that Western Buddhists and Asian teachers are merely at cultural cross-purposes, locked in a perpetual stand-off of ego versus we-go? I suppose that if I believed this to be true, I would have forsaken my own Buddhist practice and ongoing relationship with a Buddhist lama years ago. This is not to say that moments when I wished to run and spare myself the difficulties inherent in this endeavor and relationship have never arisen. They have, and at times with an undeniable vengeance. The challenges of practicing an Eastern spiritual tradition within an ego-based culture are not always easily communicated, but I have experienced them as both enlivening and worthwhile. I have come to think of this experience as a cross-cultural *projective identification* process.

In psychoanalytic theory, projective identification addresses the universal tendency to disown parts of ourselves by projecting them onto others. Object relations theorist Melanie Klein described it as a psychological tactic of early infancy, whereby a baby who cannot tolerate his own aggressive feelings toward a primary caretaker whom he also loves hurls these feelings onto the caretaker, who is then experienced as being particularly aggressive and persecutory. This imperfect solution creates new layers of interpersonal complexity, and fear is exacerbated rather than reduced. But the idea and unconscious intention is to spare ourselves consciousness of the conflictual parts of ourselves, for instance, feelings of love and hate for one person that we cannot reconcile and/or seem to endanger us interpersonally (Klein, 1975b).

Psychoanalyst and writer Thomas Ogden has described this as a three-stage process. First, the person feels compelled to expunge some distressing aspect of self, which is projected onto another and experienced as coming from the recipient of his projections. Then the person is inspired to influence the recipient in ways that reinforce behavior, thoughts, and feelings that are congruent with the projection. Finally, after the recipient has internalized the projected content, the projector interacts with the recipient of his projections as if this projected content were the recipient's defining and dominant attribute or nature (Ogden, 1979; Wishnie, 2005, p. 28). In his later writing, Ogden emphasized the dangers of this interpersonal dynamic, suggesting that it can compromise the subjectivity of the recipient. In our efforts to evacuate parts of the self onto another, a dialectical collapse can ensue such that we no longer hold the tension of intersubjectivity, of one self meeting up against the reality of another self (Ogden, 2005).

There is a further danger that the person projecting his own split-off aggression onto another would then erroneously experience the recipient as being persecutory, perhaps even dangerously so. These intrapsychic maneuvers have manifested throughout history in all manner of defensive homicidal actions that can catastrophically escalate into full blown war (see Neumann, 1969, for extensive analysis of this deadly psychic process as it manifested in World War II).

Yet, as Ogden suggests, projective identification does not always have a negative outcome. As he became increasingly interested in the psychic content that lies between any two subjects, including the analytic dyad, his theory of projective identification began to include a transformational potential. Within a successful analytic relationship, the experience of receiving another person's projection can challenge the parameters of our self-concept. As in the example of Naropa's interaction with Tilopa, one gives up a sense of individuality "in order to free oneself from oneself" (Ogden, 2004, p. 191). In tolerating the psychological burden of receiving another person's projective identification, we may discover within ourselves new ways of being that come to feel expansive.

For example, an analyst may experience and project onto the analysand more interpersonal confidence and savvy than the analysand consciously possesses. When the analyst interacts with the analysand as if he were in true possession of these foreign attributes, the latter may feel a sense of disorientation. It may feel uncomfortable, but if the analysand is induced to pick up these attributes and capacities, it can also provide a healing and expansive opportunity to wrestle with the discomfort of stretching beyond a delimiting identity and sense of self. And the same is true for the ways in which the analyst may be changed. If an analyst takes on a new capacity for skillful aggression, personal confidence, or even his or her own wisdom mind from a patient who has projectively identified this content in the analyst, they may find themselves positively changed and enlivened.

Within the Buddhist teacher/student dyad, opportunities for projective identification are ongoing. On the negative end of the affective spectrum, both parties may project unwanted sexuality or aggression (two potentially inflammatory feelings I will address in chapter 6) onto the other, setting the stage for the kind of heated conflicts and passionate boundary crossing that were played out in the American Buddhist world in the late 1980s (see Boucher, 1988). Certainly for monastics, it is not surprising that these two fraught human instincts would find themselves easily disowned and projected onto others. I think, however, that Western students attracted to the Dharma are just as likely to split off from sexual and aggressive feelings, which are not easily controlled and can leave one feeling frightfully out of control, a state Westerners have particular aversion toward.

On the positive end of the affective spectrum, Buddhist teachers may project onto their students their own equanimity, compassion, and capacity for patience. This may feel uncomfortable to the student, even creating a subtle feeling of fraudulence. It is entirely possible that the student would know better—she might remember all too well the elderly man she pushed past in her effort to make the train earlier that morning, or her curt and entitled manner with the bank teller who seemed to be moving through water in a transaction that was not too demanding or complicated. But if the projection is strong enough, which is to say if it is a projective identification and the teacher sees these qualities as being dominant in the student, there is a marvelous opportunity to let these qualities press in upon the student, to move into and around a former subjectivity that leaves the student authentically changed. The Buddhist teacher may also projectively identify in the student a capacity for empathic attunement and dependency on the Buddha, Dharma, and Sangha that allows the student this sense of dependency, which may feel as though it has landed on her like a meteor from outer space.

Alan Roland has written of the reciprocity of empathic attunement in Asian hierarchical relationships, where each person seeks to support the other in their respective roles in ways that are affirming and ensure the maintenance of self-esteem (1996, p. 103). In this way the teacher would offer students guidance and critical feedback with sensitivity and tactfulness, and students would offer their teachers deference, loyalty, and respect so that each person would reap the relational benefits that bolster a sense of worth born out of their respective relational roles.

I suggest that it is the rare Western student of Buddhism who brings to his relationship with Asian teachers personal experience that resembles this exchange of esteem within hierarchical relationships free from corrupting efforts at humiliation, dominance, or subservience. Thus, such a feeling and capacity to engage with another who is defined by his or her role as being above oneself, in ways that are mutually supportive, would *have* to be induced by another; it is introduced into the student's psyche from the experience, history, and consciousness of the teacher. In this way the teacher's projective identification onto the student becomes a gift that if received and wrestled with may enlarge the student's sense of what is possible within his interpersonal experience.

From the student's side, there may also be ample opportunity to attribute to the teacher aspects of consciousness and cultural norms of selfhood that may be beneficial and growth-enhancing for the teacher. Jeffrey Rubin has suggested that with its emphasis on no-self doctrine and dis-identification with self-experience, Buddhism may be on the run from subjectivity (1996, p. 181). He points out that detachment from one's self construct does not mean that we won't also be powerfully influenced by our particular subjectivity. Psychoanalysis is, in part, a method for addressing the impact and nature of subjective experience, particularly when it remains largely unconscious. It is a tool for helping people engage more consciously with the reality of their subjective experience so that unwanted qualities, feelings, and personal history may be integrated into one's persona, even a no-self persona, which we consciously prefer and feel protected by. It is a method that honors the impact of the unconscious as a repository for life experience that we struggle to accept.

Students who have embarked on the analytic journey may bring a heightened awareness of what is ameliorative in coming to know their psychological selves. From a Buddhist perspective, this psychoanalytic work could have real ethical implications, in that a self that is more fully known might be less inclined to engage in the potentially dangerous aspects of projection, where the unknown or unconscious aspects of self find a ready home in another person, or country, or religion. Such students might impute to their Buddhist teachers this curiosity about their own selfhood, the nuances of personal experience that give rise to difficult and glorious feelings, desires, and perhaps even the secret wish to be better known by others, psychic warts and all. Perhaps in this way the Western student might offer their Asian teacher the silver lining of a psychological self, with its potential to feel uniquely present and accounted for.

In reconfiguring projective identification as something more than being trapped by or losing oneself in another person's projections, Ogden discerned a critical means of communicating. He encouraged analysts to explore their own internal reveries as a response to the patient's efforts to communicate an important self-experience (Ogden, 1994, pp. 228–31). I believe that the same opportunity exists within the religious pair, where the pressure both teacher and student may feel to move beyond who they genuinely are may be received as a sacred correspondence pointing to truths worthy of their attention.

The interpersonal challenges between Asian teachers and their students that I have presented are formidable, but they are in no way insurmountable. While I appreciate Jung's warning to Westerners interested in Buddhism that our own unconsciously Herculean efforts at evasion may trump any real spiritual growth that comes from this cross-cultural endeavor, I believe that the answer is not to walk away from Buddhist practice but to acknowledge the challenges and seek workable solutions. Buddhist scholar and feminist Rita Gross has suggested that the idea that Westerners cannot study and practice the Dharma is as untenable as the notion that the Chinese cannot practice Christianity—one's ethnicity does not determine relationship to spirituality (2008). She does not, however, deny that practicing a traditionally patriarchal discipline as a Western feminist will pose challenges.

Spiritual challenges need not send us packing. Rather, they call for increased curiosity and a willingness to learn more about the larger context out of which our chosen faith tradition has emerged (Aronson, 2006, p. 71). So too, these cross-cultural spiritual paths require each participant to learn more about his or her own unquestioned spiritual lens. We must ask, where did our sense of personhood come from, and how has it been shaped by the dominant religious belief system of our own culture? These are fraught questions, but if they are at least fleetingly entertained, there are immense and enriching possibilities in this meeting point of Western and Eastern selves, monastic teachers and their lay students, with their different pasts and unconscious imprints: who we are may come to seem both substantial and wonderfully lithe.

transmission and transference
the role of idealization in healing

4

THOMAS OGDEN speaks of the rediscovery process that takes place in any noteworthy theoretical endeavor. We do not, he suggests, discover new truths that had previously been buried in our shared human history, but happen upon truths that are continuously rediscovered throughout time (2005, p. 65). In Buddhism and psychoanalysis, traditions whose stark differences I have emphasized, there is ample evidence of this shared rediscovery in the role of idealization that suggests a common ground worthy of further exploration. In this chapter I will compare and contrast the means through which idealization in both healing dyads can facilitate an altered and salubrious experience of interpersonal and intrapsychic relationship.

In both enterprises transformation is sought within the primary healing dyad. In Tibetan Buddhism students seek to study the Dharma with the lama's guidance and eventually to take into their own heart and mind the lama's mind of clear seeing—his wisdom mind. The objective is not to obey the lama, but to let her wisdom mix with and enliven one's own buried wisdom. In psychoanalysis the analysand is also engaged in an active learning and internalization process, in which new ways of relating to oneself and to others are modeled by the analyst and experienced between the analytic dyad. So too, if they are ever to move beyond the analytic space, the analysand will internalize experiences with the analyst that activate the emergence of newly discovered qualities and attributes. In Buddhism this process is called *transmission*. In psychoanalysis it is referred to as the working through of *transference*. These processes are not the same; they involve radically different conscious understandings of how healing takes place for both members of each dyad. In Buddhism, transmission is unidirectional, with the lama transmitting his wisdom *to* the student; in psychoanalysis, transference is bi-directional where the analyst too will (counter)transfer her own experience and beliefs onto the analysand. Yet the idealization through which the Buddhist student and analysand view their respective partners serves a similar and critical function in these divergent relationships.

In my efforts first to explicate the common ground in transmission and transference, I will focus on the psychoanalytic theories of Heinz Kohut, the founder of *self psychology* and a theorist whose interests brought him unknowingly into dharmic territory. His use of transference in the analytic dyad revealed a certain reverence for how two-person relationships infuse and make viable the individual psyche. His psychoanalytic theories underscored an essential relationship between transference and idealization as a necessary psychic avenue toward individual and relational wellness.

Throughout the many divergent schools of psychoanalytic thought that preceded and followed Kohut, there are numerous theories of transference that posit different content and psychological purposes for transference. Freud described transference as a process in which the analysand projects onto the analyst particular attitudes and feelings harbored toward her primary caretakers, alongside her experience of the caretakers' attitudes and behavior. This transference of psychic content precludes the analysand from recognizing the projections, offering the analyst insight into the analysand through her unconscious reenactment of prior interpersonal experience. Freud referred to this reenactment as the *transference neurosis* (1912), and he urged analysts to distinguish this *transference relationship* from the *analytical relationship* (Storr & Stevens, 1994, p. 111). It was and still is in many theories considered to be a necessary part of psychoanalytic treatment.

Carl Jung expanded Freud's theory of transference to include the impact of archetypal needs. For Jung, transference cannot be reduced to the analysand's personal history with primary caretakers; it includes the vast influence of archetypal figures and relationships, or "identical psychic structures common to all" (Jung, 1929, para. 259; Storr & Stevens,

1994, p. 33). Jung explored transference with particular interest in how the analysand's previously unmet archetypal needs, for a father figure or wise old man, for instance, might be projected onto the analyst. Ultimately, he valued transference for its potential to affect both members of the analytic dyad, ushering in a transformation through a total engagement of both analyst and analysand.

For Heinz Kohut, transference is the crucible through which the analysand comes to develop missing parts of the self. Through transference, the relationship with the analyst gets woven into the analysand, into her very self-structure. He modeled this process on his theory of how the infant begins to develop a sense of self, a process that is entirely dependent upon the infant's experience with her primary caretakers.

Kohut's emphasis on relationship and the dynamics between the child and his or her caretaker as the catalysts for psychological healing put him at odds with the predominant psychoanalytic theory of his time. He challenged Freud's drive theory, which posited an intrapsychic reality dominated by body-based instincts of sex and aggression that cannot be fundamentally altered by the care a child receives. Kohut acknowledged in his theories the experience of *feeling* driven, but found that these drives were the products of a self that lacked necessary cohesion and structure (Kohut, 1977, p. 74; Strozier, 2001). For Kohut, the drives of Freudian theory were not biological realities with ultimate impact on the child's psyche. Rather, the grip of a drive resulted from unsuccessful primary care that created fixations in the child's psyche, which Kohut called *disintegration products* (1977, p. 170).

Kohut did not question the presence of drives. He continued to respect the reality and influence of our instincts, particularly in regard to sex and aggression. Where he broke from Freud was in his assertion that the human need for intimacy and union with others both precedes and goes beyond the impact of our sexual and aggressive drives (Strozier, 2001, p. 25). For Kohut, the way we express ourselves through love, sexuality, and aggression manifests our deepest and most abiding need for connection to others. In this way the self drives the instincts, and not the other way around, as in Freud's theory (ibid.).

Kohut developed a self psychology that emphasized the needs of the self to feel and be intact through critical interpersonal experiences from the very beginning stages of life. For Kohut, the self was not the ego or an agency of the mind, as posited in Freudian theory. Rather it was a structure within the mind formed out of developmentally necessary experiences with our primary caretakers. It was unknowable in its essence, like all reality, but could be studied in its various forms, both cohesive and fragmented. Kohut described the self as that secure feeling of being a unit in space on a continuum in time where there is a center for the basis of our actions and perceptions (1977, pp. 177 and 310). This sense of self, argues Kohut, provides an integrated and cohesive source for ambitions and ideals that are connected to specific talents and skills we later seek to develop and implement (Kohut, 1971, p. 177). With a healthy sense of self, we experience a sense of being the same person throughout the passage of time, despite changes in one's body and mind, personality, or life circumstance (ibid., p. 180).

It would seem that with his emphasis on self that is structured in the mind, Kohut's theory would not lend itself to resonant dialogue with Buddhism and its emphasis on emptiness and no-self. In the classical Buddhist view, what we take to be the self is in actuality a constantly changing product of the *five aggregates*: the body, feeling, perception, mental dispositions, and consciousness (Smith & Novak, 2003, p. 35). There is no "there" there, but each of these elements of "self experience" are misperceived as inhering in a self, which proves to be a deeply unsatisfying and frustrating process.

In contrast to these misperceptions of fixed self attributes, Kohut was after the nuclear rudiments of self, the living, life-giving variables that allow one to move through life without the chronic and devastating experience of being and feeling all to pieces. He was not interested in positing a fixed self, and not convinced that the discrete self of Freud's theories could ever be viable in the context of interpersonal relationship. Instead, he was interested in what allowed us to wake up one morning feeling intimately in connection with the person we were the day before. What were the necessary experiences in our early childhood relationships that made it possible to feel fueled by personally meaningful and unique relationship to one's life? What Kohut discovered was that the self was by its nature an *experience of relationship* taken into one's very being.

For Kohut, the necessary structures of self are laid down early in life. He spoke of the infant's *primary narcissism*, a term Freud used to describe the baby's initial feeling of wholeness and union, in which there is no discernable separation between it and others. Kohut viewed this primary narcissism as the beginning stage of a lifelong developmental line of transforming narcissism. Unlike Freud, who defined narcissism as "the libidinal cathexis of the self" and argued that narcissism interferes with more evolved forms of love for others, Kohut sought to legitimize narcissism as a critical investment in self that ideally undergoes several transformations throughout the various stages of life (1966, p. 270). He sought to redefine narcissism as an essential attempt at restoration and a necessary psychological fuel throughout life, in contrast with Freud's view that it must be transformed into dyadic love.

In Kohut's theory of narcissism, babies' initial blissful state precludes a feeling of separation between themselves and others. But this primary narcissistic state is eventually interrupted by the invariable frustrations they suffer in ill-timed feedings or bodily care that is not perfectly suited to their needs. These manageable, nontraumatic frustrations that interfere with their sense of seamless union are not readily accepted. Children long for the feeling of safety and peace that comes with experiencing themselves as intimately and perfectly attuned with the world.

In order to restore this peaceful and profoundly comforting early experience of self—the primary narcissism—children will develop two additional forms of narcissism whose success or failure will have critical implications for the evolution of their psychological well-being or lack thereof. In the first attempt at restoration children will attribute all things powerful and good to themselves. They hold fast to the original feeling of omnipotence and omniscience, where there are no limits to what they can do or be (Kohut, 1971, p. 25). Kohut called this the *grandiose self*, by which he meant a feeling of great and limitless capacity. But young children need another in order for this steadfast feeling of ability to take root. In their primary caretaker they seek a mirror for their grandiose self, someone to affirm that they are indeed superlative and powerful, endowed with marvelous talents and abilities.

In the second effort at restored union children will imbue another with the attributes of power and goodness. They will seek the desired feelings of safety and wholeness by being intimately connected with the recipient of their idealization. Kohut thus called this psychological process the *idealizing parental imago*. In this second effort to repair their primary narcissism, children would admire the caretaker's abilities and talents, his or her purported power and great capacity. Through this union with a powerful other, the feeling of wellness, of being okay in the world, would successfully be restored (Kohut, 1971, p. 28).

With this understanding of idealization as a necessary experience for transforming primary narcissism and building self-structure, Kohut continued both to build upon and challenge Freudian theory. For both Freud and Kohut, idealization is understood as the "mental process by means of which the object's qualities and value are elevated to the point of perfection" (LaPlanche & Pontalis, 1973, p. 202). Yet for Freud, even while idealization in early childhood is necessary for establishing the child's capacity for ideals, it is ultimately suspect and used to camouflage envy and aggression (a theme Klein elaborated upon; see chapter 6). Kohut, in contrast, emphasized the critical role of idealization, particularly of the young child's parent, as the only way to internalize the capacity for ideals, and thus a necessary developmental stage of transforming narcissism. Without this process, the child would be unable to build foundational parts of the self that would facilitate a meaningful adult life experience.

Kohut further distanced himself from Freud's understanding of idealization through his emphasis on how idealization is received by the caretaker. Through this emphasis we begin to see the interpersonal focus that challenged Freud's predominant drive theory. For Kohut, the two rudimentary efforts to transform narcissism through the grandiose self and the idealizing parental imago cannot provide the child with the self-structure she seeks unless the caretaker responds in a way that allows the child to internalize these responses so that they are ultimately experienced as belonging to herself.

The child cannot give herself these necessary internalized structures, but is dependent upon others to facilitate her development and security. For this reason, the caretaker and his or her particular reaction to these critical efforts at building a sense of self is experienced by the child as a missing psychic limb, and therefore, part of the self. Kohut coined the term *selfobject* to emphasize that from the child's perspective, the parent's function in responding to efforts at self-construction is taken into the child's very self-experience. The child and the caretaker's response to the child are woven into and experienced as one being (Kohut, 1971, pp. 45–47).

According to Kohut, the wholesome process of building self-structure occurs in two steps. With the grandiose self, the child would ideally elicit a joyful mirroring from the parent, whereby the child's sense of terrific power, strength, and aptitude is affirmed. Kohut spoke of the child's need for "the gleam in the mother's eye," her loving response to the child's efforts to feel more capable than he is during that particular phase of development. With such affirmation, over time the child would come to integrate this feeling of capacity into his overarching reality. Ultimately, this sense of ability would manifest as self-esteem and ambition that would become the lifelong self-structure that allows one to take pleasure in one's pursuits and feel capable of accomplishment (Kohut, 1966, p. 252).

In the idealizing parental imago process, the child's caretakers—her self objects—would happily receive the child's need and wish to attribute to them all things grand and powerful. They would neither solicit this idealization nor reject it, but would rather, through repeated and nontraumatic frustrations, unknowingly help the child internalize her idealizations so that the qualities and capacity she has invested in the caretaker may ultimately come to be the child's own ideals (Kohut, 1971, p. 28). Kohut called these nontraumatic disappointments *optimal frustrations*. They were critical for facilitating a "passage through the object," where the child's projections onto the parent moved into and through the parent before such parental qualities, emotional attitudes, and responses came back to manifest as part of the child's very self (Siegel, 1996, p. 71).

Kohut later developed the concept of transmuting internalization, a process in which the optimal frustrations would allow the child to internalize the parent's psychological functions without his or her personal qualities (ibid.). In this process these frustrations served as a way of keeping the parent right-sized, so that the child's own sense of what is ideal, rather than merely idealized and potentially fantastical, comes to fruition within her own psyche. When this does not happen, when the parent either will not accept the idealization or shatters it through trauma or unmanageable disappointment, the child is left with a chronic object hunger, a need to find in another the missing part of her own self (Kohut, 1971, p. 45).

―――――――――――――――――――――

When students of Tibetan Buddhism enter into relationship with their Buddhist teachers, they embark on a kind of Kohutian journey of restoration to a state of union intuited as having once been experienced but somehow lost. Through the relationship, the student first recognizes in his teacher the idealized qualities of compassion, patience, insight, and wisdom. In this process it is not just the teacher but also the relationship that is idealized. The student has moved close to a source of the wisdom, clarity of mind, and compassion that he seeks.

Traditionally the student must come to feel a deep devotion to the teacher that allows him to recognize these idealized attributes that the teacher alone seems to possess (Sogyal Rinpoche, 1993, pp. 135–38). The Tibetan word for devotion, *mö gü*, means "longing and respect: *respect* for the master, which grows deeper and deeper as you understand more and more who he or she really is, and *longing* for what he or she can introduce in you, because you have come to know the master is your heart link with absolute truth and the embodiment of the true nature of your mind."

Throughout the Buddhist sutras one finds countless references to the importance of devotion as the primary vehicle for the realization of one's own wisdom mind. It is explicated as the heart's path to the necessary respect and deference to the teachings that are imparted, or *transmitted*, through the teacher. A serious student would be utterly open-hearted, feeling tremendous receptivity to the teacher so that the teachings may enter the heart more fully. As in Kohut's theory, the aim would be to introject the teachings through the teacher, alongside her capacity for wisdom and compassion, so that the student discovers her own shared wisdom within. In so doing, the student receives the teacher's blessings through their "mixing of minds." It is a process that may take many years, after a student has been readied throughout many lifetimes, and it is transformational in its impact.

In order for this transmission to take place, the student would initially be attracted to who the teacher is, rather than what the teacher does. Kohut similarly theorized that it is not what the caretaker does per se, but who the caretaker is, his or her very personality, that is a necessary precondition for the "passage through the object," or transmuting internalization, that must eventually take place (1971). In the Buddhist dyad, the student would idealize the lama for his or her unbounded compassion and wisdom. This idealization would be expressed through the student's devotion—his unshakable commitment to his teacher—which communicates in part his longing to realize his own enlightenment or wisdom mind.

There is an intimate and essential connection between the student's idealization of and devotion to his or her teacher. Devotion can be understood as a necessary precursor for the development and impact of idealization. One without the other would prevent the process of internalizing the teacher's wisdom mind.

Yet the student would also be conscious of the lama's flawed personhood, the limitations that suggest the lama is not in sole possession of the wisdom and compassion the student seeks. Devotion should not diminish the student's critical thinking skills. If it does, the student will in all likelihood be unable to internalize what she reveres in her teacher. In his sociological study of Tibetan Buddhists, Daniel Capper found that when students were unable to recognize the fallibility of their lama, they were similarly unable to integrate the lama's idealized qualities into their own sense of self (Capper, 2002, p. 196). Instead, what ensued was akin to Kohut's object hunger, whereby the student longed for the lama rather than for the teachings and wisdom the lama endeavored to transmit.

In my experience, and in Capper's study, true teachers will invariably frustrate their students. These frustrations are not typically intentional, although I believe they reveal a semiconscious and highly intuitive understanding of the students' potential fixation with the teacher as a flawless Buddha emanation. As in Kohut's theory, teachers will ideally frustrate and challenge students' idealization in ways that are not traumatic, which is to say these frustrations will be optimal (although traumatic frustrations are also an unfortunate reality in the history of Buddhist teachers in the West).

Teachers may be abrupt or harsh in manner, impatient, or even downright rude. These qualities will typically be felt by the student as a startling disappointment. One's lama can morph before one's eyes into a mere mortal, no better than any other secular lowlife skulking through life with dubious values and interpersonal skills. Yet these keen disappointments provide a necessary and felt reminder to the student that no one person, regardless of training or ostensible insight into seemingly esoteric matters, is the lucky owner of wisdom. Rather, the sought-after wisdom mind is our shared nature—our buddha nature. We come to buddha nature through its living presence in another, when we mix our minds with the mind of our teacher through the transmission of teachings and blessings, and move squarely beyond the realm of dualism and false notions of inherent separateness. As in Kohut's theory of the self-object, the teacher is experienced as part of the student; their minds become one.

Tibetan Buddhist teachers are typically amused by the Western curiosity about transmission and Westerner's awe regarding it. They recognize in this curiosity a wariness, a lack of ease with the basic vulnerability and permeability that Tibetan Buddhists simply take to be aspects of our very nature. In transmission—the dis-identification with a discrete self that allows for a receptive absorption of another—the Tibetan Buddhist teacher merely sees the reality of how we "inter-are" (Bobrow, 2003). When asked direct questions about transmission, my lama tends to shrug his shoulders, suggesting that "everything is transmission—teachings, taking refuge, talking, giving and receiving blessings, sitting with, and celebrating together. You have to trick Westerners into this process by emphasizing rituals of celebration, or the experience of simple meditation. If you use the word *transmission* they run for the hills."

I find these responses amusing, but also convincing. I suspect that the concept of transmission and Kohut's selfobject transference evoke in many Westerners the unpleasant feeling of not being in control. In such processes the Cartesian dualism that is our cultural heritage is rendered too porous and malleable. Yet these processes, according to Buddhist doctrine and Kohut, respectively, are simply shared and inescapable realities. For Kohut and Tibetan teachers alike, they simply point to our foundational, lifelong interbeing.

This mixing of minds between Buddhist teachers and their students can be understood as a selfobject relation. When students begin their studies, they are likely to feel within themselves a sense of something missing: the capacity to tolerate life's many frustrations without undue shame or despair, a curiosity about others that balances with and compensates for self-obsession, and an abiding sense of gratitude rather than the resentment and irritation that so easily dominate waking consciousness. The mixing of minds is not a process in which difference between self and other is eliminated—there is a constant holding of both conventional and absolute realities—but rather an experience of turning toward the other with total absorption. Zen psychoanalyst Joseph Bobrow evokes Wilfred Bion's state of reverie, whereby the mother "tunes into and dreams her infant" (2003, p. 206), and Winnicott's "primary maternal preoccupation" (1956), in which there is a temporary dis-identification with self that allows the mother to enter more fully into her child's reality. From a conventional perspective, there is a clear object-subject dichotomy in these states. Yet there is also a profound discovery of another being's experience through a temporary and far-reaching disinterest in one's own subjectivity.

In his discussion of transmission, Robert Thurman draws on the theories of biologist Rupert Sheldrake to demystify the process and to underscore its basic logic (1998, p. 26). Science is helpful in this endeavor, appealing to our Western Enlightenment roots, which privilege reason above feeling and intuition. Sheldrake speaks of a "morphic resonance" in which one person's feelings, beliefs, or behavior will be experienced by another without the aid of verbal communication. In his research, he has discovered scientific evidence for the human brain's capacity to transmit and receive information without the conduit of secondary-process thinking. This basic receptivity and taking in of others, says Sheldrake, is simply the way we are wired.

Thurman builds on this theory of morphic resonance to emphasize its ethical implications for the contents of our own minds. If it is more than speech and action that affect others, it follows that we need to pay vigilant attention to our mental habits, which may affect others as much as our physical actions or gestures (ibid., p. 28). The ethics of this awareness come into stark relief when we explore the potential pitfalls that exist when a parent, analyst, or teacher is the recipient of a child's, analysand's, or student's idealization—the means through which we internalize another.

For Kohut it is critical that the parent accept the child's idealizations without exploiting them. In this way the parent would be a loving recipient without being sexually provocative or overstimulating (Kohut, 1971). The ongoing opportunities for frustrations that would be unmanageable to the child are carefully navigated so that neither the parent nor the idealization is compromised. Nevertheless, Kohut suggests that the parent will inevitably frustrate the child. If, for instance, the parent cannot detect a lie the child has told, he will be diminished in the child's eyes and no longer the all-knowing godly figure he had previously been perceived to be. When this occurs, the child will retreat emotionally, but if the frustrations have been "fractionated" so that the child can slowly release her hold on others as the sole owners of great capacity and idealized qualities, the child can instead begin to internalize some of these functions and attributes. In this way the parent sustains much of the mystique the child has invested in him, but not so much that the highly esteemed qualities and attributes cannot circle back to the child's own being.

Within the analytic dyad, an analysand who has suffered traumatically the loss of perfection of another upon whom he has relied, will return to the critical selfobject experience. Kohut called this the *idealizing transference* (1971; and see Kohut, 1984). He argued that the analyst will invariably be idealized by such an analysand, and that she too will frustrate her analysand's idealizations. Whether because of separations due to vacation, the analyst's inability to remember something discussed in a previous session, or minor lateness, the analysand's idealizing transference will be ruptured and cause an emotional retreat. It is during these critical moments in the treatment that the analyst's ability to interpret empathically the analysand's regression will facilitate the process of transmuting internalization.

In such experiences, the adult patient has the pivotal opportunity to build missing self-structure that may now supplant a previous search for a perfect other. He may begin to replace chronic object-hunger and the need for perfection in others with an empathic resonance and the ability to have and be led by his own ideals. I believe that there is a similar process within the Buddhist teacher/student relationship, although the intentionality and sequence of events may differ. As in Kohut's theory, the student will typically idealize the teacher, both for his or her capacity to understand the student's experience with great wisdom and for the teacher's attributes of kindness, patience, and compassion.

This idealization will be entertained for some time, but if the relationship continues, it will be challenged and frustrated by the teacher's shared humanness—his inability on a given day to concentrate on what a student is sharing, a teaching delivered with obvious impatience for the student's questions, a missed appointment, and so on. But these frustrations, while initially troubling, will help the student reorient from the teacher toward the teachings. As in Kohut's model, this is a critical juncture in the student's spiritual journey. If the frustrations are not optimal, the student may walk away from her spiritual endeavors altogether and never integrate the qualities and capacities she had formerly idealized in her teacher. And if the teacher cannot help restore a sense of trust and connection with the student when the frustrations are *not* traumatic, the necessary reorientation toward the teachings and the student's own capacity for wisdom may remain elusive.

For this reason, it is essential that lamas accept their students' idealizations without exploitation and with empathic humility, as in my experience they tend to do. As in any relationship in which one member of the dyad is endowed with particular and enviable gifts of special interest to his or her partner, the stage is set for potential abuse.

In the teaching and practice of Vajrayana, also known as tantra, the lama is especially endowed with necessary powers to provide face-to-face oral transmission. The feeling of intimacy between teacher and student is heightened in these practices, in which students visualize the lama as a living Buddha. These visualizations are intended to move the student toward openhearted receptivity to the lama's awakened mind so that it may mix with the student's awakened mind within. The lama is the living link to the Buddha's enlightenment.

Sogyal Rinpoche describes this process in the following way:

> To see the master not as a human being, but as a Buddha himself, is the source of the highest blessing...if you relate to your teacher as a buddha, you will receive the blessing of a buddha, but if you relate to your master as a human being, you will only get the blessing of a human being...Only if you come to see your master as a buddha can a buddha-like teaching come through to you from your master's wisdom mind. If you cannot recognize your master as a buddha, but see him or her as a human being, the full blessing can never be there, and even the greatest teaching will leave you somewhere unreceptive.
>
> *Masters themselves do not need our adoration* [emphasis added], but seeing them as living buddhas will enable us to listen to and hear their message and to follow their instructions with the greatest fidelity...When your heart and mind are fully open in joy and wonder and recognition and gratitude to the mystery of the living presence of enlightenment in the master, then slowly over many years, transmission from the master's wisdom mind and heart to yours can take place, revealing to you

the full splendor of your own Buddha nature, and with it the perfect splendor of the universe itself. This most intimate relationship between disciple and master becomes a mirror, a living analogy for the disciple's relationship to life and the world in general. (1993, pp. 136–38)

These spiritual practices are potentially transformative for the student in relationship with a "true teacher" who, as Sogyal Rinpoche says, does not need the student's idealization. Rather, the teacher serves as a container for the feeling and insight that the student seeks to integrate.

When teachers are idealized in this way, a feeling of great intimacy can ensue. As a result, an absolute integrity in the teacher is called for. During the late 1980s, the idealization of the Tibetan teacher in Western practice gave rise to a slew of power abuses that ultimately came to the attention of the media and the Dalai Lama (Fields, 1992, p. 367). Western students were unaccustomed to the nature of spiritual devotion required in order to engage in Vajrayana practice. So too, Tibetan teachers new to the West were unaccustomed to engaging in these practices with Western householder Buddhists in cross-gender dyads. The necessary idealizations gave way to the same types of sexual abuse and power plays that have historically occurred in clinical settings when analysts have been unable successfully to receive and contain the analysand's idealization (Gabbard & Lester, 1995).

For Kohut, such transgressions in a psychoanalytic treatment prevent the analysand from obtaining crucial missing parts of the self. Instead, she becomes reliant upon the object—in this case the analyst—to fill in for what she cannot build within herself. In both traditions these transgressions have at times caused practitioners and analysands to enter into sexual relationships with their teachers and analysts, where I suspect a similar object hunger may have eclipsed the integration of wisdom and healing that originally inspires most spiritual devotees and analysands on their healing paths. Ultimately, some of these Buddhist students left the Dharma altogether, feeling disillusioned and unmoored (see Boucher, 1988, and my chapter 6 for fuller discussions of these issues). I can only imagine how such experiences for students during this time may have rendered the very prospect of nondualism, or mixing minds, an unsavory and altogether perilous endeavor.

The stakes are high when idealization is operative. There is a devotional quality to idealization that is a necessary emotional state that readies oneself to reinternalize what has been projected onto and identified in the recipient of one's idealizations. This powerfully open-hearted, open-minded perspective leaves the student, analysand, or child particularly vulnerable. For this reason, unerring ethical conduct in the analyst, teacher, or parent acts as a critical safety net. Such integrity would be woven into the personality of these idealized figures, so that it is not specific actions that determine the depth of their integrity, but their very personhood.

For Kohut, the most important source of a well-functioning psychological self-structure is the personality of the parent (Kohut & Seitz, 1963, p. 370), in particular, the parent's ability to respond to the child's demands for mirroring and merger with firmness that is not hostile and affection that is not seductive. If a child is in relationship with a caretaker and must repeatedly contend with responses that are hostile, immature, or overstimulating in their seductive allure, she will experience unmanageable anxiety that prevents the necessary psychic growth that she naturally longs for.

Kohut's emphasis on the personality of the caretaker asks us to consider the importance of who we idealize rather than his or her particular actions. What are the interpersonal dynamics played out over time that mix with the child's idealization? Kohut explicates the dangers of a caretaker who lacks the necessary maturity to both receive and contain the child's need to merge with an all-powerful other. The parent is entitled to his humanness; he may have a bad day or a moment of striking regression without causing undue harm to the child. In the same way, Buddhist teachers can have moments of ill temper, make jokes that are poorly timed, or be distracted by cell phones and chocolate without preventing their students from moving forward on their spiritual paths. But they must be ready to tolerate their students' need and wish to see what is most alive and spiritually generative in the teacher, to be a living Buddha in the eyes of their devotees. If they cannot—if they continuously or defensively underscore their fallibility, or seem to feel a general discomfort with idealization—students will lack the necessary mirror for their own awakening to wisdom.

I am not surprised, however, that many well-meaning and otherwise excellent teachers find it difficult to be on the receiving end of their students' idealization. As the object of idealization, one may intuit the psychic weightiness of the other's needs. It can feel burdensome, a kind of psychological responsibility one does not feel equipped to assume. So too, for the highly attuned teacher (or analyst), I suspect there is an awareness that the idealization speaks to the presence of fear as much as it does admiration. In rejecting the idealization, it is possible that teachers and analysts are saying to their students and analysands, "Do not be afraid of me. I am not that powerful; what I rely upon is available to you too."

Object relations theorist Melanie Klein speaks of idealization primarily in regard to its defensive properties. She suggests that in early childhood there is a strong correlation between the need to idealize and the child's persecutory anxiety, the fear of being harmed by another who is experienced as being all bad (1975b, p. 273). For Klein, when idealization of self or other is active, there is a need to split oneself and others into clear binary categories of good and bad objects. If children have been unable to integrate their caretakers' good and bad qualities, the ways they are both responsive and frustrating in their caretaking, they will use idealization as reassurance of the caretakers' goodness. For adults too, according to Klein, when idealization is operative, its primary purpose is compensation for the fear of being harmed by another. In this way idealization would highlight only what is good in another, in order to leave the bad safely in the shadow: the stronger the idealization, the stronger the fear (ibid., p. 274).

But all is not bleak and hopeless in a Kleinian universe. She suggests that just as the young child has the urge to split self and others into wholly good and bad objects, there is another psychic stream that pushes toward integration. As adults, we sense the missing parts of ourselves—the parts we have pushed into the unconscious—and we feel a sense of deprivation without them. This intuition of what is missing in our being pushes us toward integration despite the pain that will ensue when we seek consciously to integrate the good and the bad within. Remarkably, says Klein, we know, albeit unconsciously, that it is only love that compensates for hate, and if we do not allow these opposing feelings to meet, the integration we push for will not transpire (ibid.).

Klein posits an inherent wisdom in this theory, an intuition that our own goodness, and the goodness of others, must be tempered by its opposite. It is our urge toward integration that allows us to accept our own deficits and limitations, and those of others. For Kohut, we need help in accepting this augmented and integrated picture of self and others. The optimal frustrations he speaks of, and the way these frustrations are empathically responded to in analysis, help us continuously shift our reliance from a perfect other to a more abiding sense of relatedness that includes our ideals and shared human imperfection, which he called an *empathic resonance* (Kohut, 1984, p. 77). But we need another to model this integrated way of being, and to cultivate within our own psyches the ability to be led by our ideals rather than merely projecting them onto another.

For Klein, our need to idealize is tempered by our efforts at integration. For Kohut, it is tempered by the receptive and fallible humanness of another. Through others' ability and willingness to deal with our disappointment in their mere humanness, we take into ourselves enlivening functions and attributes. There is hope in both theories. Jungian psychoanalyst and Buddhist writer Polly Young-Eisendrath speaks of the hope that is expressed in idealization within the analytic dyad (Young-Eisendrath, 2003, p. 305). In the process of idealizing the analyst, the analysand is communicating her trust that this particular analyst can help guide her to the healing and transformation she seeks. In this way idealization suggests that the analysand has a simultaneous faith in her own capacity to transcend suffering. If the analyst is imbued with the idealized qualities of insight and the marvelous ability to help others heal, then it follows that healing is possible.

I would argue that each of these theorists has addressed one critical facet of idealization. Klein's theories are resonant for me; I am aware of the chronic fear that co-mingles with the idealization of both my lama and my analyst. In my experience, fear is indeed the underbelly of idealization. As much as I love and revere these two healers for their wisdom, kindness, and persevering curiosity about my own psychospiritual journey, I am also intermittently afraid that the work we have done together will not ultimately manifest in a life of steadfast psychic and spiritual freedom. Mostly I am afraid of disappointment, of their potential to disappoint me in ways that are not optimal—afraid that their own hidden pathologies or woundedness might one day make a shocking appearance. And to Kohut's point, I fear that if I should suffer these disappointments,

my analyst and lama will be unable to address them in ways that are healing and compensatory.

At the same time, I have experienced the ameliorative impact of seeing
them both through the lens of idealization. In perceiving my lama as an
embodiment of awakening, of joyful awareness, of all that is good and
nourishing in the world, I have deeply imagined such a lived experience.
I have come to know, albeit fleetingly, what it would be like to go through
life with constant attention paid to what is possible, and with an unshakable identification with my potential.

With my analyst, I have come to know a deeper patience for the ways
my psyche seems to tack back and forth between the good and the bad
both in myself and in others. Having idealized his capacity to be patient
with my circuitous journey, I have taken in some of this tolerance for lifelong efforts at integration. I have experienced, without being aware of it
at the time, the Kohutian "passage through the object," and I have come
to recognize in myself qualities and capacities that had formerly been
housed by another.

In retrospect, I can also discern within my own analysis the positive
nature of having experienced my analyst as being particularly insightful,
at times even a gifted healer. These perceptions were, indeed, pointing to
my own unconscious trust that our work together was valuable, that it
had real merit because of his ability to help others work through the personal nuances of suffering. These idealizations, à la Young-Eisendrath's
theory, also suggested that somewhere within my psyche was a belief in
my own ability to effectively work through suffering and create a more
joyful life. There was tacit hope in these idealizations, providing a psychic
fuel that kept the analysis moving forward.

In my spiritual endeavors and analytic work, idealization has served a critical role. It has been a necessary psychological ingredient in these contrasting efforts at psychological and spiritual transformation. In both
enterprises, idealization has spurred on processes that have actively transformed the idealization into internal resources that have felt more stable
and less ephemeral than the idealization itself, which can so easily flip into
the fear of attack or disillusionment of which Klein speaks.

For Kohut, this transformation within the clinical setting involves reactivating the archaic early childhood needs for mirroring and merger that are ultimately supplanted by the ability to be sustained by a feeling of empathic connection, which he understood to be a primary source of security in adult life (Kohut, 1971, p. 77). This affective experience of being understood by another comes about through a combination of the analyst's optimal frustrations with effective and sensitive interpretations regarding the psychological retreat that may follow such frustrations. Through this sequence of interpersonal events, the analysand builds upon her own self-structure, which has internalized this imperfect mirroring and understanding, alongside a growing belief that the feeling of being basically understood and in empathic connection may be found in the world beyond the clinical space (Kohut, 1984, p. 79).

Transformation beyond the clinical setting, for Kohut, comes in several manifestations. In its first form, the analysand experiences an increased freedom in selecting mirroring and idealizable others who can nourish her growing ability to feel invigorated by interpersonal relationship (ibid., p. 77). Kohut likened a more cohesive self-structure that throughout life needs healthy people to meet selfobject needs, to lungs that are healthy and functioning but nonetheless dependent upon clean and fresh air to breath. This need for others remains throughout our life, but it is not indicative of the total transformation of primal narcissism that fuels our ongoing psychic journey.

Kohut argued that interest in the self was neither shameful nor problematic, and further, that it was a necessary and lifelong psychological tendency. Yet he understood that this interest must undergo critical transformation from our primary self-interest, including our original grandiosity and idealization of others, to an ever-expanding sense of investment in and connection to others, and ultimately, to the world at large. He broke from Freud in suggesting that dyadic love, our capacity to enter into and sustain romantic love relationships, was not the end goal of a transformed interest in oneself.

For Kohut, the first of these transformations manifests in creativity. In creative individuals, there is a psychologically porous relationship with the world that they inhabit, a sense of constant interaction in which they are forever discovering with the fresh eyes of a child the newness that comes from each new day and new encounter (Strozier, 2001, p. 157). With a creative approach to life we maintain connection to the child within, and by extension, to the child's joyous and masterful sense of ongoing discovery.

From creativity, Kohut moved on to the development of empathy, that capacity to step into the inner life of another through vicarious intro- spection. In empathy he recognized an essential analytic tool, and also the very breath of life—the means through which we feel psychologically real to one another (1978). Kohut linked this capacity to the baby's first merger experience with the mother, particularly with her face, where the infant could gain access to and discern her emotional state. As the mother's own identity, feelings, and action are woven into the baby's self, this primary empathy prepares the child to recognize later that "our basic inner experiences" are similar; we share a psychic reality to which we can become carefully attuned (ibid., p. 451). If cultivated, empathy provides a gateway into relational intimacy and the ability to see with depth and clar- ity the lived experience of another.

I suspect that even if Kohut had stopped with the achievement of empathy as the ultimate manifestation of transformed self-interest, clini- cians interested in Buddhist doctrine would continue to marvel at the par- allels between this Kohutian psychology and the bodhisattva's path. Yet he was moved to transcend the person-to-person relationship and con- sider a more evolved state of transformation, proposing the transference of self-interest to interest in the world at large as the final stage of one's transforming narcissism. This has a striking similarity to the Buddhist understanding of impermanence that gives rise to our realization of emptiness.

At the end of Kohut's developmental line was the recognition and acceptance of our transience. For Kohut, a healthy person will transfer his interest in himself to the world he has been in relationship with. He called this transformation a move into *cosmic narcissism*, in which one accepts fully his own impermanence and the continuation of the world he will leave behind (see interview with Robert L. Randall in Jacobs & Capps, 1997, 178–79). He called this the *curve of life*, in which we under- stand without undue despair that we are part of a life continuum that does not start with us and will not end with us. The world is something more than our own individual experience, and our capacity to move into this graceful recognition, argued Kohut, is our greatest psychological achievement. With this reconciliation to impermanence and connection to the larger rhythm of life and death comes wisdom, the final transformation of our primary self interest.

In the Buddhist teacher/student relationship, there is a comparable development from the dualism of self and other to the nondualism of shared wisdom mind. In the beginning stages of learning the Dharma from a Buddhist teacher, the student will bring an (often unconscious) grandiosity and idealization to the relationship. There is a wish to be perceived as a student supremely capable of navigating an arcane spiritual, psychological, and metaphysical system, as well as a need to idealize the teacher and impute to her great and powerful attributes. This stage may be long-lasting, and the student's ego may swell as he imagines that his insight, patience, and compassion rival that of the teacher. In this way the student of Buddhism may for a period of time simply revel in the gleam of the lama's eye.

Eventually, however, a good and true lama will start plenty of fires that the student will be asked to jump into (see Finn, 1998). In the Tibetan spiritual biographies, these "fires" are set with teachers' clear intention to continuously challenge their students' ego-identification and ready them to hear and integrate the Dharma. In years past I have experienced such fires as innocent "requests" that in retrospect I do not think have been so intentional. Rather, they seem to me more in line with Kohut's description of the analyst's or parent's inevitable shortcomings.

The teacher's requests may at first simply play into the student's grandiosity—the vestiges of the students' delightful feeling of exceptional competence, where no fire is too wild or too hot to touch. Eventually, however, such fires will likely serve as optimal frustrations (although they will not feel optimal) that over time chip away at the student's idealizations. If the lama is Tibetan, chances are he will make all manner of last-minute requests—to run errands; to pick up a visiting rinpoche at a far-away airport; to attend that evening an important event planned more than a year ago, where the student should also help out with the cooking and cleaning ("and by the way, do you know how to cook a goat?"). Such requests will often come without warning or apology. They may put the student in a situation that causes terrible anxiety—for instance, asking her to secure visas for a group of visiting monks who are scheduled to travel within 24 hours. In such requests there is plenty of opportunity for disaster, both internal and external.

If the student shares any of my personality attributes, she will likely contemplate finding another teacher—perhaps even another religion that will spare her these ongoing frustrations. She will question the teacher's judgment, maturity, even his basic psychological wellness. And indeed, there may be parts of the teacher that are relatively underdeveloped (e.g., an ability to plan ahead, to be pragmatic and organized). However, if the critical psychospiritual components of the teacher and the student are intact, the relationship will in all likelihood continue, moving the student into a more integrated sense of herself and her teacher. Perhaps suddenly, owing to her frustration with the teacher, she will feel only intermittently compassionate, and even occasionally short-tempered or moderately homicidal.

These decidedly human feelings will temper the grandiosity that may have initially spurred the student on the Buddhist path of study and contemplation. She may come to question whether she is in fact a secret arhat, a fully-realized wise being planted to model enlightenment in the midst of mere mortals, or perhaps rather just a garden variety neurotic with interpersonal problems. Chances are these compromised self concepts will accompany deteriorating idealizations of one's teacher. That said, I suspect that the average Western student of Buddhism will initially be more inclined to suffer a loss of idealization than to willingly take a conscious blow to his or her own grandiosity. After all, if a student finds himself in a situation in which he feels unbearably vulnerable or incompetent, he can always blame the teacher first. I have tried this often and it works—for a time.

Eventually, however, there is another path that awaits the Buddhist student after the mirroring and merging they have sought prove to be unachievable. It is a merging of a different order, with more elbow-room for the humanness of both teacher and student, that mixes with their shared buddha nature. But first, there is much that must be given up. And the wish to be glorified via association with high lamas or other Buddhist teachers, to participate in the mystique of an Eastern religion, or to strengthen one's ego-based position is usually the first to go.

Buddhist teacher and writer Joseph Goldstein tells a story about such a pivotal turning point in his relationship to the Dharma and his Buddhist journey (see Epstein, 2007, pp. 222–26, for analysis of this story using Winnicott's theory of unintegration as it pertains to the meditative state).

Many years ago he was on a silent Zen retreat, or *sesshin*, with the formidable Zen teacher Joshu Sasaki. They were engaged in the practice of the Zen koan, where students are asked questions with no clear answers, that seem to defy logic and therefore challenge the limits of discursive thought.

Several times a day, in interviews with the teacher, Goldstein was asked to solve the koan at hand (such interviews—opportunities to address one's experience with spiritual practice—also take place in the Tibetan tradition, but koans are unique to the Zen school). Despite his every effort to provide wise and cogent answers, the teacher would dismiss him, saying that his answers were "very stupid," or "okay, but not Zen." Eventually the teacher gave him a seemingly less elusive koan: "How do you manifest the Buddha while chanting a sutra?"

Leaving the interview, Goldstein began to prepare two lines of a sutra that he would chant for the teacher. He rehearsed endlessly, determined to get it right. Yet, with the mounting pressure of the interview and the backdrop of a childhood experience in which a singing teacher had told him to "just mouth the words," he became increasingly ill at ease. When the bell rang for the next interview, he entered and began to chant, bungling every word. It was a disaster, and one that touched upon an old and tender wound. When he finished, the teacher looked him dead in the eye and said with great affection, "Very good" (Goldstein, 1994, pp. 21–23).

This poignant story reminds me of many moments when I expected my own shortcomings and tender spots to meet with humiliation or something comparably unfortunate. These moments can unexpectedly reveal vestiges of our archaic grandiosity, our need to be supremely capable, to execute any task at hand with ease, and to be free from struggle. Despite great maturity and spiritual devotion, the urge to repair our earliest experience of perfect, unfettered being can and usually will make an appearance in the presence of a great and powerful other, someone whom we wish to be mirrored by.

Good teachers, however, will sense this unconscious desire to bolster oneself and to reify an identity based on one's own discrete acumen, talent, or prowess, which ultimately serves as a kind of psychic and spiritual armor. Because they are not analysts (or parents), they have pedagogical license to apply psychological heat through harsh or clumsy tactics, to step on toes and provoke their students when they unconsciously make these maneuvers. They may swat at such efforts as if they were bothersome flies. But if their primary goal is to help the student recognize his or her own wisdom and compassion, these harsh methods will skillfully burn away the student's defenses. The teacher will also intuit and respect the limits of these defenses. When this happens, a Kohutian empathic resonance replaces the need to be seen as exceptional and to see the teacher as beyond human fallibility. There is a deeper stream that flows between the teacher and the student when these barriers are removed, one which can carry our own humanness and that of the teacher.

One of the Buddha's primary goals was to help people engage reality and to do so free from reactive feelings of disinterest, aversion, or desirous attachment. His path was one of acceptance of our impermanence and the transience of all phenomena, but also one of joyful discovery, where we might come to find the endless potential for connection with others via our shared human vulnerability. He proposed a method for this discovery process that used interpersonal relationship between teachers and students as a model for the proliferating sense of union he hoped his path would facilitate.

The Buddha proposed that our view of others as inherently separate is flawed. As a result, we misperceive things and ourselves as discrete and existing without connection to each other. As adults, we cannot recognize the infant's experience of total union with the world beyond itself, and even forget our own prior experience of this unfettered being with others. Yet in the Buddhist teacher/student dyad and in the analytic one, we find ourselves and our relationship to the world around us through union with another.

In both relationships there is a reclaiming of lost bits of self and self-experience that come to us after we have projected them onto someone else. We seem to need another to come up against "in love and in friction" in order to build a cohesive conventional self and to remember that our true self, which both self psychology and Mahayana Buddhism agree is a fluid and ever-changing construct, is intimately bound in human relationship (Horney, 1945). In both systems, the "I" that we take at face value is in reality an ever-expanding gathering of others that starts with an essential *we*.

We cannot find ourselves, or be ourselves, alone.

culture and suffering 5

THE BUDDHA said that he had only one thing to teach—suffering and its end. The Buddha lived during a time of great turmoil, when radical changes in economy and government resulted in warring kingdoms and an eroding social structure. These dramatic conflicts and the tumult of nature—monsoons, drought, and flooding—left masses of people vulnerable to chronic deprivation, disease, and hunger. The prevalence of human suffering became the Buddha's sole focus. His method was one of profound internal exploration so that one's mind might more effectively mix with the world.

The Buddha posited the ultimate impact of the mind on one's environment, but he remained attuned to the specific challenges a given setting might create. He sent his disciples out into various communities with instructions to speak in the local dialects, to bring the Dharma to people in the ways that were most accessible to them. As the practice of Buddhism spread, it mixed with cultures that fastened upon the specific elements of the Dharma that most closely mirrored the dominant reality of their people.

Legend has it that throughout his youth Siddhartha Gautama had been spared any exposure to sickness, death, and material deprivation. As the son of a wealthy king, he was raised in a luxurious palace with private Brahmin tutors, instruction in the arts and archery, and beautiful young women. Twelve years prior to Siddhartha's birth, his father had been told that the young prince would ultimately become either a great monarch or a sage. With a strong wish that his son become a ruler, he made every effort to protect Siddhartha from the outside world and prepare him for a future of skilled leadership. But in his twenty-ninth year Siddhartha left the palace and viewed four sights that brought him up against the reality of suffering—an elderly man, a sick man, a dead man, and a monk. This was the beginning of his awakening. After his enlightenment under the legendary Bodhi tree, the Buddha spent the remaining forty-five years of his life teaching about suffering and its end.

What unfolded was a calculus of the causes and cessation of suffering, a lavishly enumerated blueprint of the mind. His view on suffering, while expansive and inclusive of the great variability in human experience, was nevertheless specific to the time and culture in which his enlightenment unfolded. Today this cultural legacy has begun to mix with the changing circumstances and life experience of the millions of Westerners practicing this ancient Eastern spiritual tradition. I propose that contemporary Western culture has created specific forms of suffering that Western students attempt to address in their Buddhist practice and with their teachers. And it is in this particular experience that another lens through which to explore the challenges of cross-cultural spiritual practice may be useful.

Psychoanalysis, like Buddhism in all its traditions, is also a culture-specific approach to lived experience. With its emphasis on individual experience, where the boundaries between self and other are taken to be absolute, it is perhaps less inclusive of the variability of human suffering than Buddhist doctrine. Nevertheless, with its exploration of how suffering is created *within* an individualistic culture, it can provide illuminating insight into the experience of Western Buddhists who bring their discrete, Western selves to their Buddhist practice and their spiritual teachers.

From a Buddhist perspective, suffering is intimately bound up with our basic misperception of reality. What we take to be real and fixed—ourselves, our bodies, the discrete existence of ourselves, others, and the world—is in actuality the endless interactions of changing causes and conditions. When we grasp on to things—ourselves, other people, feeling states, or situations—we suffer. Nothing stays the same, and nothing is sufficiently *there* to be grasped on to. Yet we try again and again, exhausting ourselves and frustrating others in the process.

This approach to suffering can seem rather straightforward when boiled down to its foundational elements. But the Abhidharma, a body of literature that emerged shortly after the Buddha's passing and synthesizes the psychological insights presented in the course of his 84,000 teachings, offers an intricate, enumerated portrait of the human mind and its endless capacity for suffering. In the Abhidharma one finds, for instance, references to the three marks of existence, three poisons, three forms of suffering, ten fetters, four faults that prevent us from realizing the nature of mind, six major afflictions, ten impediments, five hindrances, five groups of grasping, four delusions, and so on. One learns of twenty-eight physical phenomena that co-arise with fifty-two mental factors, leading to eighty-nine manifestations of consciousness, which evolve into a series of seventeen mind moments that are fueled by twenty-four forms of causal relations (Olendzki, 2008, p. 15). When we suffer, some element of this system has mixed with one of the fourteen unwholesome mental factors that ensure our suffering.

I have attended intensive Buddhist retreats at which these various facets of human suffering were systematically addressed. I noticed in my own initial response, and in those of my colleagues, an eager appetite for the marvelously concrete science of these lists, although there were also comical moments when eyes rolled back into weary heads. After so many years in psychoanalysis, which some Buddhist students have integrated with decades of support groups and endless twelve-step meetings, it can be exciting to discover a system that has clearly identified only three forms of suffering generated by six major afflictions. In the larger morass of healing methodologies available to my fellow Buddhist students to address every aspect of life that may be associated with one's sense of disease, ten impediments to freedom doesn't sound so insurmountable.

While it is beyond the scope of this chapter to address the breadth of these many teachings on the nature of human suffering, I will offer a cursory exploration of the central teachings that inform the responses of Buddhist teachers, particularly those in the Tibetan and vipassana traditions, to their Western student's various life struggles. I'll begin with the tale of Kisa Gotami.

This story is a favorite among Buddhist teachers and writers. It offers an emotive entry point into the Buddha's teachings on suffering and its end, allowing us to visualize our own relationship to the suffering we actively defend against. It asks: What or who do we hold on to in times of loss? Do we lose sight of our relationship to others in the midst of pain? Can we keep our hearts open and minds alert when engulfed in suffering?

It is said that during the Buddha's time, a young woman's only remaining child, an infant, had died. Out of her mind with grief, she clung to it, running from person to person for help. Nodding heads and sorrowful eyes left her only more bereft, until someone mentioned that a great sage, a buddha, was teaching in a nearby village. Perhaps he could offer the healing no one else could. She ran off to find the Buddha, sat through his teaching, and then approached him, still carrying her dead child.

"Please, Buddha, can you make a medicine that will return my child to life?"

He saw the grief in her eyes and the limp child in her arms. "I know of such a medicine; it is special and very pure," he said. "I need mustard seed from a household where no one has died—not a servant, a grandparent, or a friend."

Buoyed by this response, Kisa Gotami quickly left in search of the needed mustard seed. She knocked on door after door, begging for this missing ingredient. Those who answered were happy to offer her the mustard seed she needed, but no household had been spared the death of a family member, a servant, or a friend. Every household had known the suffering of loss and death.

Later that day Kisa Gotami returned to the Buddha, profoundly moved by the realization that the suffering she faced was everywhere around her. It could not be escaped. With this realization she grappled anew with the reality of her child's death and the increasing compassion she felt for all those who had suffered similar loss. The Buddha performed a special ritual and blessing for the child, and in the years that followed, Kisa Gotami became a great and wise devotee of the Buddhist path. She was ultimately seen by the Buddha as a fully realized being, an arhat, and came to be known as the Great Compassionate One (Unno, 2006, p. 142; see also Dalai Lama & Cutler, 1998, p. 109).

This story brings to life the Buddha's four noble truths, his three marks of existence, and the three forms of suffering. The first noble truth states the truth of suffering. With the reality of old age, sickness, and death, the stage is set for immense loss. It is for this reason that Buddhism is often mistakenly viewed as a pessimistic philosophy that harps on pain and suffering and seems to pay little attention to the joy and endless discovery of a creatively lived life. Yet there are three additional noble truths—something many Westerners interested in the Dharma tend to forget. The Dalai Lama is quick to remind students that the second noble truth identifies the *cause* of suffering—our efforts to cling to what cannot be clung to. When we grasp at a phenomenon that is by its very nature impermanent, we will suffer. When considering this second noble truth it is often said that pain is unavoidable, but suffering is optional. How we relate to the losses we will invariably endure, whether we feel cut off from the world at large or more intimately connected through the shared experience of loss, will either soften the heart and sensitize us to the shared human condition, or generate yet more suffering through the corrosive impact of resentment, entrenched grief, and aversion to mourning.

The Buddha identified three forms or aspects of suffering: the fact of sickness, aging, and death; the impact of change to ourselves, our environment, and other people; and the resultant suffering from all conditioned mental states—our tendency to link reactive behaviors and thoughts to our fleeting responses of pleasantness, unpleasantness, or neutrality. It is the last of these that the Buddha wished to emphasize, and as implied in the poignant story of Kisa Gotami, this is where we see that suffering can be optional. Aging, sickness, and death cannot be avoided. But grasping at what changes and avoiding the reality of what cannot change—the truth of impermanence—is a sure-fire method for suffering that seems to have no end.

The third noble truth states that there is an end of suffering, and the fourth noble truth identifies the way to this end: the eightfold path, a roadmap for the critical actions and thoughts that will alleviate suffering. In this roadmap, the Buddha offers specific behaviors and moral guidelines designed to help us reduce optional suffering. Through these tools and guidelines, students of Buddhism are reminded that happiness is a tangible option in life—despite the pain of loss and impermanence—but such happiness is never a random occurrence. It takes training, effort, and a clear wish for its development.

From the Buddhist point of view, suffering has a root cause. Just as happiness is no accident, neither is our suffering. In our efforts to be free from suffering, it makes sense to pull out this root from within our own minds, rather than merely snipping at the toxic weeds that otherwise endlessly proliferate (Dalai Lama & Cutler, 1998, p. 117). In this way the teachings seek to integrate the calculus of mind I referred to above into one pithy statement: *Gather all blame into one*. This *lojong* mind-training slogan serves as a reminder to those on the Buddhist path that when suffering arises there is a precious opportunity to explore the nature of this root cause. Seen from this perspective, the Dharma posits a quite hopeful approach to suffering—that if we examine its nuances with great attention, we may uproot it from our very being and come to live in the happiness and equanimity that is our birthright.

In his efforts to point others toward this birthright, the Buddha emphasized the primary roadblocks to happiness and internal freedom. The Buddha spoke of these psychic roadblocks as the *three poisons*. They are anger, sometimes thought of as ill-will or feelings of aversion; greed, also thought of as grasping or desirous attachment; and ignorance. Anger was identified as the first poison for its ability to sabotage and corrode our ability to feel and express compassion. Greed was taught as the impulse that binds us to all illusory sources of happiness—a process that ensures suffering as can be seen in the fallout of addiction, violence born out of romantic attachment, and present day acts of war fueled by attraction to power, global territory, or natural resources. (See chapter 6 for discussion on Buddhist doctrine of desire.) The last poison, ignorance, is posited as the root cause of human suffering.

In this foundational teaching, ignorance refers to a "fundamental misperception of the true nature of the self and all phenomena" (Dalai Lama & Cutler, 1998, p. 117). This misperception of reality is the root cause of suffering in the Buddha's teachings. When we hold on to feeling states, substances, jobs, or relationships that seem to generate happiness, we will sense the inherently ephemeral quality of all situations and objects. But if we do not consciously recognize and authentically accept that they are impermanent by their very nature, the happiness we seek will forever elude us. It is for this reason that the Buddha suggested that when we suffer, we should gather all blame into one, that is, recognize that all our suffering arises from one source—the ignorance of reality that is our shared human tendency.

When Buddhist teachers listen to their students recount stories of pain and suffering and the depression, anger, or frustration that result from these experiences, they will likely hear narratives of inner affliction, where negative mental states have prevented their students from moving toward reality. These negative mental states are called *nyon mong* in Tibetan and *kleshas* in Sanskrit (ibid., p. 199). These *nyon mong* are also referred to as obscurations, in that they obscure the true nature of reality, distorting the lens through which we view a given circumstance. In two of the kleshas—mistaken perception and wrongly placed affection—we erroneously perceive phenomena to have an inherent and abiding nature, and then focus our desire on these fleeting phenomena (Payne, 2006, p. 49). These negative states may be emotional or cognitive. From the Buddhist view point they are considered delusional because of their tendency to interfere with our true buddha nature—that subtle but abiding internal state of clear seeing freed from all negative emotions or thoughts (ibid., p. 37).

A teacher listening to a student express his ensnarement in the kleshas would be well versed in the antidotes to these negative and clouding mental states. Here the science of Buddhism enters in as a kind of spiritual medicine, a way to correct the mental defilements that are understood as illusory, and not our real and true nature.

In the Dhammapada, a treasure trove of clear and simple statements of the teachings, the Buddha says that there are six major afflictions. They are greed, hatred, delusion, conceit, doubt, and arbitrary opinion (Cleary, 1994, p. 9). Since these states are not considered to be intrinsic to the true nature of mind, their antidotes are sought in the concerted application of particular mental qualities and actions that can restore one's true nature. With this in mind, a Buddhist teacher might remind his student of the *six skillful actions*: generosity, morality, respect, service, listening to the Dharma and sharing it with others, and meditation (Goldstein, 2003, p. 75).

This approach to difficult emotions and thoughts is designed to help students restore their place of inner rest. When they are lost in greed and grasping, they might be reminded to find ways to give, so that they strengthen the part of themselves that is concerned for the welfare of others, and is generous and emotionally abundant. When furiously angry or suffering a feeling of righteous indignation, they might be encouraged to remember times when the object of their fury elicited in them genuine feelings of affection and love. These feelings, too, were strong but fleeting. They might be counseled to settle their minds on another facet of the story they have told.

Ultimately, as the Dalai Lama suggests, one might be encouraged to apply the antidote of wisdom to his or her clouded state of ignorance, to contemplate the true nature of reality so that one is freed from the hooks of delusion. To be present for these core teachings from the Dalai Lama and other great Buddhist teachers can feel like a much needed balm for a troubled soul. They provide a method for reframing the various manifestations of human suffering, so that we might begin to withdraw the power external circumstance is so easily infused with. These teachings are designed to help students shift the focus of their attention from the perceived to the perceiver.

In the Buddhist view, it all comes down to the quality of our own minds. If we change our minds, we change our world.

———————————————————

We begin to see how this approach to suffering challenges dualistic notions of internal and external, self and other. From a Buddhist perspective, a settled and peaceful mind will experience even a turbulent environment through a lens that both colors and creates what is seen. This nondualistic understanding of how we create our worlds through our perception is perhaps most readily seen in children, where a laughing and happy child ready to play might turn to a dour person sitting next to him on a train and thrust a toy into his hands. Because children see the world through a playful mind, they turn everyone—even the unwitting recluse—into playmates. So too, a miserable child who has entered into a full-blown tantrum will reject even the most enticing toy, or her favorite ice cream; when children's minds are troubled, the world becomes a troubling place.

For adults, the same is true. An agitated person will likely perceive fellow pedestrians on a busy city street as maddening irritants who interfere with his efforts to get where he's going. A curious and compassionate person may perceive the same pedestrians as "precious human lives," or simply as other sentient beings making their way through life. From a

Buddhist point of view, the important point is that divergent mental states interacting with the same external reality will result in radically divergent behaviors, and these in turn cause different circumstances. It is in this way that our minds change our worlds.

Given this emphasis on the nature and state of one's mind, meditation is seen as the primary Buddhist vehicle through which the mind may be trained. In vipassana practice students are encouraged to take note of the fleeting mental conditions—the many passing thoughts, fantasies, wishes, plans, and memories—that make up a given meditation session. These efforts to note the ephemeral nature of our internal worlds are designed to cultivate insight into impermanence. We may try to grasp on to one of these fleeting states—the memory of a great romance or even the bitterness of disappointment, which can fill us with a gratifying sense of righteousness—but over time, we begin to realize that these stories, feelings, and thoughts are insubstantial. There is indeed nothing that we can hold on to.

It sounds rather straightforward, but as any long-term meditator will have experienced, it isn't easy. It can be difficult to accept the painful losses we have suffered, or that fleeting chance for happiness that seemed not to materialize. While one meditates it is common for these places of fixation to dominate efforts at noting, or coming back to the breath, or touching a thought and letting it go. Instead, one may touch a thought and hold on for dear life. If the memories are painful, if we are reliving the tragic death of someone we loved, the frightening diagnosis we have recently received, or a trauma that left us with unhealed psychic wounds that seem beyond repair, these meditation sessions can feel as though they have the power to kill. It is remarkable just how painful a quiet period of sitting can be.

The Buddha made countless efforts to address the nature of these internal struggles. He taught that when we are in the grips of a wily mind with a tendency to ruminate, to fantasize about a better lot in life, or to get lost in efforts to keep itself entertained and distracted from the reality of the human condition, meditation can be utterly ineffectual. These difficulties, which the Buddha called fetters, hindrances, and impediments, interfere with the meditation practice that if properly engaged would ultimately ensure our freedom.

Briefly stated, the five hindrances (which are also the first five fetters) are sense desire or grasping, states of aversion that include anger and ill will, sloth and torpor (including feelings of sluggishness and laziness), restlessness, and lastly, doubt and uncertainty (Rubin, 1996, p. 132).

Joseph Goldstein describes the impact of these hindrances in this imaginative teaching:

> Imagine a pond of clear water. Sense desire is like the water becoming colored with pretty dyes. We become entranced with the beauty and intricacy of the color and so do not penetrate to the depths. Anger, ill will, aversion, is like boiling water. Water that is boiling is very turbulent. You can't see to the bottom...Sloth and torpor is the pond of water covered with algae, very dense. One cannot possibly penetrate to the bottom because you can't see through the algae...Restlessness and worry are like a pond wind-swept. The surface is agitated by strong winds...Doubt is like the water when muddied; wisdom is obscured by murkiness and cloudiness. (Goldstein, 1976, p. 53)

This teaching speaks to a most valuable gem that is easily buried or camouflaged by our habituated mental tendencies—our mind of clear seeing. I have always found it helpful to remember that the point is not to control one's thoughts, feelings, or doubts, but simply (or with continued struggle) to come back to the wisdom and clarity that lies hidden beneath these fleeting internal states. It is said that when our mind is troubled, peace has not gone away—we have. The point is to come back to the place of rest that resides within.

The remaining fetters that can impede this return to our wisdom mind include mistaken views of self, practicing wrongful rites and ceremonies, attachment to realms of form, and conceit or self-obsession (Rubin, 1996, p. 132). These additional fetters underscore the many pitfalls of the Buddhist path, where practitioners might unknowingly sustain belief in an enduring "I," confuse the rituals of prayer and meditation with actual enlightenment, lose themselves in mystical states of consciousness, or identify with some notion of self, despite the Buddha's directive that "nothing is to be clung to as I, me, or mine."

The ten impediments to meditation include "worrying about the maintenance of one's dwelling; concern about one's family; obtaining gifts or reputation that result in spending time with admirers; being occupied with students or teaching; involvement in projects; travel; caring for family or co-residents, pupils, preceptors, teachers, or fellow students in a monastery; any kind of affliction or illness; theoretical studies that detract from one's meditation practice; and attachment to supernormal powers rather than involvement in meditation (Rubin, 1996, pp. 133–34; from *Visuddhimagga*).

The Buddha's vision was remarkably inclusive of a broad spectrum of human experiences and mental states that might interfere with one's practice. Contemporary Buddhist teachers working in the West bring this vast and inclusive perspective on the many challenges of a Buddhist practice to their students. Often their insights into the hindrances and fetters help students work more deeply into areas that have given rise to frustration. Certainly, it is rare that sloth or torpor, restlessness, or distraction with one's family or professional projects will not affect the experience of Western Buddhist practitioners. For these issues, and for so many more, their teachers may provide invaluable insight into a troubling meditation session or a recurring struggle with a central Buddhist teaching.

Increasingly, however, Buddhist teachers across traditions have found that Western students bring particular difficulties to their spiritual practice and their teachers that transcend or at the very least challenge the basic parameters of the Dharma. As Buddhist writer David Loy has said, the Western individual functions with a clearly delineated sense of separation from the world they inhabit, which results in ongoing efforts to influence and manipulate others to get what we imagine is needed and desired (2003, p. 107).

Western Buddhists do not typically grow up in a communal culture in which one's ego identification is intimately bound with an extended family or community. For this reason, they may experience their meditation practice quite differently than a native Tibetan, Korean, or Japanese Buddhist. They may find that their practice emphasizes personal content more than ontological or metaphysical experience (Engler, 2006, p. 22). They may also find that their practice generates particular challenges as a result of the interface of a Western self-construct and a practice that is predicated on interbeing and emptiness of self.

I am interested in the various psychological elements that arise out of the Western cultural mores that typically influence our early childhood development of self. Jack Engler, Jeffrey Rubin, and Mark Epstein have all written extensively on the many psychological issues that Western Buddhists seek to address in their spiritual endeavors. They include depression, low self-esteem, and the unconscious wish, greatly influenced by Western Enlightenment values, to be invulnerable, a wish that manifests in myriad interpersonal difficulties. These are some of the more pressing issues that have historically been greeted with bemusement by Asian teachers.

The Dalai Lama openly acknowledged several decades ago his confusion about the "low self-esteem" to which his Western students repeatedly refer. It was an idea that didn't translate into a cultural system in which self-esteem was inextricably bound to deference and devotion to others in a reciprocal esteem-giving matrix of relationships (Roland, 1996, p. 107). In the cultural environment in which the Dalai Lama was raised, feelings of self-worth were not a locus of conscious attention. The individual was supported and infused with a sense of importance by participating in a larger network. It was the group that one considered and valued, and by virtue of this belonging, the self seemed not to suffer as it did in the West.

In the many conversations I have had with Asian Buddhist teachers, these "psychological issues" have caused much head-scratching. It has been tempting to try to explain my sense of these cultural fault lines, wondering if increased attunement to the history of Western values as they have manifested in the individual psyche might help teachers understand what otherwise can seem illogical. Western Buddhists, after all, tend to be people of affluence who are well educated and have sufficient time to study the Dharma. I have heard several lamas indicate that for these reasons Westerners are particularly well suited for a meaningful and spiritually fruitful Buddhist path. With their material wealth and relative comfort, they are ideal candidates for committed and long-term Dharma study and practice. Typically, however, these statements are soon followed by a rejoinder: Unfortunately, there is the small problem of Westerners' undisciplined and unsettled internal world.

Buddhist teachers usually understand well the complexities of Western society and the difficulties that can arise for students who have been relentlessly schooled in the virtues of individual achievement but are spiritually malnourished. They see clearly in many students the schism between hubris camouflaging a tenuous self-confidence that is part of the Western (particularly urban) persona and the desperation for wellness that has so often driven them to the Dharma. This cultural insight is particularly nuanced and deep among teachers who have been living and teaching in the West for decades.

That said, I have at times sensed that the interface of early childhood development—the many factors that influence the individual psyche of their students—and culture has remained largely amorphous. Nowhere in the Dharma is attention paid explicitly to the impact of early childhood experience. It is simply not addressed as a pressing spiritual or psychological reality, an omission that in part seems informed by the communal culture from which it emerged. Perhaps the pervasive scarcity that defined the period in which the Dharma evolved—the lack of food, stable home lives, and stable governing bodies—provided psychic fuel for teachings that de-emphasized subjectivity and attachment (Rubin, 1996). This was not a time in which the stability of family life could easily be relied upon.

The absence of attention paid to one's subjective experience and family of origin can create much confusion for Western students new to the Dharma. It is not uncommon for students to bring their struggles with family members to their Tibetan Buddhist teachers, only to sometimes be told that their wish to set boundaries with a difficult parent with whom they have a history of abuse, or even to detach from the parent altogether, must be forsaken. One's parents, from a Buddhist perspective, should be viewed as precious human lives and loved accordingly. Students may leave these conversations feeling increased shame about their ostensible inability to be loving and tolerant—to be Buddha-like. Yet they may have received such counsel from teachers who were forced to leave their good and caring parents early in life for monastic training, or due to war or sickness. In other words, the teacher's own subjective and early childhood experience may remain largely unconscious. But if a student is new to his spiritual studies and in the throes of idealizing his teacher and the teachings, this larger perspective that includes the psychological may be totally eclipsed by a wish to please the teacher.

I would argue that in order to understand the spiritual capacity of the Western Buddhist one must also consider the influence of family life. For many Western Buddhists, the experience of early childhood family life is distinctly influenced by our heritage of Western Enlightenment values. It can serve as a kind of boot camp in the ethics of individualism, a cultural training ground for a society that will demand a viable, discrete self in all its citizens. American families tend to live in units that have grown increasingly smaller as divorce rates have risen, and the ability to study and work in distant states and countries has created a trend among American adults to build lives for themselves far from their families of origin.

The overarching ethic of these Western family units is the primary division between self and other that David Loy speaks of. The family is structured, by and large, to be self-supporting and not intimately connected to or dependent upon its larger community—thus the symbolism of the Norman Rockwell white picket fence, which over time gave way to the current proliferation of gated communities. In the urban milieu in which I write, it is possible to live next door to fellow apartment dwellers for years on end without ever knowing their professions, their places of origin, or even their first names.

This clear division of self and other can also manifest *within* the family, so that children come to feel objectified by their caretakers, or fundamentally outside their caretaker's primary concern of self-care. These experiences of Western culture mediated through the family have resulted in serious psychological conditions that can easily influence the spiritual processes of Western Buddhists. Psychoanalyst Karen Horney wrote extensively about the severe and potentially devastating effects of intrafamily competition (1945, p. 284). Most notably, she discerned the schism between Western notions of brotherly love and the drive toward individual success (ibid., p. 288).

This competition, argued Horney, gives rise to a basic anxiety in children, whose feelings of being unsafe and ill at ease influence their efforts to cultivate certain psychological coping mechanisms. These adaptations ensure their psychic survival within the family but wreak havoc in their adult interpersonal experience. For the child exposed to such intrafamily dynamics, the inherent contradiction of being cared for by a person who is also experienced as oppositional or competitive cannot be reconciled.

Underneath this foundational anxiety, Horney discerned the child's *hostility* toward the caretaker with whom he felt unsafe and insecure. Because the hostility only made the child feel more vulnerable, since it was projected onto the caretaker and thus increased his perception that the caretaker was unsafe, he pushed it underground—into the unconscious.

These two fraught concepts—anger and the unconscious—have often left Asian Buddhist teachers bemused and uncertain about their Western students' experience. Mark Epstein tells the story of a retreat he attended led by a young Tibetan lama, during which the lama expressed confusion about the discrepancy between the parental doting on children he observed in Western cultures and the anger his adult students so often felt toward their parents (Epstein, 2005, pp. 122–126). From his perspective this made no sense. In the Tibetan culture of his youth, children were not coddled or catered to when suffering the myriad frustrations of childhood— impatience, overexcitement, or simple fatigue. Yet they did not typically grow to feel conspicuous anger toward their parents. Where, he wondered, did this anger stem from in the West?

Epstein explained to the curious lama that in his psychoanalytic practice he found that many patients had not felt accepted or loved for who they were, but rather objectified and made to fit a proscribed model for childhood that the parent had imposed. This objectification resulted in feelings of emptiness that were not ontological in nature, but a feeling-based sense of being hollow and without a genuine personhood. As a result, the patients came to feel that they had a *false self*, and that they were cut off from the real self they were meant to be. With the passage of time, the patients could no longer feel an authentic connection with their sequestered spontaneous aliveness, feeling only the legacy of anger that preceded the development of their false self (ibid., p. 124).

D.W. Winnicott discovered this false self in children he treated who had not been permitted in their earliest infancy an uninterrupted sense of *going-on-being*, or existence that is unfettered by one's environment. What Winnicott found in his extensive work with mothers and their children was the profound importance of a mother (or care provider) that could remain utterly sensitized to the needs of her infant in its earliest stages. This maternal attunement would grow within the child an abiding sense of we-ness that he would carry throughout his life.

As in Kohut's selfobject paradigm, basic health was predicated on a central experience between parent and child that would be woven into the child's psyche. In such a scenario, says Winnicott, the baby would be able to relax into being. Over time, this relationship between the baby and her "environment mother" would manifest itself as a kernel of beingness deep in the center of the child (1952, p. 99). It is this kernel within the baby's psyche that would allow her real self to evolve. Simultaneously, the baby would learn to allow the environment in as she continued to develop this experience of unique meaning from within her own depths (ibid.).

The psychological suffering that ensued when this structural we-ness did not take root was potentially life-wrecking. Without the "good-enough" care of the baby, where the baby's needs were not perfectly met but *were* carefully and sensitively attended to, the baby would feel this locus of being lodged in her shell—the hard and uninviting membrane of false self that separates the outside world from within. In his remarkably intuitive work with young children, Winnicott found terrible psychic fall-out among children who had not been cared for on their own terms, but rather on those of their parents or their culture, which may have emphasized rigid schedules that made for ill-timed feedings and other basic schisms in childcare. What he found missing was not the parental doting noted by the young Tibetan lama but a necessary in-tune-ness with infants' hunger and their need to be held physically and psychically—to be cared for in the full spectrum of their bodily and emotional needs so that their primary feeling of connection with the mother, and with the world at large, was not prematurely interrupted, giving rise to a false and fixed "I" that could never experience authentic connection with another.

Winnicott, however, did not stop with the two of the mother-infant dyad. He wrote of the father's critical role in supporting the mother, and that of the society at large, which must step up to care for children when their parents cannot do so (1986). His vision began with a critical dyad that was supported by a larger societal web. There was no viable "I" without a "we" at its center and an "us" that held them both (Guntrip, 1968, pp. 265–67). In this way Winnicott was unusual in the brief history of psychoanalytic theorists.

For Freud, we are by our very nature autonomous beings driven by body-based instincts of hunger, sexuality, life, and death. Concern for others outside our nuclear family units was suspect, an indicator of neurosis (1986). Freud was largely interested in twos—the interplay of secondary- and primary-process thinking, the fraught relationship between the conscious and unconscious with the warring factions of id, ego, and super-ego, and the almighty biological father and his woefully rivaling son.

From Freud's perspective, human suffering had everything to do with our basic instinctual wiring: we longed for total gratification of our id-based urges of sexuality and aggression while simultaneously negotiating the ego's need for our caretaker's love and societal protection. This internal, largely unconscious maelstrom of love and hate was at odds with our conscious desire to meet our caretaker's expectations, the very thing that would ensure our survival within our families and society at large. The key to alleviating this suffering was to bring our unconscious desires and experience into consciousness. Healing traveled along this clear path from primary-process thinking—that unconscious and voraciously desirous place within—to the privileged secondary-process realm where we might consciously acknowledge the truth of our buried internal reality. Consciousness was *the* Freudian antidote to suffering.

Much to Freud's dismay, this emphasis on concrete binary systems gave way to Carl Jung's sea of archetypal imprints that is our *collective unconscious*. Heavily influenced by Freud's research and his devoted mentoring, Jung struggled with Freud's view of the self, with its binarism of conscious and personal unconscious. In his psychiatric practice, he had begun to take note of certain behavioral tendencies that transcended the scope of an individual frame of reference. He did not deny the presence or importance of the personal unconscious, but he found a deeper, more inclusive and potentially life-altering unconscious that operated within every individual psyche. This was our collective unconscious, our psychic inheritance of myriad behavioral patterns and tendencies that existed from the beginning of time. But Jung has remained the exception in the history of psychoanalytic thought. The expansive internal world has left many Western psychoanalytic theorists uncomfortable with the porous boundaries of self and endless others.

For Jung, our most pressing internal psychic mechanism plants us in otherness—both within and with others (Jung, 1939). He posited an internal gathering function, which he called the Self, that pushes us to integrate our many split-off and lost parts. This integration happens only when we wrestle with the way our particular life experience and struggles intersect with the collective human experience. He proposed that our personal complexes were a royal road to the deepest stratum of our collective unconscious (Jung, 1948).

From the analytic two and the essential conversation between our ego perspective and the Self, that organizing internal mechanism that pushes for wholeness, Jung moved toward a vital third that results when we suffer consciously the opposites within ourselves and between ourselves and others (Ulanov, 2007, p. 163). This third thing might be a symbol or a solution that seems to come to us as a gift from beyond ourselves. Working with this new third thing was, for Jung, a central pathway to freedom from suffering.

Jungian psychoanalyst and writer Ann Ulanov describes the Jungian depth psychological approach to suffering in the following way:

> Jung discovered in his descent into the psyche that opposites comprise the unconscious. When neurosis unbalances us, consciousness carries some of these opposites in conflict with their counterparts in the unconscious. Treatment amounts to gathering into consciousness the opposites split between conscious and unconscious so that we suffer consciously what before warred interminably between our conscious reason and our unconsciously derived symptom, our conscious resolve and our unconscious compulsion…
>
> On the way to such expanded consciousness, moments arise in the field between analyst and analysand that illumine the reality that holds us in being. We are transplanted to a depth where we see the radical congress this reality conducts with us. We still keep mindful of the tasks of analysis…But alighting it, making an entry through this ego work is a spark of the divine come into the human, a tiny fish eye in the vast dark of the cosmos, that yields glimpses of unending light existing there in the depths and in the heights all the time. One is moved to act in surprising ways. (Ulanov, 2004, p. 370)

Jung was not uninterested in the impact of consciousness, but he paid a greater respect to the power of both the personal and collective unconscious. He posited a wisdom in the psyche, an inherited psychic function that required our willingness to explore the depths of both layers of the unconscious without losing consciousness in the process (see Ulanov, 2000). This transcendent function was for Jung a masterful antidote to human suffering, which for him was a life lived without real and integrated connection to the riches of our deeply buried psychic parts.

As psychoanalytic theory evolved, Jung's insights into the unconscious interbeing that so many contemporary Buddhist psychoanalysts have noted was conspicuously ignored (Finn, 2003, p. 125). This has something to do with his interest in religion and his novel suggestion that we come wired not only with instincts for sex and aggression, but also for belief in God. I suspect, however, that his continued ostracism has even more to do with his suggestion that we share the same deepest layers of psyche—we are, from a Jungian view point, jewels in a vast and ancient Indra's net of archetypal patterns and tendencies. We do not and cannot exist with impermeable psychic boundaries, a concept that flies in the face of Cartesian logic and individualism. For Jung, at our deepest level of being there is a shared human stream of existence that informs, nourishes, and troubles us all.

Jung's approach to suffering evolved along with the object relations school of psychoanalysis, led by Melanie Klein. A devout follower of Freud, Klein built on Freud's theories but did not dismantle the basic focus on the individual psyche. Her insight into the infant's internal landscape, with his efforts to take into his psyche the representation of his caretaker, fleshed out Freud's emphasis on the discrete psychic mechanisms that would operate regardless of the infant's environment. On the one hand, Klein challenged the totally self-contained discrete individual of Freud's theories by positing a constant introjection, projection, and re-introjection between the infant and his or her caretakers. One can think of this process as a red ball that the baby takes from within his own imagination, tosses to the parent, and then catches again as if it weren't his own creation; or, in the case of its own hostility, a monster it has conjured from within but which seems to come from the parent. The baby, argued Klein, was engaged in ongoing efforts to internalize the good aspects of the caretaker and defend against what he experienced as the bad or frustrating aspects of the caretaker. In this way relationship between the baby and the caretaker was the very foundation of the baby's later psychological development.

Nonetheless, Klein was not primarily interested in the specificity of care the child received, the parents' personalities, or the nuances of family environment. Instead, she posited a baby who would invariably internalize what was unconsciously projected onto the parent—the red ball and/or monster he has created but mistakenly perceives as coming from the parent (Klein, 1975b). She followed a largely internal psychic progression that would ultimately facilitate the child's capacity to express concern and gratitude for others. In this way she underscored an empathic connection with others as a great psychological achievement, but one that happened predominantly within the confines of the child's own psyche (Roland, 1996, p. 10) Her interest in how the child comes to recognize the importance of the *two* came through an intricate analysis of the self-contained *one*.

From Klein, psychoanalysis evolved into an exploration of suffering that continued to pay homage to the foundational thinkers and their emphasis on the young child's relationship to his unconscious world as it intersects with the world around him. Yet this respect for the influence of the individual unconscious would evolve into a keener curiosity about the potential for healing that might be realized when this unconscious was explored within the analytic dyad. There was a collective push into an area of exploration that challenged Freud's pessimistic view that, because of problematic and problematizing internal psychic mechanisms, the most we could hope for was a "common unhappiness."

An analysand of Melanie Klein, Wilfred Bion would emerge as a psychoanalytic thinker with a marked interest in how full psychospiritual aliveness might be achieved. His theories moved well beyond the resolution of early sexual fixation and adult neurotic symptomatology. Instead, he found himself drawn to what he called *ultimate reality*, which he symbolized by O. For Bion, O represented the full reality of ourselves and all phenomena (Bion, 1965, p. 147). Because it made up our very being and all that surrounds us, it could not be fully known, yet it begged to be grappled with. Bion developed a mathematical blueprint of the psyche that has induced as much weary eye-rolling within the psychoanalytic community as I have observed in Buddhist circles in response to the Buddha's enumerated mosaic of the mind. But like the Buddha's teachings, his insights are worth the struggle.

For Bion, another letter, K, represents our thinking capacity, which is necessary in order to talk about our beta elements—the things we have lived through but have not processed into symbols, images, thoughts, or feelings (1970, pp. 9–30). We need K to help us move toward O. But when K, or thought used in the service of shielding oneself from ultimate reality, creeps into the picture, distracting us with memories and desires, we miss the life-changing impact of O. When this happens, we cut ourselves off from certain parts of ourselves and our life experience, our true feelings and thoughts, which results in nothing short of psychic deadness. Impacts with O, argues Bion, are shattering, but they are also enlivening (1965 and 1970; see also Eigen 1998b for illuminating discussion of Bion's theories). Knowing and consciously being in the reality of pain suffered, of having lost loved ones, or never having been received by our loved ones with the affection and care we have longed for, is ultimately nourishing *and* devastating work.

It was the laborious but potentially liberating work of the analytic dyad to help both analyst and analysand move into their own realities as they continued to discover just how real they, their work, and the world at large, could be (Eigen, 1998b, p. 81). Bion spoke of the potential destructiveness of thinking or theorizing that was used in the service of evading the truth of one's past and present being. In this way he mirrored the Buddha's many caveats regarding metaphysical speculation. He was not interested in merely surviving the psychic depletion that can result from suffering. Like the Buddha, he asked analysands to walk closer to the nature of suffering, to enter into it, and to see what happened if this courage eclipsed our customary default to evasion of pain and suffering. For Bion, a far-reaching acceptance of suffering was the critical determinant of mental growth (Symington, 1996, p. 6).

Bringing us to present-day psychoanalytic thought, the intersubjective and relational schools (e.g., Robert Stolorow, George Atwood, and Thomas Ogden) have continued to move beyond the Freudian drive model of the human being, in which conflict looms large and autonomy is dominant (Rubin, 1996, p. 22). Instead, this latest group of psychoanalysts has focused on what lies between the analyst and the analysand. In the classical Freudian model, transference and countertransference are considered to be almost exclusively the products of the analysand's personal history. The intersubjectivists posit a third subjectivity that results when the subjectivity of each member of the analytic pair mixes together—a kind of analytic mixing of minds (Ulanov, 2007, p. 160).

As in the Buddhist dyad, this is not an unconscious merger, but rather the discovery of an augmented sense of self through what is experienced between two people. Through the analyst, and through the space between the analyst and analysand, one may come to feel less tethered to or constricted by prior notions of self. And, as in the Buddhist dyad, such a process does not erase difference between the two partners; it suspends the conventional orientation toward what George Atwood and Robert Stolorow call "the myth of the isolated mind" (1992; see also Bobrow 2003, p. 267). Within this theoretical framework, suffering is explored as it manifests in the interplay between the analytic dyad.

Thomas Ogden encourages analysts to pay close attention to their own internal reverie as a central method for sustaining awareness of this inter-subjectivity, as it houses key information about their interpersonal experience with the analysand (1994). His focus on the internal state of the analyst offers an interesting application of Buddhist mindfulness in the clinical space, a way to sustain awareness of both members of the analytic dyad, so that analysts' neutrality does not slip into a denial of their own potentially illuminating internal reverie.

This school of theorists suggests that the antidote to suffering is to break through the isolation of our own ego perspective and reconnect with the subjectivity of the person we are in relationship with. This happens when we can sustain a commitment to repairing the ongoing ruptures of connection that happen in any interpersonal relationship (Ulanov, 2007, p. 162; see also Benjamin, 2005, p. 197). Healing happens within each person when the relationship is continuously restored and kept alive.

What these divergent theories have in common is a respect for the unconscious as it manifests in the realm of interpersonal relationship. Some of them are more focused on the unconscious as it impacts the analysand, and others seek to explore how the unconscious, mined and unmined, may influence the people in our lives and the world at large (Bion, 1970; Jung, 1971; Neumann, 1969; Ulanov, 2004).

In the classic Buddhist point of view, the unconscious is like a small room in a psychospiritual Ramada Inn compared to the total experience of past lives, which might be likened to the vast unfolding spaces of the Taj Mahal (Dalai Lama & Cutler, 1998, p. xvi). When asked about the role of the unconscious, the Dalai Lama has said that it is overly emphasized in Western thinking, which he notes, is largely a "this life" philosophy (ibid.).

These suggestions are interesting and worth careful consideration, particularly for those of us vexed by psychological or spiritual difficulties that seem not to budge despite our diligent efforts to work through them, or for those born into life circumstances that are by their very nature shaming, painful, or inherently frustrating. A Buddhist perspective that takes into consideration the imprint of countless "previous lives" from the beginning of time, and anticipates countless "future lives," offers another lens through which to explore painful life experience, one that may replace the pressure of "getting it right." This is not a call for "this life" defeatism, but rather a way to consciously link our current wholesome efforts at happiness with an abiding trust that these efforts will eventually flower.

However, as someone who has been engaged in the psychoanalytic process, my appreciation for the unconscious rivals my curiosity about past-life imprints and future-life potential. In his marvelously lucid essay on some of the more prevalent psychological pitfalls of the Buddhist path, particularly as they pertain to Western practitioners, psychoanalyst and Buddhist teacher Jack Engler speaks of the Abhidharma's emphasis on oppositional mental factors that cannot simultaneously co-arise (Engler, 2006, p. 27). This Buddhist theory suggests that when in the grips of a negative mental state, one must apply its antidote, a contrasting positive state. Thus in order to transform the three poisons, for example, one must apply generosity to greed, compassion to anger, and wisdom to ignorance. There is truth to this method. Current neurological research indicates that the problem is not that we utilize a small fraction of our overall brain capacity, but rather that as we use one brain function we shut down others. There is wisdom in reinforcing mental processes that facilitate happiness and reduce suffering.

From a psychoanalytic perspective, however, this is but one aspect of our struggle to heal from suffering. Engler invokes another Western psychological principle, referred to as the principle of multiple determination (ibid.). This theory proposes that we have myriad and simultaneous motivations for our various behaviors, feelings, and thoughts. Some of these motivations will be conscious, while others will be entirely unconscious. This is a critical insight that psychoanalytic theorists can offer to Buddhist practitioners and teachers: that the rub of the unconscious is that it is *unconscious*—we simply do not (typically) know, and continuously forget, that it exists and informs every facet of lived experience. As a result, we tend to behave as if the unconscious—that small room in the Ramada Inn—does not and cannot provide precious psychic information about our spiritual lives and our many hidden motives for seeking spiritual freedom on a Buddhist path. It is my contention that when this psychic content is not explored, we may unconsciously sabotage the spiritual freedom that might otherwise be achieved.

For example, while we may express conscious feelings of affection for our teachers, these feelings may be a defense against unconscious anger or hostility that we feel unsafe expressing or merely harboring, as if it were a dangerous fugitive whom we imagine should be sequestered or even snuffed out. This can lead to difficulty with meditation, or to passive aggression that gets acted out in other ways. We may consciously pursue meditations on no-self in order to move toward spiritual freedom from a discrete "I," when unconsciously we wish to hide from all relationship and belong to nobody in particular (Storr, 1996, p. 220). So too, our conscious desire to be free from all mental defilements may belie an unconscious wish to be invulnerable to all forms of pain and suffering, to be superhuman and fulfill the Western Enlightenment ideal of total self-containment (Engler, 2006, p. 25).

Western Buddhists have historically suffered from the full range of hindrances and impediments explicated in the Dharma. We are no strangers to the laziness, restlessness, and conscious ill-will that the Buddha identified as three of the five hindrances. Yet difficulties on the Buddhist path that seem to be so much laziness, sloth, and torpor may also point to unconscious psychic feelings and wishes that sabotage our conscious spiritual yearnings more effectively than mere laziness. In his clinical work with Buddhist practitioners, Jeffrey Rubin has at times discovered the presence of unconscious guilt in his analysands that results in the "resistance to wellness" that Freud posited in his initial analytic endeavors (Rubin, 1996, p. 129). What looks like a meditation practice that is sporadic and neglected due to mere sluggishness and poor concentration may in reality be one that is undermined by the meditators' unconscious belief that they do not deserve the happiness and freedom such a practice might bring about. In this scenario, sluggishness might serve as a defense against a move toward wellness, a resistance that is neither without meaning nor a universal phenomenon free from personal content.

Melanie Klein has suggested that we have a dread of not adequately mastering our destructive impulses (1975a). The guilt we feel about our hate for the people we also love, resulting from the frustrations and fears suffered during our earliest stages in life, may give rise to an endless effort to make reparations. For Westerners pursuing a Buddhist spiritual path, it seems plausible that our unconscious guilt about feelings of hostility toward our caretakers and all beings (including our teachers) who have ever frustrated our need to be viable individuals in this compulsively individualistic society may fuel the wish to atone for these "poisonous" mental states and to make reparation for decidedly un-Buddhist aspirations. These unconscious efforts at reparation may appear as a wish to cultivate compassion—to "be a bodhisattva"—that masks a deeper ensnarement in chronic caretaking that lacks the genuine warmth of a more integrated capacity for compassion.

What I have observed within the many Buddhist communities I have participated in is a pervasive wish to have one's spiritual practice effectively address and resolve the full spectrum of emotional and psychological challenges beyond the spiritual realm. It is not uncommon to hear Western Buddhists say, with some small hint of unconscious pride, that due to their spiritual practice, they no longer need psychoanalytic treatment or therapeutic support. Or, conversely, Buddhists may suggest that spiritual practice and psychoanalytic treatment are the same—they both seek to eliminate suffering and increase happiness.

Yet, as any Buddhist psychoanalyst (and many Buddhist teachers) will readily state, it is very possible to have a deep and rich spiritual life that reaps all manner of spiritual rewards while core psychological patterns and struggles remain untouched. Furthermore, if these psychological issues and emotional patterns are not addressed in a system designed to explore their personal meaning and impact, spiritual practitioners may unwittingly use their spiritual endeavors to camouflage their existence and bypass the hard work of addressing the reality of the psyche, with its conscious and unconscious halves (Engler, 2006, p. 23).

A Buddhist teacher, after all, is not primarily interested in or trained in facilitating the student's conscious confrontation with his psyche. If she is a true and good teacher, she often will provoke in the student powerful feelings and longing, strong emotional reactivity, and the wish to be seen as worthy and precious. But this wealth of emotionality and psychological data in the student can easily remain altogether unconscious, or conscious but not worked through or understood. The process of working through what transpires between two people is typically the domain of the psychoanalyst.

It is often obvious to Buddhist teachers when their students are suffering from preexisting psychological issues that the teachers may not be equipped to handle. And if they are quite sensitive, they will intuit when students have projected their prior experience in life onto the teacher or lama. Yet the nature of these struggles, composed as they are by a confluence of culture, psyche, and spirit, may be somewhat or entirely elusive.

Teachers will not turn students away or avoid efforts to address their students' difficulties. They may offer an intuitive counsel, which is often quite insightful and soothing. They may also remind their students that suffering provides opportunities to reinforce their sense of connection with all suffering people. Some teachers, especially in the Tibetan tradition, may suggest the practice of tonglen, in which the student breathes in the pain of others and breathes out all her good will, compassion, and wish to alleviate collective suffering. The universal nature of the student's suffering would likely be addressed with interest and kindly support. And I would argue that this broader, spiritual perspective—if it is integrated into the particularities of the student's personal history and psychic reality—can be invaluable. But if students bring their psychic realities to their Buddhist teachers—including failed or frustrated efforts at romantic intimacy, struggles to defend against an abusive family member, or addictions to sex, food, or people—without working through these formidable challenges in a system that understands the complexities of the human psyche, a more universal spiritual approach may fail to help such students heal.

Buddhist teachers may sense that such students are somehow "missing the point" of the Dharma (Fields, 1992, p. 282). It is in these efforts to address psychological issues in a spiritual enterprise that many teachers I have spoken with have experienced their students taking the Dharma on their own terms. Many high lamas speak of the Western struggle to settle the mind on any one healing tradition. From their perspective, we seem unable to surrender to the Dharma, to let it take root within our minds. Instead, our "personal matters" reign supreme. As a result, we unknowingly use the Dharma—consume it—to bolster our egos and reify identity. Yet from a psychoanalytic perspective, the student's ego—which is both conscious and unconscious—may be in dire need of healing so that it can become more malleable and dis-identified in its spiritual endeavors. In this way students would be readied for the experience of devotion to their teachers, and readied for "mixing minds," without becoming vulnerable to unconscious merger or object hunger, which are helpful to neither teachers nor students.

Every Buddhist student will be on a spectrum of relative unconsciousness about his or her own efforts at spiritual healing and wellness. I agree with Engler that pure and wholesome motives for studying and practicing Buddhism may mix in with unconscious motives (Engler, 2006, pp. 25–27). When this happens we may simultaneously seek a true and lasting liberation from suffering on the Buddhist path through relationship with our teachers *and* use the Dharma to defend against the psychological work, thus ensuring the pain of confronting Bion's O. It seems likely that when Western practitioners hope to address in their spiritual practice the psychological fallout of growing up in families in which the worst elements of Western culture were harshly inculcated, or when childhood trauma has been denied and quietly reverberates through our adult lives, they will indeed miss the point and the fruit of the Buddhadharma.

From my experience, it is folly to imagine that one's spiritual practice alone can uproot the morass of psychic defenses that have resulted from early childhood experience, former trauma, or even constitutional predispositions that have set the stage for addiction, interpersonal difficulty, or severe psychological maladjustment.

In the Insight Meditation tradition, in which mindfulness practice is the foundation of one's spiritual path, I have found a great potential to confuse spiritual freedom with psychological well-being. With its emphasis on mindfulness of the five aggregates, the components of what we take to be our "self," there is a slippery slope between careful investigation of these ephemeral elements and disowning subjective experience. For example, one of the aggregates, feeling, which in this instance is not our capacity for emotion, but rather the pleasantness, unpleasantness, or neutrality associated with any given experience, is a locus of mindfulness teachings that can create real dissonance between psychological and spiritual growth (Goldstein, 2003, p. 160).

In vipassana practice students are encouraged to investigate the way that the feeling aggregate conditions our seemingly automatic aversion in response to unpleasantness, grasping in response to pleasantness, or lack of concern in response to neutrality. There is much wisdom in these teachings that points to what neurologists have come to find in recent years. In our perceptual processes there are critical, albeit fleeting, gaps between the times in which we perceive, process, and respond to information or perceptual content (Goleman, 2003). Mindfulness practice can help students unlink their purportedly instinctual responses from the perceptions of pain and to pleasure that occasion them, offering a wider range of options in painful scenarios that they would prefer to avoid or in pleasurable circumstance from which they can't stand to part. On a global scale, the potential for mindfulness training to support individuals and even whole nations in working more skillfully with these precious moments in which reactivity becomes optional could stave off endless manifestations of unnecessary human suffering. These are remarkably powerful teachings, and I in no way wish to undermine their importance.

Yet these teachings are easily misinterpreted, particularly by Western students, whereby all feeling states are considered to be mere distraction from the more noble pursuit of spiritual purity. With the backdrop of Western Enlightenment values that privilege reason over feeling, Buddhist students may translate mindfulness teachings to mean that all feeling states, particularly those of real depth, should be quickly relinquished, like hot potatoes that will burn the tender fingers pointing to our placid buddha nature. Furthermore, the Buddhist mindfulness teachings do not address the personal meaning in feeling states, either as they exist in aggregate form or in the broader spectrum of emotionality. The signposts these feelings may provide to unconscious or seemingly forgotten experiences with primary caretakers or other loved ones are simply not acknowledged.

From a psychoanalytic perspective, feelings may pose a healthy challenge to our preferred ego position, reminding us that all is not well, even though we would like to imagine it so. An upsurge of boiling rage while standing in line at the supermarket, if analytically engaged before it is "let go," may remind us of a moment or a lifetime where we were kept waiting for key ingredients necessary for a nourished psyche. Unexpected tears while watching an "after school special" with one's son or daughter might speak to painful beliefs we have carried about ourselves or our world that were conceived during a long ago, forgotten episode in our lives.

I propose that mindfulness training can sometimes encourage practitioners to "let go" of mental content too quickly, before it is mined for the gold it offers when honored as valuable psychic information. I suspect, too, that for practitioners who have not benefited from psychoanalytic or psychotherapeutic work, it is an ongoing temptation to confuse mindfulness of one's emotional states with fully felt and integrated feeling. It seems plausible that this confusion may have something to do with the jarring discrepancy that can exist in practitioners who simultaneously exhibit an almost saccharine spiritual persona, which seems to float loftily above the human realm, and undercurrents of passive aggression, depression, and compulsive sexual desire, which may come out sideways when these psychological and emotional states are unconscious and therefore unintegrated.

If one seeks to appreciate the nuances and meaning of any psychoanalytic theorist, from Freud to Klein and Winnicott, one must grapple with the world that informed their insight and their particular locus of attention. Similarly, Buddhist writer George Elder suggests that Buddhism can be understood only when evaluated in light of Siddhartha Gautama's life experience (Elder, 1998). Psychoanalytic theorists and Buddhist teachers do not write or gain insight in a vacuum. Freud lived through two world wars, lost a child and a grandchild to diseases that are now preventable, and was forced to flee his country of origin while leaving behind four sisters as an eighty-three-year-old man living with cancer. That he would fasten upon a conflict model in which the most pristine parts of the psyche are both at war with one another and under siege from within and without is not surprising when one considers the world he had known and suffered through. Perhaps it is also unsurprising that as an analyst he preferred to avoid eye contact with his analysands, to be spared the discomfort of human interaction that was too intimate and too fraught with potential hurt and loss (see Gay, 1998).

Siddhartha Gautama, in contrast, for the first twenty-nine years of his life knew nothing but pleasure, luxury, and a life of ease. During the first half of his lived experience, life *was* pleasure. It is not without meaning that after his shocking foray into life beyond his Indian Garden of Eden he would posit desire as one of the three poisons. For the young prince, a life in which every desire was met had precluded his ability to know, understand, and address the reality of people who suffered terribly within yards of his protected domicile. Yet ultimately, happiness and freedom—our collective goal and most basic nature—remained his primary domain. As the very first Buddhist teacher, the Buddha asked his students to look within and find the peace and clarity that is our birthright.

The meaning each of these founding healers and philosophers happened upon grew out of their own cultural milieu and life experience. Today, whether a person seeking wellness is drawn to Buddhism or to psychoanalysis, and furthermore, whether or not these healing endeavors prove to be effective, will have as much to do with the individual and the culture from which they emerge as the system they have chosen (Cooper, 1998). To suggest otherwise is counter to my understanding of emptiness—that all phenomena, including healing systems, are empty of inherent meaning and are rather a constant flux of changing causes, circumstances, and conditions. What Buddhism and psychoanalysis are and can provide will mix with the setting, the consciousness, and the unconscious of the practitioner.

David Loy asks an important and pressing question: What is Buddhism adapting itself to today (2003, p. 16)? Within the larger Buddhist community there has been a strong and healthy tradition of *engaged* Buddhism, whose practitioners have attempted to bring the Dharma to particular crises in the secular world. For example, Joanna Macy's efforts to heal the environment through Dharma-influenced endeavors, and Thich Nhat Hanh's renowned efforts to heal the painful split between Israelis and Palestinians living in the Middle East, have grown deep roots over the past thirty years. Psychoanalysis has some catching up to do, but it too is starting to bring its healing tradition to where it is most needed (see Altman, 1995; Illovsky, 2003; Layton et al., 2006).

Each of these traditions is forever changing, as are all phenomena, influenced by the particular historical era and cultural setting in which it finds its ready participants. In the cultural environment in which I have practiced Buddhism and psychoanalysis, people continue to bring an ever-changing set of struggles and difficulties to their efforts at healing. While the more universal conditions of aging, sickness, death, fraught family relations, financial stress, and the psychic fallout of war continue to be ever present, there are also new and culturally specific forms of pain and suffering that call for an unshakable humility in both spiritual and psychoanalytic circles.

Contemporary Buddhists (particularly urban) now face the pervasive loneliness, fear of terrorism, the continued rise of childhood diseases including autism and leukemia, the impact of technology on far-reaching attentional deficits, and the fallout of postmodernism with its dismantling of discernable truths. I believe it will be increasingly useful for both Buddhist teachers and psychoanalysts to explore how these present-day Western realities mix with the Western Buddhist mind. And most relevant to this work, to be mindful of how these Western students address these experiences with their dharma teachers and their analysts.

Is it too much to expect either one of these healing endeavors to address fully the total spectrum of these changing needs and difficulties? I believe so. Ideally, I would like to see more Buddhist teachers support their students by encouraging them to seek out any additional psychoanalytic or psychotherapeutic support that may serve them, and their spiritual path, well. So too, I would like to see more clinicians honor the limits of what they can do for their clients (see chapter 8). Psychological insight, after all, can be a heavy load to carry without a method for connecting one's personal experience to the larger web of human reality. Buddhist meditation practice can offer analysands a way to contextualize the personal content that may otherwise reinforce feelings of isolation, of having had a childhood or adult experience that is too traumatic, too deviant, or simply too problematic to allow active and joyful participation in the world.

A Buddhist viewpoint, with its emphasis on the universality of human suffering, can serve as an antidote to the ego-strengthening and (potentially) reifying effect of psychoanalysis. With this critically important perspective, Buddhist teachers remind their students that we are all joined in our suffering, merely finding personal roads into the collective experience of being incarnate, vulnerable, and impermanent beings. As a method of honoring the particular ways in which each one of us suffers this incarnate experience, psychoanalysis may step in to mirror the preciousness of each individual psyche that meets the Buddha with its own history, its sense of what is meaningful, and its conscious and unconscious wish to be free from suffering.

It is my hope that healers in both traditions may continue to develop their own curiosity about the nature and nuances of human suffering in this particular time and place with appreciation for the limits of what any one healer or healing system can offer.

desire and aggression
two of the three poisons

6

As any Buddhist teacher or psychoanalyst will readily confirm, desire and aggression are key players in the human mind. We come into this incarnate existence primed with overpowering desire for the things we want and equally powerful feelings of aversion toward the things we do not want. We are not a species of moderation, nor have we ever been. Our distant ancestors used every ounce of aggression at their ready to spear their meat: they created special tools to smash bones so that they might gain access to brain-enhancing bone marrow and eat it with frenzied delight. They were stocking up for long winters when food was scarce—something we still do some 100,000 years later despite, for instance, the twenty-four-hour deli on every New York City block. When animals or other hominids approached, posing danger, our ancestors were neither inclined nor physically equipped to sit down and "talk things through" (Horrobin, 2001). More likely, the adrenal glands, with their potent cues for fight or flight, kicked in at full force, with two choices: kill or run for your life.

Today we struggle mightily with this physiological hardwiring. When there is something pleasurable on the scene—say, a person or a piece of cake—our inner caveman wants to pin it down and claim it. Similarly, all things eliciting aversion seem to provoke a comparable degree of reactivity—we want either to destroy what we reject or get as far away from it as we possibly can. Now that our brains have evolved into the big fatty masses they are, our capacity to reflect on these seemingly instinctual responses, with their lower primate dynamics, has given rise to much guilt. From where I stand in the psychoanalytic and Buddhist worlds, this is the stuff of psychoanalysis *and* spiritual practice. Seekers are looking for another way to be human—to want and love and desire without being destroyed or destroying another. So too, we want to find another way to work with our anger and our rage.

Human beings are for the most part aware of the ramifications if we do not find another way: there is a penal system in place that has evolved into a kind of Dantean inferno, or perhaps a kind of social Gulag. Prisons are not typically places of reform, as they were intended to be, but vast warehouses where one's sense of humanity can too easily suffocate. Even when incarceration is not the likely outcome, our inability to work through anger, for example, can have equally serious ramifications in the interpersonal realm: hearts can be pierced, family ties ruined, and good and loving marriages destroyed. For these reasons, learning to relate to desire and aggression in ways that are workable, both for the individual and for the society in which we live, has been the focus of psychoanalysis and Buddhism from their inception.

In previous chapters I have referred to the three poisons as they are identified in the Buddhist sutras: anger or ill-will, desire or grasping, and ignorance. The third poison, ignorance, commonly taught as a basic misperception of reality, is considered to be the corrupt psychospiritual soil out of which anger and desirous grasping grow. As a long-term Buddhist practitioner, I know that these two human emotions are rightly identified as potentially toxic. On the more innocuous side of anger, I have had endless experiences of standing on subway platforms railing at the train that simply would not come, even as, ironically, I was on my way to hear a great rinpoche talk or impart blessings at my desired destination. On the more serious side, I have watched anger pushed underground come out passively, either in a customary wish to hide from the offending object, to isolate and spare myself the difficulty of these feelings, or in a round of intellectual sparring with a tacit subtext striking for its absence of intellectual nuance: *You're a big meany, a jerk. I hate you and I hope you die!*

According to some Buddhist writers, angry feelings serve no useful purpose (Dalai Lama & Cutler, 1998, p. 77; Thurman, 1998, p. 177). Anger results when we do not skillfully engage the reality that is before us. When we have become ensnared in feelings of frustration, either because we have not gotten what we want or have gotten what we don't want, anger and perhaps aggressive behavior will follow. There is no Buddhist doctrine on aggression as a mere form of physiological movement, a feeling-neutral stance. Instead, aggression is understood as an offensive or hostile action. It is anger in motion.

Buddhist teaching depicts anger as an emotional defilement, or *klesha*, with a problematic conceptual component that differentiates it from a pure energy source (Thurman, 2005, p. 43). It is viewed as a destructive mental habit predicated on a deluded sense of inherent separateness. The early Buddhist "psychologists" spoke of *anusayas*, dormant tendencies in the mind that are easily triggered during times of distress or upheaval. Anger was identified as an anusaya that typically left a path of destruction in its wake (Bennet-Goleman, 2001, p. 69). Buddhist teaching acknowledges that it may be experienced within the body, but its inception is in the mind, where it is fueled by dramatic, often one-dimensional ideas and storylines.

The goal, stated by the Buddha, is to skillfully conquer our anger, to recognize that it is never useful to others or to our own efforts at well-being. He instructed his followers to "Abandon anger…Overcome anger by nonanger" (Cleary, 1994, pp. 76–77). In his teachings, giving in to feelings of anger was compared to "licking honey from a razor." He taught that feelings of righteous indignation, of being slighted or offended, or attributing to another person unseemly motivations that they may not actually have, can offer an illusory satisfaction. To place ourselves in the right and make the other clearly in the wrong can be satisfying. In this way anger can provide a gratifying sweetness that is not easily forsaken.

In Buddhist teaching, however, when we act on anger or have the urge to act on it, we have become ensnared in a fundamental misperception of reality. There is the delusion of *inherent existence*, which evokes a strong, erroneous feeling of basic separateness. Operating within this delusion, we are likely to feel alienated by a situation or person that appears to be disconnected from our own consciousness and inherent existence. When this occurs, efforts to protect self from other result, and we assume a defensive posture that sets the stage for hypersensitivity about what is rightly "mine," and who "I" am, and whether these self-experiences are appropriately honored. This root delusion of an absolute, independent self justifies the need for defensive and offensive protection, standing by its very nature in opposition to the rest of the world.

In this dualistic paradigm, where the fluidity and impermanence of all beings is forgotten, it becomes easy and tempting to invest inherent meaning in others and to exaggerate certain qualities that seem to define their very being. From a Buddhist perspective, anger arises because we have focused our attention on the object of our anger—an object that is perceived as coming from "out there"—and exaggerated their negative qualities (ibid.). In this way anger defends our delusional experience of having a fixed and independent self.

The problem with anger, says the Dalai Lama, is that it is simply not part of our most basic nature (Dalai Lama & Cutler, 1998, p. 39). In Buddhist doctrine we are, in our deepest being, good-natured. When we are free from the various defilements that result from unskillful actions and changing causes and conditions, we are compassionate, gentle, and kindly. Anger results when our efforts at loving others have been frustrated and we have given way to that frustration, or when we simply lack a realistic attitude. In his teachings on anger, the Dalai Lama encourages students "to be sensitive and respectful to the concrete reality of your situation as you proceed on the path towards your ultimate goal" (ibid., p. 195). He underscores the need to differentiate between our ideals and the realistic standards by which we assess our progress.

In other words, he is calling for a deeper engagement with our own reality at any given moment. Rather than surrendering to powerful feelings of frustration when we cannot get what we want, or when we get what we don't want, he encourages students to alter their perspective. In this way his teachings illustrate a central theme of Buddhist wisdom—that we are happiest when we hold our reality gently and with patience, knowing that everything changes, the good and the bad.

The great eighth-century Buddhist philosopher Shantideva states that we are only "rightly angry with anger" (1979). When in the throes of angry feelings, students on the Buddhist path are encouraged to carefully examine their intentions. Is our intention to hurt others as we have been hurt? Or perhaps we wish to display our basic power, which has been called into question through some deprecating remark or action. The Dalai Lama teaches that when the intention is pure, and when anger is driven by compassion, it *can* be an agent for change (Dalai Lama & Cutler, 1998, p. 209). But this is very much the exception. The Buddha underscored this teaching when he pointed to the subtle but important difference between circumstances that call for a fiery action, a wrathful capacity that blazes its way to a positive outcome, and anger predicated on the misperception of self and others.

When a small child endangers himself, running toward a wild animal or a moving vehicle, a caring parent will raise her voice and swiftly grab the child before he is harmed. The intention in this use of aggression is critical. It is based on the wish to spare another being avoidable suffering. That said, students on the Buddhist path are encouraged to discern the motivation behind our anger and aggression, because anger, as stated in the doctrine, is mostly poisonous and thus is itself a grave danger that should be rooted out whenever possible.

The antidote to anger is to cultivate a deep and abiding compassion for all beings. In the Mahayana tradition, students are reminded that anger and resentment are counter to the bodhisattva ideal of holding dear all sentient beings and learning from our enemies, who are also within the sphere of precious human life (Dalai Lama, 1995, p. 82). Many Buddhist students practice cultivating loving kindness. Students begin by developing this attitude of kindness first toward themselves, then toward friends and family, and next toward people for whom they have neutral feelings. This practice ultimately includes one's enemies, or people with whom conflict has arisen. The idea is to build an open-hearted receptivity for all beings, so that we can remember our shared buddha nature even in times of anger and conflict.

Renowned Vietnamese Buddhist monk Thich Nhat Hanh suggests that anger must be cared for as a mother cares for her baby (2001, p. 32). When we explore our own anger, he encourages us to do so with sensitive precision and gentleness of spirit. Like a mother who cherishes her baby, soothing him and showing him her greatest attention, so too should we care for our own anger with mindful attention. Nhat Hanh recommends an intensive focus on the experience of anger that is neither invasive nor impatient. He proposes that mindfulness will act as both a receptor and a mirror to contain affectively charged experiences (ibid., p. 164). In this way, it makes room for the presence of anger without thoughts of remedy or resolution.

Relying heavily on mothering imagery, Nhat Hanh suggests that mindfulness mirrors the presence of anger just as an effective parent lovingly mirrors what the infant or young child may feel. Mindfulness is therefore the means through which we ultimately become relational in the midst of anger. Buddhist teaching explicates the process of replacing aversion toward one's own anger with a meticulous and friendly curiosity (Bennet-Goleman, 2001, p. 37). In this way a healing relationship with anger is cultivated as a necessary challenge to the aversion we typically feel when anger has arisen.

Yet even Nhat Hanh acknowledges that in a conflict between two people the mindfulness of one person involved cannot by itself manage the impact of anger. For Nhat Hanh, anger can be effectively worked through only if it is acknowledged and addressed by the parties involved, with swift and conscious intentionality. In the sutras, the Buddha gave a twenty-four-hour time limit for confronting the people who have triggered our anger (Nhat Hanh, 2001, p. 55). He emphasized that no more time should lapse and that we should vigilantly adhere to the condition of loving speech. Nhat Hanh puts an interpersonal spin on this Buddhist doctrine, recommending that the angry party ask the object of their anger for help in resolving this difficult feeling. With great insight, Nhat Hanh notes that when we are angry we long to shun those who have angered us, to show them how ineffectual they are and how meaningless they have become (ibid., p. 41). We easily become withdrawn children with folded arms, closed to feelings of warmth or affection. We aim to hurt others as we feel we have been hurt. Thus, the Buddha offered his directive to push through this place of aversion and restore the interrupted connection.

For Buddhist students, these teachings on anger offer necessary support when their relationships with lamas and teachers have become difficult and frustrating. Through cultivating a compassionate and curious approach toward her own anger, the angry party may come to understand that she has unknowingly tethered herself to an unrealistic expectation. The Dharma offers students a way to work through difficulty with their teachers with reduced opportunity for blame or outright rejection that could sabotage the longevity of the relationship.

Having studied the Buddhist philosophy of anger, students might be more inclined to investigate the nature of their own minds rather than the shortcomings of their teachers. They would be encouraged to keep the focus on their perceptions rather than on what they have (perhaps erroneously) perceived. In bringing such equanimity to their experience of anger, the teachings say, students are better able to keep conscious of their interbeing and shared inner wisdom mind, breaking down dualistic notions spurred on by the emergence of anger.

The contrast between this rather optimistic view of anger and aggression and the stark early psychoanalytic views becomes imminently clear. In a famous essay, "Instincts and their Vicissitudes," Freud states that "hate, as a relation to objects, is older than love" (1915). As a dualist who explained all mental processes as conflict between opposing instinctual urges, Freud discovered that hate was closely connected to the ego's efforts at self preservation (Storr & Stevens, 1989/1994, p. 44). The ego railed against all the unwanted stimuli from the outside world, wishing to return to an earlier state. It was during this time that Freud posited an *aggressive instinct* that existed in its own right. With his devotion to the influence of instinctual processes on the mind, whereby the instincts seek return to an earlier unstimulated state, Freud found himself moving toward a theory of a universal wish to be free from stimuli, to return to the place from which we come. This was his "death instinct," from which all aggression toward the external world was derived:

> After long hesitancies and vacillations we have decided to assume the existence of only two basic instincts, *Eros* and the *destructive instinct*...The aim of the first of these basic instincts is to establish ever greater unities and to preserve them thus— in short, to bind together; the aim of the second is, on the contrary, to undo connections and so to destroy things. In the case of the destructive instinct we may suppose that its final aim is to lead what is living into an inorganic state. For this reason we also call it the death instinct. (SE, XXIII 148)

Freud recognized the death instinct and its aggressive derivative as the greatest threat to civilization. There was an ongoing conflict between life and death, as he saw it, that played out on a global stage and within his individual analysands. It should be stated that not many future analysts gave much credence to his death instinct. Melanie Klein, however, took up his death instinct and reveled in the theoretical nuances of our destructive nature. I agree with Michael Eigen that Klein was "more Freudian than Freud" (1996, p. 27). Klein, Eigen suggests, stood on Freud's shoulders and looked death squarely in the eye (ibid.).

Central to her theories is the notion that the infant's primary source of danger is "a destructive force within" (ibid.). For Klein, the infant's hatred toward the frustrating mother or toward a part of the mother—the bad breast—is felt as a frightening force and is thus hurled outward and projected onto the mother or mothering figure. Alas, this doesn't help much, as the bad mother is now experienced as being even more terrible and potentially dangerous; thus the child reinternalizes this badness.

For Klein, the baby must also work to internalize the good mother—the good breast—so that she can pass through this early stage of persecutory anxiety and move toward the more advanced "depressive position." In this way she moves toward the parent as a good object and internalizes this parental representation. As one might suspect from the Kleinian jargon, this is not a hugely optimistic model in regard to our basic human nature. Yet there is hope. Ideally, the child comes to feel bad for the hostility she feels toward the parent and makes efforts at reparation. In other words, if she is progressing, she feels depressed by her own anger and hate toward a person she also loves, for the harm she may have caused. In a Kleinian world, there is tumultuous internal conflict between love and hate from the very beginning of life. Hatred does not come in response to our external environment but rather is mobilized through the infant's frustration.

Until recently, I was troubled by Klein's insistence that even newborn babies are capable of hating others. This seemed to me a grand projection onto the infantile psyche, about which we can only rightly conjecture. Yet through a more careful review of her theories I have come to appreciate her emphasis on this lifelong struggle to integrate the oppositional feelings of love and hate we feel toward our loved ones. Klein paid an abiding respect to the impact of unprocessed and unintegrated feelings of hate on the psyche and on our efforts at relationship. She plotted the nuanced progression from our initial rejection of hate to a place where love and hate coexist through a more dominant and evolved feeling of gratitude. Her theories underscored the importance of understanding the aggression that drives our psychic development toward wellness or toward immense internal and interpersonal suffering.

Heavily influenced by Klein, D.W. Winnicott wrote extensively about the intrapsychic roots of aggression. While I have come to appreciate the importance of Klein's theories, I find in Winnicott a multifaceted perspective on aggression that evokes a broader spectrum of our human potential, the ways in which aggression may be generative and creative as well as destructive.

For Winnicott, aggression is in its earliest form a manifestation of motility (1987). When the baby kicks or bites or throws a tiny fist into the air, he is utilizing his aggression. At its origin, aggression is activity. As the baby discovers that he has muscles that can be engaged and used, he throws his foot in the air, where perhaps a caretaker will be there to catch it and playfully kiss a toe. The baby discovers that there is a world beyond himself. He meets up against another reality. In this way "aggression makes us feel that objects are real, that they exist outside us, in their own right. Aggression links us to the reality of the environment and opens its riches to us, if we can endure the necessary transformation of aggression" (Ulanov, 2001, p. 108; see book for a splendid exploration of Winnicott's larger body of theory and its relevance to religious practice).

This transformation in the experience of aggression comes when the baby grows and feels frustrated by her caretaker's imperfect efforts to meet her needs. Eventually this frustrated wish to control others will result in the experience of hatred and destructiveness. In its earliest stage, however, aggression is an expression of primitive love (Winnicott, 1988, pp. 133–34). Winnicott speaks of our ruthlessness, in which loving is not yet restrained or socialized. The baby loves with her whole self, her body and heart, without consideration of cultural norms or how her love will be received or rejected. This is fully unselfconscious loving, and it has the energy of aggression mixed into its expression.

Ultimately, in this developmental line the baby would come to reach the "stage of concern" through his ability to consider the impact of his aggression. When this stage is successfully reached, the child can integrate his ability to love with the vestiges of ruthlessness and aggressive instinct still at play, alongside his confidence in not harming himself or others. This crossover, however, necessarily involves caretakers who can accept and tolerate the child's ruthlessness *without retaliation*. If the mother becomes emotionally distant after the child playfully bites while breastfeeding, or if she handles the baby harshly in response, the child will learn that his instinctual aggression is not welcome.

But Winnicott was not looking to blame mothers or hold them to impossible standards of equanimity. He showed tremendous empathy for mothers and for the long list of formidable challenges they face with their young children. He even went so far as to suggest that mothers hate their babies before the baby hates his mother (1947, p. 201). He provides a long, highly amusing, and very resonant list of reasons why mothers would understandably hate their babies, who unknowingly demand endless sacrifice without offering thanks, who hurt and endanger the mother during pregnancy, and who can be impossibly difficult only to smile winningly at the next stranger they pass (ibid.). Yet he is equally emphatic that mothers, or "the mothering ones," must hate their babies without doing anything about it. For the baby to develop and successfully integrate his primitive aggression, he *must* interact with a nonretaliatory adult (Winnicott, 1971, p. 150).

It is at this juncture in Winnicott's theory on aggression that psychoanalysis and its healing potential within the analytic dyad come alive for me. In a complex paper he delivered in 1968, Winnicott spoke of the child's need to cross over from "object relating" to "object usage." He explained that when a child can express her ruthless, unrestrained love to a parent who does not retaliate and survives the attack, she discovers the parent's own reality. Such a parent becomes more than something that can be manipulated or organized on the basis of the child's faulty sense of omnipotent control. The parent has her own adult reality, which will come into clear focus for the child if she can sustain her own more mature and integrated capacity to tolerate her child's aggression.

The implications of this capacity as it impacts the child's interpersonal experience are profound. Winnicott described this process as a part of destructiveness, in which the child destroys his fantasy object and comes into contact with reality. This is *not* exploitation, but the process through which children learn to integrate their instinctual life *and* make space for the reality of another to emerge. A mother who survives her child's destructiveness will allow the child to see her own objective reality (Winnicott, 1968). In so doing, the child discovers a whole world beyond himself that can be known, related to, and enjoyed.

Psychoanalyst Christopher Bollas has written about the implications of this pivotal journey within the analytic space. Bollas writes of his psychoanalytic treatment of analysands who could not express aggression without fear of harming the analyst or calling forth the analyst's persecution (Bollas, 1996, pp. 27–31). Such analysands could not operate in a space beyond concern, with trust that the analyst could tolerate their aggression. Instead, it came out sideways, through icy silence and cold remarks meant to leave the analyst feeling diminished and unworthy. Bollas invites the reader into the analyst's experience with the example of one such analysand, someone whose primary caretaker had been rejecting and intolerant of the young child's ruthless capacity to love. Month after month of stone-cold silence and intermittent eviscerating commentary had taught Bollas about the interpersonal devastation that results when someone's aggression has gone underground.

In his evocative description of his treatment of this young woman suffering from split-off or repressed capacity for conscious aggression, it becomes clear that aggression is powerfully operative even when indirectly expressed. Despite his best efforts to offer interpretation of the analysand's covert aggression, the way her early efforts at loving were likely received, how she may have learned to communicate anger as a result, and most importantly, the ways she surely suffered through this learning process, the analysand remained in unyielding, punishing, and indignant silence. After several months of such treatment, when his irritation had grown into full-blown anger, Bollas simply told her in an even tone, "You are a monster" (ibid., p. 38). Stunned, she balked at this outrageous statement, but he continued. "You are being monstrous and this is inhuman behavior on your part!" Jolted beyond belief, the analysand, with whom he had hit an impenetrable impasse for months on end, burst into tears.

This stark admission of his own aggression was not so neatly worked through with her, but it was a start in which she could learn about the toxic effect of aggression that is disowned. She also learned of her own ability to tolerate another person's aggression, and even to be enlivened by it. Through her relationship with Bollas, she experienced aggression consciously felt and directly expressed as a strengthening component of relationship, rather than its demise.

Within the analytic dyad, Bollas has noted that analysands who were unable to express their ruthless love to primary caretakers, to risk "use" of their parental objects, had a tendency in treatment to self-analyze rather than "use" the analyst (1996, p. 26). In this way their split-off aggression kept them locked in a one-person system that bypassed the connectedness of risking anger toward the analyst and so discovering who and what the analyst was really about.

As an analysand, I have seen the contrasting results of both positions. In earlier stages of my own analysis, I experienced the fear of destroying my analyst through a less controlled "use" of his presence and capacity to tolerate and withstand my anger. Such fear tended to fuel a great deal of intricate self-analysis that rendered the analyst a mere observer in my own efforts at self-cure (Khan, 1974, p. 97). In later years, this began to shift. For example, after the events of 9/11, I found myself revisiting a fairly chronic fear that something even worse would transpire. Who else would die, and in what grizzly ways, I wondered with no small amount of dread.

During one such session my analyst rather flippantly suggested that my fears of future attacks indicated my covert hope for impending catastrophe. I winced, and knew in my bones that this interpretation was based on faulty logic. I shook my head and told him that saying this to me was tantamount to telling a holocaust survivor who fears future genocide that they in fact genuinely wish for more genocide. His response struck me as thoughtless and insensitive, and worse yet, totally ego-based—the product of his need to make an interpretation, to take back our space and make it his own. In that moment, I really hated him for it—for judging and distancing himself from my fears rather than sharing in them and holding them (and by extension, me) as an understandable response to trauma.

After telling him so, he was quiet and soon admitted that upon hearing my analogy he knew that he was wrong. He hadn't thought it through. He was sorry, and I felt that his apology was sincere. In retrospect, I see that because I was able to risk direct expression of anger, our exchange did not slip into the trap of familiar defenses that I would have resorted to in years past. I did not muse on the history of trauma survivors. Nor did I need to punish him by making him feel intellectually subpar, by dancing around his interpretations while throwing cerebral darts at his "faulty logic." Instead, there was a real exchange of feeling—my anger, his regret, my hurt, his empathy—and through this we moved into a heightened consciousness of our intimacy, our interbeing if you will, that emerged out of this direct communication of anger and his capacity to respond without retaliation or withdrawal.

Winnicott wrote that "the danger is not in aggression, but in the repression of aggression" (1950, p. 204). My analyst could tolerate my aggression and angry assertion that he was doing "bad therapy." Bollas could tolerate his analysand's honest fury, her clear statement that he should not have called her a monster, that he was a terrible person for having done so. He could not, however, continue in a relationship in which unconscious aggression with psychically lethal impact was played out without end. Nor could I gain much or grow from my analysis without risking expression of the anger and aggression that was part of a thriving and dynamic relationship with my analyst. For this reason, Winnicott called our conscious aggression a psychological achievement. It is a call to grapple with "all of our inner reality," so that it does not hurt the self or others, but allows us all our fullness of objective being (1960a). In her book on Winnicott and psychic reality, Ann Ulanov suggests that "knowing we hate makes us more responsible and less dangerous" (2001, p. 107; see also Neumann, 1969).

There is an ethical component to exploring and utilizing our own aggression. It is a necessary relational fuel, a way to keep our own being more fully alive, alongside the ability to recognize the aliveness of others. In contrast, the psychic retreat that can occur when aggression has gone squarely into the unconscious can be emotionally and physically deadening. It is a sure-fire way to sever human connection or to keep it tepid, to render both people in the human dyad two-dimensional.

For this reason, Karen Horney referred to the whole psychic process that renders our aggression unconscious as an essentially amoral endeavor. In her depiction of the young child's response to an environment in which he feels fundamentally unsafe, she explores the pervasive interpersonal and intrapsychic fallout of unconscious hostility. For Horney, the full spectrum of hostile impulses provides the main source from which neurosis evolves (1937, p. 60). She broke from Freud's intrapsychic locus of aggression, troubled by his fatalism, which posited an inevitable collision between self with its ongoing instinctual urges for aggression, and society with its threatening penal system (1939, p. 191). Instead, she sought to understand the environment in which the child was reared and its impact on the child's internal world.

She was not uninterested in the psyche and the unconscious, as some theorists have suggested, but rather sought to investigate those environmental conditions that seemed to cause tremendous intrapsychic suffering in the child. In fact, she challenged Freud's instinct theory because it reinforced "an acceptance of a conflicted self and thus, unwittingly, a dependence on external circumstances for finding happiness" (Horney 1939, p. 290; see also Westkott, 1997, p. 76). Instead, she proposed a healing process (for the adult) that underscored the need to explore one's own capacity for generating happiness and reducing suffering. Horney brought her keen insight to the ways we manipulate our conscious minds in order to control the unconscious. Her theories proposed an analytic process of bringing these two halves of the psyche into a realistic embrace.

For Horney, if the young child is in an environment with caretakers who are distracted with their own lives, biased toward one sibling, domineering, erratic, overindulgent, or simply unable to conceptualize the child for the person she is, feelings of insecurity and anxiety will ensue. Horney suggested that it was never one factor that elicited this anxiety, but a larger mosaic of "adverse influences" that leave the child feeling basically unsafe and ill at ease (1950, p. 18). The child will also feel immense hostility for feeling so isolated. But à la Freud and Klein, the hostility will typically be repressed and projected onto others. This split-off hostility sets the stage for evolving interpersonal experience where fear of others and exacerbated anger may reign supreme.

The young child seeks a solution to her dilemma. She wishes to find a way to co-exist in an unfriendly environment where she may more effectively elicit the love and security she so desires. Horney identified several key methods and particular attitudes that the child might adopt to bring about these more favorable conditions. Depending upon their personality and the personality of their caretakers, they would either move toward others as the *self-effacing type*, move against people as the *expansive type*, or move away from others as the *resigned type* (ibid., p. 76). These types served several purposes—to provide the child with a more unified sense of identity, to allow her increased viability within the family, and most poignantly, to keep her real and unloved self in a lifelong stranglehold.

The most beastly forms of aggression, in Horney's view, are toward our real but unseen and unknown selves. For Horney, the real self was not a fixed entity but "a set of intrinsic potentialities, including talents, capacities, and predispositions that are part of our genetic makeup…It is everything that a person is at a given time: body and soul, healthy and neurotic" (ibid., p. 157). She posited an evolution of the personality types described above in which the child comes to feel that she should be more or fundamentally different than she is. Horney called this the *tyranny of the shoulds* (ibid.).

This ferocious regime of being is designed to cultivate and sustain an idealized image of oneself. For Horney, this idealization of a particular self-image was a neurotic solution to the child's feeling of basic anxiety. As it took hold, the child would come to feel overpowering hostility toward her real self, which would invariably make itself known when she was unable successfully to manifest a particular idealized image. In this way a person would come to live between the two alternating tides of neurotic pride (in the idealized image) and a nearly lethal self-contempt (ibid., pp. 90–100). Such a person is bound to hate her real self for interfering with the life plan that ensured psychic survival within her family of origin. But as her adult life evolves, this unconscious self-hatred will continue to render the world an unsafe place, where she must forever "lift herself up" over others and simultaneously keep her real and despised self fully underground.

Horney suggested that we do not hate ourselves because we are without value, but because our idealized self-image continues to reach beyond itself. It strives for nothing short of perfection. "The hatred results from the discrepancy between what I would be and what I am. There is not only a split, but a cruel and murderous battle" (ibid., p. 113). This self-hate fuels the idealized image, spurring it on to achieve even greater heights of perfection. When it cannot, or will not, there is a tidal wave of hatred toward the real self for sabotaging these efforts. Of course, this hatred can also be directed outward at the many people who seem not to recognize the person's idealized image, or whose more innocuous criticisms are misinterpreted as affirmation that the person is indeed a contemptible, unworthy being.

In this process of idealization, there would be no developed internal resource to allow one's real self to interface with this idealized image and to spur on its integration. This is in contrast with Kohut's *idealizing parental imago* (see chapter 4), where the idealization of the parent's image is tempered by the parent's tolerable shortcomings and circles back to the child as the capacity for ideals. Horney's idealized image is driven by neurosis rather than a healthy developmental desire to build into one's own psyche the functions of others. It is a way to keep others out rather than a way to bring them squarely within. In this way Horney's idealization severs relationship between one's real self and others, and serves as a kind of psychic armor against a world perceived as hostile and unsafe.

In the Horneyan analytic endeavor, the analysand must first consciously feel and express some genuine compassion for his or her own suffering. This necessary presence of warmth and care toward the self would allow the analysand to develop an increased curiosity about his own reality, who he is and what he feels at a given time. In this way he would begin to withdraw the energy that he has invested in an illusory self and slowly develop an increasing consciousness of the person he is in that particular phase of his life. Of critical importance for Horney were a move toward conscious suffering and a willingness to accept one's limitations without using them as fodder for self-attack.

As a clinician increasingly interested in Buddhist practice, Horney proposed a way of exploring the complexity of human aggression and anger that honored the extent to which we suffer when they are denied, ignored, or merely meditated away. She called for a true bare attention and friendly curiosity toward all manifestations of aggression, so that we might come to know ourselves and the people around us better and with open hearts and minds.

I think of the children I see as a clinician and play therapist. They are all delightful, loveable children with terrific imaginative lives, big hearts, and lots of unprocessed rage. I think it is fair to say that very few of them have encountered the Winnicottian nonretaliatory acceptance of their unbridled capacity for ruthless love. Thus, *à la* Horney's theories, many of them seem to feel that they should be somehow different from who they actually are. A big part of our work together involves their delight in taking toy swords and hacking me to pieces, week after week. They revel in my willingness to ham it up, with bulging eyes, and a drooping head after I've been ritually decapitated. They shriek with laughter as they scalp me, cut off my ears, and gouge my eyes out. So too, they seem thoroughly to enjoy "giving me my body back." When I thank them, they tend to nod or say casually, "You're welcome," or "No problem."

At bottom, I believe they need to know that each week I will be there awaiting their arrival with pleasure, despite having been dismembered the week before. They need to know that I can take it, that their ruthless destruction does not in fact kill me off, but simply makes me more real. I believe they need their aggression, as it mixes with their immense capacity to love, to be fully embraced. Through my willingness to be destroyed, I become a separate, older, and more mature person who can let them be totally alive children—anger, ruthless love, and all.

In these encounters I have also learned about the close relationship between anger and desire. When the children I see have had ample time to gouge my eyes out, to roar with rage, and delight in my "death," they are more willing to accept that the session will end. They seem fulfilled and somehow at peace. While it is never easy for a child to stop doing what is fun, they are more able to say goodbye when the session is over. In contrast, when these ritual killings are too rushed, when we've run out of time and they can only destroy me once and quickly at that, it's never easy to end the session. Sometimes they simply refuse to go.

———

Having offered this cursory review of Buddhist and psychoanalytic approaches to anger and aggression, I consider now how these contrasting theories manifest in the two primary healing dyads. In each dyad, what is most helpful in these differing approaches to anger and aggression?

In the Dharma, students are taught a method of coping with anger that is "cooling" in nature. We see the concerted application of friendly curiosity and mindfulness, both toward one's own anger and toward the object of one's anger. There is a clear emphasis on remaining in connection with one's capacity for equanimity, and for conscious belief in all beings as precious and worthy of our efforts to work through conflict with a peaceful attitude. In this way the Dharma does not suggest a radical dichotomy between emotion and intellect. There is a certain assumption that the two are necessarily in relationship and can inform one another.

In thinking back to Engler's discussion of multiple determination (see chapter 5), and the myriad factors—both conscious and unconscious—that can simultaneously motivate our behavior, I question this assumption in the Dharma, particularly as it pertains to our behavior in relationships. I think, too, of Klein, Horney, and Bollas, whose analytic experiences underscore how powerful unconscious anger and hatred can be. What they are suggesting as a result of their experience within the analytic space is that the intellect (a conscious function) may fasten upon notions of self and others that are in profound and unconscious conflict with one's genuine feelings. Authentic emotions and radically divergent intellectual perceptions can coexist within the same person, who may not have any conscious awareness of this dissonance.

For example, Buddhist students may consciously perceive their teacher as offering them important opportunities to "practice" patience, loving kindness, and unshakable devotion when the teacher is behaving in ways that are frustrating, mean-spirited, or seemingly disrespectful. They may consciously focus on the teacher's buddha nature, which is at its core placid and clear-seeing. But unconsciously students may feel fury for having been disrespected or humiliated in some way that left them questioning their basic value. And if these feelings remain unconscious, they may manifest as a kind of compulsive caretaking and tolerance for bad behavior that is in actuality an unconscious atonement for these split-off feelings of anger. As Horney suggests, they will find a way to cope that utilizes idealization of teacher and teachings, or of themselves as *spiritual* people, in the service of keeping their genuine and unseemly feelings unconscious and thus safely camouflaged. Worse yet, if students cannot tolerate their own feelings of anger toward the teacher, or vice versa, the relationship may rupture with great loss to both teacher and students.

Simply put, I am suggesting that mindfulness does not account for the power and potential impact of the unconscious. Bollas' analysand, in all likelihood, had no conscious intention to become so punitive with her analyst. Chances are that, like most analysands, she sought analytic treatment to soften her defenses and to become more at ease in relationships. Unless she was suffering from full-blown psychosis, which was not the case, such behavior would have caused her both horrendous shame and increased intrapsychic suffering. But when unconscious feelings and beliefs about ourselves are triggered—as they invariably are in the psychoanalytic process—one's greatest and most heartfelt intentions can be easily overshadowed by entrenched behaviors and defensive psychological maneuvers.

Bollas' analysand needed an analyst who could risk expressing his own aggression directly, to make conscious for her the toxic impact of passive aggression or anger gone underground. Through this experience, she learned of a very real integrity in aggression expressed with honesty and courage, for it lacks the vengeance and potentially punitive spirit of covert anger. It has a clean intentionality that is resonant with the Buddha's reference to wrathful compassion, where heat is used in the service of reducing suffering and sustaining connection.

The theories of Winnicott, Klein, and Horney all attempt to explicate the necessary preconditions for our learned ability to express aggression with this clean intentionality. From their perspective, it does not happen via adult belief systems but through essential early childhood experience. In this way they recognize critical differences between the child and the adult, alongside pronounced differences between psyche—with its conscious and unconscious parts—and the intellect. When those early life experiences do not transpire, these psychoanalytic theorists propose a treatment process that allows people the opportunity to engage in intimate relationship where "object usage," idealization, and unconscious hate may all risk encounter with another. The psychoanalytic dyad creates an unusually healing space where our most suffering selves can safely make appearances without being vulnerable to retaliation or retraumatization.

Yet I do not wish to suggest that a psychoanalytic understanding of anger and aggression is necessarily more effective in facilitating healing than Buddhist spiritual training. For ultimately I believe that the experience of sustaining mindfulness in the midst of overpowering affect is what allows us to make use of, rather than merely to act out, one's feelings. In the Dharma one finds a critical insight regarding anger: that it easily induces feelings of aversion that cause us to turn away both from the very experience of feeling anger and from the object of our anger. This conditioned response of aversion can leave people locked in unconscious anger and aggression even in the course of psychoanalytic treatment with skillful clinicians for years on end. In other words, the automatic response of aversion toward anger and aggression, without conscious understanding of this universal mental tendency, may sabotage even the most skillful analyst's efforts to help an analysand work through and integrate feelings of anger or aggression.

Buddhist teaching emphasizes one's capacity to remain alert to reality, even when this reality entails negative experience, loss, or injustice. And while I am not suggesting that this spiritual training alone can adequately address the impact of aggression that is unconscious to the spiritual practitioner, I believe that it can serve as a great boon to one's general interpersonal experience, and certainly to the psychoanalytic endeavor, with its near constant exploration of painful psychic reality. Understanding that turning away from unpleasant sensation is a habituated mental tendency and a universal phenomenon can support both members of religious and psychoanalytic dyads. It is a call to staying wakeful, even while in the throes of suffering, that can deepen the psychoanalytic process and help both dyads tolerate sustained periods of interpersonal difficulty.

Just as we turn away from what is painful, says the Dharma, we grasp on to what we imagine will eradicate our pain and suffering. So it makes sense that many foundational Buddhist teachings on anger are closely linked to desire. In the three poisons of Buddhist doctrine, desire or clinging takes its prominent place alongside anger and ignorance. The Dhammapada, the Buddha's book of principles, says the following:

> Do not be intimate with attachment to desire…Never cleave to what is pleasing or what is displeasing; not seeing what is pleasant is painful, and so is seeing what is unpleasant. So do not take a liking to anything, for loss of what is liked is bad. There are no fetters for those who have no likes or dislikes (Cleary, 1994, pp. 14 and 74).

These statements may reinforce a common perception of Buddhism as an austere tradition populated by skinny monks and dour practitioners. Yet the full body of Buddhist doctrine on desire and grasping is quite rich and nuanced. It is true that throughout the sutras, desire or *tanha* (thirst) is depicted as the foremost impediment to enlightenment. It is identified as the cause of suffering in the second noble truth, and as the second of the three poisons. Buddhism teaches us that we are wired with powerful sense perceptions that mix with each other into what are referred to as the "thirty-six streams" of total potential sense experience. We are forever tempted to pursue these senses for our happiness and deepest sense of gratification. When in the grips of a particular sensual pleasure, it is easy to imagine that it is indeed *the ultimate* source of happiness and fulfillment. From here, addiction can easily become a defining dynamic in one's life. That delightful sense of choice, a decidedly adult feeling that we can choose whether or not to see a desired person, to eat another piece of chocolate, to work throughout the night, or to purchase an illegal drug, is easily lost when we are consumed by the pull of sensual desire.

The Buddha, however, understood the necessity of teaching others not to demonize their desires, but rather to reorient their perception and to encourage others to wrestle with the universal feeling of not being enough, not being whole, and thus not being satisfied. In his efforts to identify the real culprit of this feeling of dissatisfaction, he made the following statement: "Do not despise the six senses, for they are not bad; after all they are the same as true awakening" (Cleary, 1994, p. 22).

This intriguing proclamation was, I suspect, intended as a reminder that the incarnate path is one of potential freedom. We are not shackled by virtue of having bodies that come wired with senses. As the Heart Sutra says, "form is emptiness; emptiness is form." Even this very body, with all its built-in limitations, is pregnant with possibility for an abiding happiness and equanimity. What causes our suffering are basic misperceptions that result in a problematic *relationship* to the senses.

The Buddha was familiar with the temptation to locate the hook of desire in our physiological needs and experience. He came to recognize before his enlightenment that strict asceticism would not ultimately facilitate the transformation he sought. More likely it would either kill him or leave him too distracted by hunger and malaise to enter into the deep concentration necessary for an awakened mind. No, he said, with much compassion for his many followers similarly inclined to reign in the body's many needs. There is a *Middle Way*. The Buddha indicated that *this* world and our incarnate place within it was the perfect place for awakening (Thurman, 1998, p. 25).

The challenge, from a Buddhist perspective, is to alter our perception of the world through steadfast and vigilant mind training. This is why we have teachers—so that we can internalize their wisdom mind and have it mix with our own and thus come to experience and create happier relationships to our external environments. Without this engagement, we are vulnerable to chronic feelings of dissatisfaction.

In Buddhist cosmology there are six realms of existence inhabited by six kinds of being. This is often represented visually as an aid for students to imagine the various conditions of potential rebirth. One such realm is populated by the hungry ghosts, terribly disfigured beings characterized by their swollen bellies, long skinny necks, and pinhole-sized mouths. With their voracious desire for nourishment and tiny mouths, they can never get enough (Epstein, 2005, p. 98; Goldstein, 2003, p. 68). They are beset with perpetual unmet needs, always trying to take in to themselves the "food" of the external world.

In Western Buddhist circles, stories of the hungry ghosts abound. Western students are often regarded, by both Western and Eastern teachers, as people lost in this realm of unquenchable thirst, where we repeatedly consume products that cause harm and cannot be digested and used for the real vigor we so desperately need. Joseph Goldstein calls this ensnarement in the desire for more products, food, or stimuli, "catalogue consciousness." He is referring to the pull we so often feel to buy something, or take something into ourselves that would somehow make us feel better, and happier. This is the experience of "wanting to want." When these chronic efforts to consume products that cannot nourish our most basic feeling of lack leave us feeling beleaguered, anger is the likely result.

In the realm of the hungry ghosts we seek what doesn't work for our particular being. We become addicted and then rail against the person, situation, or product that fails to satisfy us. Or, à la Horney's theories, we loathe ourselves for not achieving the satisfaction that the "shiny happy people" in commercials and fantastical films seem to experience with unfettered ease. Instead, when we are gripped by desire, frustration invariably ensues, often leaving us in a boiling pit of anger or some other variety of mental dis-ease.

Even in our spiritual lives, said the Buddha, desire can covertly dominate. He called this "affliction by the dust of religion" (Cleary, 1994, p. 18). I have observed this tendency in myself: the wish to be perceived as an "advanced" spiritual practitioner, or someone endowed with "special insight," has at times left me with residual feelings of loneliness, of not fully participating in the human realm. Distancing myself from the banal realm of the unenlightened, I have watched this desire render my capacity to hear sacred teachings somewhat narrow, becoming like the pinhole-sized mouth of the hungry ghost. In those moments, I get the few bits meant for "special" practitioners while the real and basic nutrients are rejected as belonging to "beginners" whose needs are more all-encompassing.

But as I have come to see, the problem was not in my desire for noteworthy insight. Indeed, a strong wish to be enlightened is encouraged in most traditions—we hold dear that precious capacity to awaken our own minds and hearts for the benefit of all beings. Where I struggled with desire was in my unconscious wish to grasp on to a bolstered sense of identity that would necessarily spare me any future pain. I wanted to know the Dharma so that it might fill in the woeful holes in my ego. There is irony in this unconscious process of reifying identity in a tradition designed to burn through identity, but apparently from the very inception of the Buddhist path, I have had company in this off-putting tendency.

For monastic Buddhists teaching in the West, desire is a complicated topic. They are typically quite sensitive to the cultural set-up for chronic frustration that Westerners must negotiate. On the one hand, we are besieged by promises of orgiastic satisfaction through endless delectable foods, and on the other bombarded with images of enticing men and women, muscular and striking for their absence of unseemly fat. If we live in a large city, we will walk by endless stores promising unfailing happiness through products we cannot afford or to which we are already addicted. From the perspective of many monastic teachers, we are like tiny boats out to sea, perpetually thrown about by powerful waves of desire for ultimately ineffectual products.

Lamas tend to watch television and have cell phones. They know what this culture is peddling in its consumerist frenzy. They too get irksome calls from telemarketers, and they customarily have a certain fascination with technology. As my teacher says, with a mile-wide smile, "A lama without a cell phone is like a cowboy without a gun."

The lamas I have studied with express a combination of hopeful compassion and a quiet, occasionally humorous resignation about this predicament. They recognize the spiritual toll that it takes on their students, and

162 : mixing minds

that it leaves people feeling constantly malnourished, as if they have been fed the wrong foods. Yet they also recognize in the Dharmic path a way to address this ensnarement, a way out. But it takes work and commitment, and a firm conviction that the work will reap rewards. One rinpoche recently told me that he felt Westerners had "trouble settling their minds." He felt that we should pursue Buddhism, but that we would not get much out of it if this unsettled mind didn't settle down, which it seemed unlikely to do.

This path of a "settled mind" involves careful and thorough study, contemplation, and practice of the Dharma, something many people don't have the time for or don't trust in. Yet without the willingness to undertake this, practitioners may easily misinterpret the doctrine as a sanction for simply exorcising any behavior, person, or idea that triggers strong feelings of desire—the dreadful "grasping" of the hungry ghosts. We may hear teachings on renunciation as a call to move further away from the secular world, and to practice the Dharma sitting on cushions in quiet meditation centers while never quite integrating it into the secular experience and interpersonal relationships that make up our waking days.

The Middle Way proposed by the Buddha's living example involves a more expansive and reverent approach to our capacity for desire. It asks for a depth of curiosity about what we seek when in the throes of desire. In this way desire is presented as a "mode of appreciation" and not a "prelude to possession" (Epstein, 2005, p. 177). In his book on desire, Mark Epstein suggests that desire's most important task is to point out the gap that desire brings (ibid., p. 95). The Dharma encourages practitioners to contemplate this gap between our purest feeling of desire and what the conventional objects of our desire actually deliver.

The problem is not in the desire but in identifying with and becoming fixated upon an external object through our misperception of its substantiality. As a result of this obsession, we forget what desire is capable of delivering and where it can take us. When students decide that their earthly desires should simply be renounced and rooted out, they often, because of unconscious fear and anger, demonize the experience of wanting rather than recognize that they must simply (or with much concerted effort) discern what is worth wanting and learn how to relate to what probably isn't.

In a sangha that I participated in when I was younger, buttons were made that read *"Happiness begins where self-cherishing ends."* This had a certain ring to it, reminding us that desire for one's self did not deliver the spiritual goods. Instead, such grasping at self lands us in a dreadful ghostly realm where happiness forever eludes us. In this sangha there was an emphasis on renunciation of all things, people, and circumstances that we might wish to possess. I couldn't help but notice that the teacher was a particularly handsome man, a Westerner who took to Buddhism in his teens. Throughout his teaching endeavors, he had managed to put together a community of mostly young and attractive men and women who seemed either openly or covertly desirous of this appealing teacher, who was a lay person but contemplating monkhood. I found myself distracted by my growing curiosity about his relationship to desire. Here he was, surrounded by fans, many of whom were young, single, and seeking partners with an interest in the spiritual realm. It seemed meaningful that his teachings were conspicuously and relentlessly focused on renunciation.

So too, I noted how we all clung passionately to the idea of attachment of any kind as a sure-fire means to suffering. We collectively deemed self-grasping to be the ultimate route to some kind of Buddhist hell. In the fervor of our appetite for these teachings, I sensed a certain attachment to renunciation as a safeguard against the fear of being pulled into a scenario of desire that we could not handle while sustaining our spiritual personas. For a student to have a romantic relationship with the attractive teacher or with someone comparably desirable, or for the teacher to have a romantic relationship with an attractive student, would throw open the floodgates of desire.

I am not suggesting that teachers should pursue their students romantically. The consequences of such liaisons in Western Buddhist circles in the 1980s were disastrous; clear boundaries between teachers and students are essential for the well-being of both. My point is that in this community there was a childlike aversion toward sexuality in general, and all things sexual were denounced as base, unhelpful distractions from the more virtuous path of spiritual practice. We erred on the side of passionately desiring renunciation over the more tangible objects of our desire, despite the nonstop current of sexual curiosity that ran through the community like a bubbling brook.

In psychoanalytic parlance, the expression of a belief or feeling that belies our true beliefs or feelings is referred to as a *reaction formation*. This psychic maneuver reverses the original unwanted affect to a conscious development of its opposite. In this process there is always an element of overcompensation in the mix (Pruyser, 1968, p. 170): thus the bright orange buttons reminding us cheerfully that we could be happy, if only we could stop *grasping*, and the almost intoxicated glow of the participants after a particularly incisive teaching on renunciation.

Reaction formation typically announces itself through an intensity of feeling that belongs to the original, split-off affect. In Paul Pruyser's exploration of the psychology of religion, he came to discover that this psychological process is common among the religious, in whom there is typically a clear divide between feeling states that are sanctioned for their spiritual purity and those that are not (1968, pp. 139–54). High on the list of feeling states valued for their religiosity are reverence, gratitude, compassion, remorse, mercy, and bliss. Not surprisingly, feelings that are considered impediments to religious practice and belief include lassitude, coldness, sloth and torpor, anger, anxious clinging, and, yes, lust.

I agree with Pruyser that the religious (and here I include those who self-define as spiritual) tend to take quite a selective approach to emotion. Given that religious practice is typically experienced as a feeling domain, a space where one becomes more heart-centered and less tethered to one's thinking capacity, there is a strong pull to associate certain feelings with virtuous efforts on the religious path and others with the baser reality of the secular world. Pruyser suggests that the whole realm of feeling, since it typically includes the passions of lust and anger, can become problematic for many religious practitioners. This, he says, is a classic earmark of asceticism (ibid., pp. 147–49).

I am not proposing that the decision to take monastic vows in any religious faith is always indicative of split-off anger or sexual desire. I am confident that this is not the case; I harbor great respect for monastics who devote their lives to the religious and spiritual practice of supporting others on their spiritual journey. While it is beyond the scope of this chapter to discern the myriad psychological and cultural factors that inform the monastic experience, I wish simply to clarify that psychologizing all religious experience strikes me as being unhelpful and often entirely off the mark. That said, I hope there might be a middle way in which we can observe and take note of religious communities and teachers that seem more integrated, and on friendlier terms with the broader spectrum of human emotionality that includes anger, sexual longing, and desire.

In the Tibetan Buddhist community in which I participate, monasticism is considered the very foundation of the Dharma's continuation. Interestingly, there is also open discussion about marriage, loneliness, and the ongoing challenge of balancing family life and spiritual practice among Western lay Buddhists. Within the first few months of studying with my lama, he asked me if I was married. "Why not," he wanted to know. "Is this your choice? Do you think you will ever get married?" More recently, I was asked in a private interview with a woman Tibetan Buddhist teacher whether I had a boyfriend, despite my intention to discuss a complex spiritual issue.

I told them both that these were 64 million dollar questions and that if they could figure them out, I'd stop seeing my analyst and fork over my future inheritance. We had a good laugh, but in these exchanges I felt them acknowledge the broader reality of my life in the secular world, where romantic partnership is common and prized. Like all good teachers, they were more interested in what was best for me, given my particular circumstance, than in prioritizing growth in one facet of my life at the expense of another. This, I believe, is the bodhisattva's way—helping others claim lost parts of themselves so that their very fullness of being can in turn inspire and support others.

There was also implicit in these conversations an important reminder that spirituality and desire are not mutually exclusive. In fact, they necessarily go hand in hand. Epstein writes that "desire is the energy that strives for transcendence" (2005, p. 8). When we can use desire as a roadmap toward relationship with our own buddha nature, that most basic place of internal peace and clarity, we will have found the source of happiness that desire wishes us to find.

Carl Jung put forward quite a resonant theory of desire. He posited a religious instinct that called us to be in conscious relationship with the "numinous." When we ignored this instinct, or found substitutes in food, sex, or work, neurosis ensued (Ulanov, 2005, pp. 20 and 76). Or worse yet, we would take our own egos to be substitutes for a divine source of wisdom, steadily moving toward egomania and into the territory of mental illness (ibid.; Ulanov, 2005, p. 149). In the twenty-first century, struggles with addiction saturate the adult realm and have begun to pervade childhood, as evidenced by the rise of childhood diabetes and the impact of ubiquitous computer games and cell phones on now legendary attention deficits. Given these conditions, Jung's theories may be worth increased consideration.

While Jung spoke of belief in God, and not one's buddha nature, he stated emphatically that it was this belief and its impact on the psyche, not the truth of God's existence, that he wished to examine. For Jung, God imagery came in all forms. But at their root, these divergent images all served a shared purpose of helping people come into conscious relationship with the deepest parts of themselves. This connection gave meaning to life and was the antidote to suffering. Ann Ulanov calls these God-images "clusters of emotion-laden symbols that operate within the psyche as the unifying centers of psychic life" (2005, p. 20).

In the clinical realm, the contrast between conscious desire and desire that has either been disowned or channeled into a relationship that causes addiction and immense suffering is clear. For Buddhists, the issue is framed as clinging or nonclinging. Buddhist teachers often give the example of holding an infant. We do so gently, but also with firmness and concentration. To hold too tightly is to do harm to a vulnerable and precious child. Not to hold tightly enough is to let something precious fall. Students are encouraged to relate to desire with a comparable reverence, one that does not grasp whatever we are holding but rather allows it to show us its own reality. If we are holding the wish for happiness through the Dharma, this will make itself known. If we are holding a person, a substance, a job, or even a political conviction or psychological theory, it will reveal its inability to provide the happiness and freedom from suffering we seek.

For Karen Horney, relinquishing this grasping urge comes from the willingness to engage our own inner reality. She discovered that relationship to false notions of the self is often compulsive; when we find an identity or personal quality that seems to ensure our happiness, we cling to it with a fervor that rivals our attachment to the most pernicious of addictive substances.

In her analysands, Horney found that the worst forms of clinging came in response to alienation from one's true self (1950, p. 161). When they had developed personality types that were used as so much psychic armor against a world found to be unsafe, they lost touch with that living center within. She argued that this alienation from our inner reality was the nuclear problem in all neurotic development (ibid., pp. 21–26). When that fluid, ever-changing being within was squelched, we would grasp on to coping mechanisms that ensured suffering for ourselves and, in all likelihood, for others. Healing was always possible, but it required a willingness to let go of the tight hold on fantasy self-images and to know the psychic mosaic of our real selves.

In both Buddhism and psychoanalysis there is a root cause for suffering and an antidote to the clinging that camouflages the healing potential inherent in desire. In Buddhism the root cause is a basic misperception of inherent separateness that leaves us feeling irrevocably disconnected from all others. With this faulty view, we feel a sense of profound emptiness that is not the ripe space of possibility depicted in the doctrine but a meaningless void into which we fall and cannot get out. In psychoanalysis the root cause is early trauma or an insufficient "holding environment" that did not allow a sense of peaceful merger with the environment, our own "going on being," owing to neglect or care that was invasive and/or anxious (Winnicott, 1960b; Epstein, 2005, p. 105). When this happens we keep trying—repeatedly and compulsively—to get the love that is not to be had either from our original caretakers or from people in our lives who help recreate the traumatizing relational dynamics of our youth. In both traditions the interruption of our basic need to feel and be in meaningful connection with ourselves and others fuels a painful relationship to desire.

Polly Young-Eisendrath writes that in Buddhism and psychoanalysis, compassion spurs on the transformation and healing we seek. She describes compassion as a "kind and loving response to the distress and suffering of another or oneself" (Young-Eisendrath, 2003, p. 303). The Dalai Lama defines compassion as "positive thoughts and feelings that give rise to such essential things in life as hope, courage, determination and inner strength" (1995, p. 64). I envision my teacher's face as I hear this description; it is an open mirror for another person's experience that reflects back his or her very best qualities and circumstance, offering an altered and happier perspective.

Young-Eisendrath refers to the many Buddhist practices designed to help people cultivate a mind of compassion. These practices abound in all traditions. In the Tibetan tradition we practice *tonglen*, where we visualize the suffering of all beings and include this collective experience in our own suffering, so that the happiness we seek may too be a shared experience. People in the Insight Meditation tradition practice cultivating loving kindness for all beings, including those we love, those we struggle with, and those for whom we have no conscious feeling. As we practice compassion and kindness toward all sentient beings, we begin to recognize our foundational interbeing. Through an authentic feeling of another person's suffering, we see that this suffering is shared, and that there are no impenetrable boundaries between self and other. In the Mahayana teachings this is the meeting of the awakened heart and emptiness; it is a perfect union of wisdom and compassion (ibid., p. 24).

Young-Eisendrath suggests that there are two ways in which compassion is cultivated within the analytic dyad (2003, p. 304). The first involves the analysand's transference onto the analyst, those thoughts, feelings, and wishes that cannot be seen as distinct from the analyst's own objective reality. When the ability to transcend suffering and move toward happiness is projected onto the analyst, it points toward the patient's own compassion for self and for others. In the earlier stages of treatment this may only be seen as a capacity belonging to a gifted and insightful analyst. But over time, if the projections are withdrawn and made conscious, they will reveal the analysand's own formerly unconscious compassion for himself, which was mirrored by a caring analyst.

In the second method of cultivating compassion, both members of the analytic dyad continue to express a deep and abiding curiosity about the patient's suffering (ibid.). Through this process of discovery, the analyst and analysand realize that they have depended upon each other for insight and for a deeper awareness of the analysand's inner world, even when the work was painful and the relationship conflictual. I agree with Young-Eisendrath that this feeling of being joined in a shared and intimate venture can usher in a profound sense of interdependence that is both psychological and spiritual in nature. It is the breaking down of illusory boundaries that prevent us from recognizing that we depend upon each other for every facet of our move toward healing and wellness. In this way happiness comes to be seen as a joint effort, a truly relational process that can heal even the most dire and ancient experience of being a perpetual "stranger in a strange land."

In visual depictions of the realm of the hungry ghosts, there is the small figure of a bodhisattva who has come offering nourishment. The Buddha taught that when we are hungry for a sense of fullness that will last beyond one feeding, we must engage with another who can point us toward the right foods. We cannot learn to feed ourselves without a kind and caring person who recognizes our hunger and who knows where nourishing food may be found. Such a person helps us understand that we are forever filled with the fruitful possibility of even more substantive connections with our deepest nature and with this nature in others. Such a person clarifies that the emptiness we feel needn't be filled with food that wears us down and exhausts our endless potential. If we can learn to tolerate the discomfort of not always knowing and not always trusting that this emptiness can be filled with the truth of our vast connection to all beings, then desire can be our greatest ally. Buddhism teaches that we cannot learn this alone.

In both traditions and within both healing dyads, coming to this realization requires a willingness to relinquish substitutes for real and abiding happiness. In psychoanalysis this is a process of mourning, where the original rupture, the places where we were psychically dropped or unloved, must be felt. It is potentially heart-piercing work, where whatever pain has been stored within may be experienced as a kind of emotional tsunami. But it is the only way to bypass the grip of false gods—objects or people who offer an illusory compensation for the pain and anger we unconsciously harbor.

In Buddhism, this is where one's capacity for renunciation becomes an authentic means toward awakening (Epstein, 2005, p. 111). This is something different from an unconscious attachment to renunciation that spares us frightening confrontation with the objects of our conventional desire. Instead, it is a willingness to clear space within our minds for insight into a truer and more reliable source of happiness and internal rest. It is a call to give up what hasn't helped and to embrace the wisdom and compassion whose union softens the heart and sharpens the mind, allowing us to be carried by a desire to help ourselves and all beings be happy and free from suffering.

I find myself reflecting on the critical ways in which my own psychoanalytic experience has helped me appreciate the Buddhist understanding of aggression and desire, and how my spiritual practice has allowed me to do the hard work of mourning and facing the losses suffered in the analytic process. I think of my analyst, who is forever inclined to remind me that anger pushed underground is likely to come back in some manifestation of self-attack. Even if it is a Buddhist poison, he is apt to say, it cannot be denied. In fact, it becomes poisonous only when it is denied. In this way I have learned to develop curiosity about my personal relationship to anger and aggression so that it can be known rather than unconsciously acted out or reactively engaged. Through this exploration, a sense of authentic mindfulness comes into play, where repression is not the only option.

Yet I have also found that the insights gained and feelings felt through psychoanalysis can be overwhelming. If they come in waves, one can feel adrift in an endlessly turbulent sea. There is nowhere to put this intensity, no place in which it can be cared for as life continues. One's whole identity can unknowingly merge with a sea of affect and insight, as if we were nothing more than old wounds, anger, and split-off desire. I have felt the need for a container to hold this tumult of feeling and painful memory.

I think too of a trip I took last year with my lama. As we drove together, the city traffic slowed our entry onto a narrow and congested highway. We crawled along, and in the distance could hear a police siren growing steadily louder. But there was no way for us to move aside. My lama was driving, and he is a slow driver in the best of conditions. He tried somewhat half-heartedly to push his way toward the right as the police car moved behind us, honking madly. When we were eventually able to pull to the side, the policeman driving the car swooped in beside us, rolled down his window, and, red with frustration, yelled, "What the *hell* are you doing? Pull over! Jesus *Christ!*" before zooming off into the distance.

With wide eyes my lama looked at me and said, "Now *that* pisses me off." I nodded, feeling stunned and embarrassed for the cop who had just chewed out a Tibetan Buddhist monk. I felt a wave of shame on his behalf, and for my lama who had been on the receiving end of clear ire and was now feeling it himself. Before long we carried on talking about an upcoming Tibetan language exam I planned to take. Together we chanted the prayers that I would be required to know, slowly and repeatedly, bringing our attention back to what soothed the mind, and to what the Buddha taught: compassion for all beings, our total interdependence, the end of suffering. There was a sense of real anger and real desire commingling. Neither was split off, and both were held by a ready container for feelings that have always been challenging to the psyche and the spirit. There was a sense of starting from our most present, human experience—driving cars in city traffic and coping with flaring tempers and our own frustration—and coming back to the deeper and more continuous reality of interdependence, precious human life (including the nasty cop), and the capacity to awaken to this reality in every moment.

when analysts meditate and buddhists analyze

7

IN RECENT YEARS I have found myself fielding numerous questions from clinicians and Buddhists interested in my approach to analytic work as a practicing Buddhist. They wonder if mindfulness training influences the way I listen to clients, or if I integrate a meditative state into the analytic attunement? Do I encourage my clients to pursue a meditation practice?

What I glean from these many questions is both a genuine curiosity about the analyst's relationship to religion and/or spirituality and its influence on her clients, alongside a real difficulty imagining how these aspects of the clinician might coexist within the established parameters and boundaries of the analytic space. I hear in their questions another set of implicit questions: What did the Buddha know of sexual anxiety, or children raised by narcissistic parents, or teenagers who shoot heroin because they are only marginally or intermittently loved, or because they have witnessed acts of terrorism? What does spirituality have to do with psychological problems anyway? And why should it matter if the analyst has a spiritual life if her role is to serve clients who suffer primarily from psychological problems resulting from relationships and experiences in the secular world?

My initial response to such questions is that everything about the clinician matters. It was for this reason that Freud insisted analysts be well analyzed, that they come to know the nuances of their own psychological and interpersonal histories, their places of fixation, and their hidden wishes and fears, so that they could tease out the differences between their own psychic content and that of their analysands. With his emphasis on transference and countertransference as the primary means through which the analyst can come to know the client's psychological and relational history, it became critically important for the analyst to know herself well enough that she not confuse what the client transferred or projected onto her with the reality of her own psychic content.

Building on Freud's theories, Melanie Klein wrote about the impact of projective identification, whereby we (in this case the analyst) identify with what has in actuality been projected onto us by another person. This is a constant pitfall in psychoanalysis, where the analysand's temptation and tendency to recreate past interpersonal experience becomes a kind of psychological theater, a fiction of the mind that can feel as real to both partners of the analytic dyad as the chair in which one sits or the paintings on the wall.

For these reasons and more, the analyst's own analysis was and remains an essential part of analytic training. Simply put, who the analyst is, what he believes in, who and what he relies upon, how he has been loved, who he loves, and who he has lost are as influential to the analytic relationship as the analysand's history and lived experience. The analyst and the analysand have a dynamic and present-day relationship. And while the experience of the analysand is indeed privileged in the analytic dyad, the analyst's perspective, beliefs, and history will be just as operative and influential. For this reason, Freud believed, and I fully agree, that what remains unconscious in any relationship, will get acted out—it will show up in ways that are surprising, and depending on the nature of what has been denied consciousness, at times limiting and destructive.

So what happens if what has remained unconscious in the analyst are feelings about religion and the concept of God, or belief in God, Buddha, or Allah? In theory, the analyst will have been trained to sustain an open-minded, nonjudgmental attitude toward the analysand, regardless of the psychic material they present. Freud wrote passionately of the analytic space as a morally neutral ground that invited the analysand to speak freely and openly about whatever memories, thoughts, or feelings arose. This analytic neutrality, said Freud, allowed the analysand to follow Freud's golden rule: to express without censorship whatever came to mind (1933).

But anyone who has ever traversed the realm of human relationship knows that mere invitation to speak freely is never enough. We are remarkably sensitive creatures, with layer upon layer of perceptual capacity. We "pick up" on tacit beliefs and feelings that may belie another person's verbal expression of open-minded curiosity. Teenagers throughout the globe know well when a parent cannot in reality tolerate the truth of their child's experience, despite the parent's plea for honesty. Lovers sense when duplicity is in the air, even as proclamations of undying love are offered. We may opt to deny what we have intuited, but the reality remains that our intuitive capacities allow us to perceive even deeply buried, totally unconscious beliefs and feelings.

Conversely, the history of human relations suggests that we are able consciously to perceive in others only what is conscious in ourselves. To return to the parent/child dyad by way of example, if the parent has never wrestled with his own secret experience in childhood—the part of himself he felt he could not share and must camouflage at all psychic costs—he may become particularly oblivious to those aspects of his child's identity or experience that have been withheld from the parent/ child relationship. In Jungian language, the parent would be able to acknowledge the reality of the child's shadow—that hidden container for split-off attributes, talents, and wishes—only if he has acknowledged his own.

This reality is well known to psychoanalysts; even the most gifted analysands may function as if whole swaths of their own and other people's reality do not exist. So too, we often marvel at what clients intuit or pick up in regard to the analyst, despite the analyst's every effort to stay attuned to the analysand and to sustain firm and appropriate boundaries. The same is true in the realm of religious belief, both in terms of what is intuited and what is denied.

The analyst will be able to consciously recognize and enter into the complexity of a client's religious experience only if she too has embarked on a conscious relationship to the spiritual realm. If she has not—even if she has encouraged the analysand to "speak freely"—the analysand in all likelihood will have his intuitive feelers out, picking up the closed-off or undeveloped parts of the analyst's own psyche. He may thus opt not to bring his religious experience into his analytic work, even if it is a part of their belief system and social life. Or, if he does attempt to talk about religious and/or spiritual experience, he may feel quietly judged or evaluated. Yet another possibility is perhaps just a sense of not being understood, as if he is "barking up the wrong tree" for insight and answers.

The religious experience, in other words, will have nowhere to land in the relationship with the analyst. If religion and spirituality are murky territory for the analyst, the analysand is likely to feel a "return to sender" phenomenon, despite an ostensible analytic neutrality and the analyst's genuine wish for an open channel of communication.

Buddhist psychoanalyst Paul Cooper calls this dynamic in the analytic space the "disavowal of the spirit" (Cooper, 1998, p. 234). It is the unfortunate process (for the analysand) whereby the analytic space may become small and unknowingly rigidified through the impact of the analyst's unconscious disavowal of the religious realm. What happens, then, for analysands who in addition to their analytic treatment have a spiritual practice or a strong faith life, and whose relationship to religion and spirituality has a significant impact on their psychological experience and well-being or entrenched struggles? Where are they to explore this interface of psyche and spirit if the analyst does not recognize the spirit as meaningful or even reality-based?

In his investigation into the psychology of religion, Paul Pruyser makes the emphatic statement that it is only the analyst who knows God's love who can honor this experience in the clinical setting (1968, p. 18). This would not be much of an issue if it weren't for the fact that over 90 percent of all Americans as of 2006 self-identified as religious and people of faith (Bader et al., 2006). Some studies suggest the number is even higher, with close to 99 percent professing a belief in God (this surprising number is confirmed by the even more surprising statistics ascertained in a comprehensive study published in *Science*; Miller, Scott, & Okamoto, 2006. Approximately 60 percent of all Americans question the veracity of evolution, privileging biblical literalism and "theistic evolution" over science).

I don't know what percentage of analysands are among the minority of nonbelievers in the United States. But it's a fair guess that a sizable percentage of people seeking psychotherapeutic and analytic support are also people whose psyches have in some significant way been influenced by their childhood and adult experience in the religious realm. Even for those who self-identify as nonreligious or atheists, chances are they will have been influenced by a primary caretaker's belief in God or a particular culture's emphasis on religious belief. In one way or another, either through attraction or aversion, notions of the divine will have found their way into their psychological and familial experience. This is one primary reason why the analyst's own conscious awareness of religious experience matters in the analytic space.

Another way of assessing the relevance of the analyst's spiritual or religious belief and practice is to ask who they are, as opposed to what they do. Psychoanalyst Neville Symington suggests that the healing agent in the psychoanalytic process is the analyst's state of mind (Symington, 2003, p. 190). Kohut had a similar insight, suggesting that what matters to the psyche of the young child is not what the parent does, but who the parent is (1977, p. 187). Interfaith scholar and activist Paul Knitter discovered that this axiom holds true in peace-making efforts, where the mindset of the peacemaker is the mutative agent. Says Knitter, "If peacemakers *are* peace, then what they do will make peace. If they *are not* peace, then what they do will either be ineffective, or it will be counterproductive" (2009, p. 197; his italics).

In Buddhist practice, the emphasis is almost entirely placed on changing one's own mind and heart. There are, of course, clear guidelines for moral behavior outlined in the eightfold path, which includes right speech, right livelihood, and right conduct. But the focus always comes back to the nature and state of one's mind. The basic idea is that a vigilant attention to the mind will challenge our conventional ways of perceiving the self and the world in which we live. There is an end goal (which I will explore in chapter 8) that involves dissolving fictive boundaries that only serve to generate unnecessary suffering for ourselves and usually for the people in our lives.

In the following pages I will ask the reader to consider how the psychoanalytic process is influenced by analysts who have moved beyond a speculative appreciation for the impact, both positive and negative, of Buddhist practice, into their own direct experience as Westerners whose minds and hearts have mixed with the Dharma. I will also explore whether a Buddhist analyst, or for that matter an analyst of any faith tradition, is better equipped to discern the subtle ways in which religious and spiritual belief/practice may be co-opted as a place of psychic hiding.

Are such analysts in a unique position to bring a truly analytic ear to the religious experience without missing either its psychological riches or hidden pathology?

I'd now like to turn my attention to analytic attunement and the Buddhist clinician. By way of entry into this expansive topic, I will start with what the analyst does most: listen—which some might suggest is *the* central analytic tool.

Clinicians who are friendly to the idea of the spiritually attuned analyst but who do not themselves practice a religious tradition tend to imagine that experience with meditation may help the analyst stay focused on the client and on what is happening within the analytic dyad. And I think they are right—but the nature of this spiritually influenced attunement, however, is perhaps somewhat different than what it is imagined to be. It is not the product of effort to control one's thoughts, or to push away distraction, but rather another way of being with and observing one's own mind that allows the analyst to be with and relate to an analysand in a highly attentive way.

British psychoanalyst and Buddhist practitioner Nina Coltart speaks of this altered means of perception and listening as the *third ear* (1996, p. 63). Implicit in this analogy is a reference to the Buddhist concept of the *third way* of being and relating that does not surrender to attachment, aversion, or mere neutrality, but rather engages reality with mindful attention and friendly curiosity. Coltart speaks of this mindful attention and heightened listening as a capacity for love (1992, p. 117). In the analytic space, this would be love that does not manifest as affect, but rather as a transcendent function whereby real tenderness, sensitivity, and the willingness to be perceived by the analysand (through whatever projective lens they use) can emerge. For Coltart, this capacity comes from an analytic attunement where there is no longer a pressing need for theoretical musing or premature interpretation, which may be clung to as defenses against taking risks, showing real emotion, or showing one's own vulnerability in a way that is respectful of the analytic boundary.

This relational image of the analyst being with and actively relating to others suggests both personal and clinical integrity. It is not a cerebral hiding place for the analyst that may gratify the analysand's conscious or unconscious desire to remain unknown. Coltart depicts an analytic space that invites the most tender, vulnerable, and alive aspects of both members of the analytic dyad to move slowly into sight. It is the kind of analytic space that gives time for this emergence to transpire but does not enable "clinical lifers" who may wish to hide out in an endless process of theoretical musing and unconsciously guarded self-revelation.

Influenced by the theories of Wilfred Bion, Coltart reminds the analyst to relinquish memory and desire, two faculties that are often merged with an unconscious wish to control through one's cognitive ability. The intellect, says Coltart, tends to be possessive—of perceived truths, of timetables, and of expectations about how a given treatment should evolve.

> Merely thinking about something can harden it up and confirm its importance to our conscious self, as well as leading us to make irrelevant judgments, such as believing that we need it, or that our attachment to a certain pattern is indissoluble. However hard we may "work" at being analysts, I think it is this intellectual component that can get in the way. (1996, p. 133)

Her efforts to transcend the shackles of discursive thought point to the Buddha's emphasis on *direct experience*. As exemplified in the "poison arrow" story discussed in chapter 2, in which a dying man demands endless information about the weapon that has wounded him before receiving treatment, the Buddha encouraged his followers to relinquish the distraction of metaphysical theorizing and engage more fully with their own experience, to "know" what was true and real through a heightened attunement with their own reality. For Coltart, to take refuge in psychoanalytic theories that the analyst has internalized from past studies, or to wed a patient to an expected outcome, is to miss the "slouching beast" within the analysand awaiting emergence. It is also the means through which the analyst misses his own slouching beast, or lively and honest countertransference, the ways they have felt in response to an analysand's behavior, thoughts, or split-off desires. Coltart believed that such mindfully attentive listening would lead the analyst "into and through the inner worlds" of his patients (1996, p. 30).

Coltart's "willed attention" is not an invitation for the analyst to zone out, to hide in lofty spiritual pretense, or to self-disclose endlessly. It is the hard stuff of knowing one's own mind so that the analyst can offer a vigilant and genuine "evenly hovering attention" to the analysand. This, I believe, is something quite different from knowing the source of one's psychological complexes, one's childhood wounds or traumas—insight that would result from the analyst's own analysis. Instead, it is a capacity for willed attention that results when the analyst has come to consciously experience *how* her mind works, and to watch this mind in action.

The mind and its tendencies, in Coltart's meaning, are not personal in nature. As in Buddhist teaching, the mind here refers to the combination of consciousness, and a response of attachment, aversion, or neutrality (Rubin, 1996, p. 17). In treatment, this heightened relationship to the nature of the mind as it is understood in Buddhist doctrine might help the analyst recognize that attachment to psychoanalytic theory or interpretation that is used as a corrective to a patient's wounded psyche is something very different from spontaneous insight born out of a vital and engaged relationship. It can usher in an increased sensitivity to the analyst's own habituated aversion or flat-line neutrality to particular themes or behaviors in the analysand that might otherwise go unrecognized and yet be continuously acted out in the analysis.

Most importantly, Coltart suggests that the ability to listen with mindful attention is a clinical and spiritual tool with the express purpose of alleviating suffering (1992, p. 184). It is not another acquisition used to bolster the analyst's sense of professional acumen, but rather a primary way to serve the analysand as she reaches toward more joyful and engaged living. It is a critical means through which the analyst can help others unfold into their own realities, to live their own destinies and not feel pushed about by the powers of fate (ibid., pp. 2–5). Lastly, this mindful listening and attention is a way to receive hidden parts of the analysand that have been waiting, sometimes for decades, for a mind with the space and the loving attention necessary for their emergence.

Karen Horney called this process of mindful analytic attunement *wholehearted attention*. She described it as the analyst's capacity for "self-forgetting" while being fully present. This was a way of "having the highest presence and the highest absence," which was "not just cold detached observation, but unlimited, nonjudgmental receptivity, the kind of matter-of-fact acceptance of experience and the feelings they produce" (1987,

p. 20). As Horney's interest in Zen Buddhism grew, she became increasingly curious about this analytic ability to listen wholeheartedly. But she also imagined that this combination of being fully present yet without one's customary ego-based and intellectually dominant position might be difficult for Westerners to comprehend (Westkott, 1997, p. 83).

> That attention should be wholehearted may seem banal, trite, and self-evident. Yet in the sense that I mean wholehearted attention, I think it rather difficult to attain. I am referring to a power of concentration…Wholeheartedness of attention means being there altogether in the service of the patient, yet with a kind of self-forgetfulness…self-forget, but be there with all your feelings. (Horney, 1987, pp. 19–21)

As she continued to develop her own interest in Buddhism, Horney grew ever more curious about how analytic treatment approached from a Buddhist perspective might address the experience of psychological pain and suffering. She began to emphasize the importance of accepting oneself not only with one's cognitive faculty, but with a deeply feeling attention that does not indulge in embellishment, condemnation, or moralizing (Westkott, 1997, p. 82). In contemporary Buddhist parlance, this is the process of "dropping the storyline" that we tend to attach to any strong feeling while gently *leaning into* the direct experience of such feelings without habituated aversion, attachment, or disinterested neutrality.

In an analytic treatment, the analysand might, for example, be encouraged to stay focused on the actual feeling of humiliation resulting from a rejection suffered—the way it is experienced in one's body and the various sensations that result from this particular affect—while staving off the temptation to lapse into well-worn narratives about oneself and others that may defend against the conscious and felt experience of suffering through humiliation and loss. In so doing, the analysand may begin to learn about his habituated responses to strong feeling and the particular ways he has learned to utilize the mind in the service of remaining unconscious of and protected from feeling deeply.

With her growing interest in how we engage our own emotional reality, Horney began to shift her focus from the content of her patient's struggles to the ways in which the patient related to such struggles. The key, for

Horney, was in the nature and quality of our attention to whatever reality served up at a given moment or in a given lifetime. In her analytic treatment, healing came from the analysands' willingness and capacity to allow themselves to feel deeply their real selves (see chapter 6 for reference to her theory of self) without grasping on to fossilized notions of self and identity that distort the truth of one's ever-changing reality.

Horney's emphasis on relationship to one's reality-based self, which trumped her focus on personal content, speaks to the way in which a Buddhist perspective can augment the analytic purview. I am not suggesting, nor was Horney, that personal content is unimportant. I am fairly certain that any worthwhile analytic treatment will carefully and exhaustively examine the many facets of the analysand's personal history, her current relationships, and the specific factors that consciously influence her decision to seek analytic treatment. But ultimately the analyst cannot undo what has already occurred, the losses the analysand has suffered, or the traumas she has survived. Nor can the analyst in good conscience reassure the patient that even more devastating losses and traumas won't be suffered in the future.

Psychoanalysis cannot stave off reality or redo the past. It can, however, help people radically alter their felt understanding and relationship to what has already happened and what may happen in the future. It can, with much patience and a kind of reverent willingness to allow analysands the time and attention they need, challenge and alter their perspective of their lived experience and so to discover healing truths even about the suffering they have endured and will likely endure as life continues.

This emphasis on perception of what and how we feel about our internal and external realities is a central theme in Buddhist philosophy. One could argue that introducing this approach to healing and wellness in the analytic space would take on an educational intention, something that is largely frowned upon in psychoanalytic theory. I would argue, however, that utilizing a spiritual teaching in the analysis is an example of how the two larger theoretical paradigms of Buddhism and psychoanalysis may remain squarely within appropriate psychoanalytic boundaries while simultaneously introducing another way for the analysand to make use of and integrate her psychoanalytic treatment.

In other words, the analysand is well served if an analyst can maximize the depth of the analytic process by allowing the analysand the time and space to mourn whatever personal losses have been suffered without losing sight of the universal nature of such losses. In this way she will be sanctioned to rage at injustice, to lament the pain of missed opportunities or the terror that prevented her from taking advantage of precious opportunities, *and* to contextualize these personal losses in a larger framework that includes the universality of mourning, loss, and frustration. Through this augmented view, the analysand may begin to appreciate our very human tendency to distort our perception of personal experience with habituated tendencies of the mind that react with aversion toward pain and grasping at pleasure.

One may rightly ask whether it is necessary that the analyst have spiritual training and experience in order for the analyst to bring this larger human context into the analytic space. Might this not also result from plain old humility and insight rather than from an overarching theory?

In his heart-warming "open letter" to the new generation of analysts, Irvin Yalom speaks of a memorable moment in his own analysis when he suffered acute self-condemnation for anticipating the inheritance he would one day receive from his father. His analyst, who customarily refrained from any personal intrusion or interruption of Yalom's analytic musing, jumped in to state that engaging such fantasy of prospective inheritance was just what *we* humans did (Yalom, 2003, p. 215). Yalom was profoundly touched by his analyst's efforts to normalize an experience that can so easily cause tremendous shame and self-doubt by placing his wish in a larger context of the human mind (and in this example, I discern his analyst's reference to the mind's response of attachment). In subsequent years, Yalom made note and attempted similarly to depathologize any "shadow" experience that left an analysand feeling stuck on a treadmill of self-flagellation by sharing similar struggles or offering the roomier context he gleaned from his analyst's use of the word "we."

While I do not know whether Yalom's analyst was a person of faith or religious belief, I would suggest that this humility and conscious awareness of the pervasive nature of core human struggles we all—healer and those seeking to be healed—suffer through is a central part of religious experience. In the Buddhist tradition, this appreciation for the universality of suffering manifests in the emphasis on changing one's perception through mindfulness, and through understanding the nature of mind, in order to bypass the otherwise tempting assumption that if only we could alter our external circumstances, pain would cease.

How might a Buddhist analyst attempt gently to reorient an analysand's perspective so that even personal suffering comes to have real and valuable meaning as a way of experiencing connection to others? I suppose the ways in which this might happen are as varied as the personalities of each individual analyst. But in my experience there are certain foundational Buddhist teachings that are likely to inform the analyst's perception and will therefore also have an impact on the analysand's changing perception. In this way the analyst's spiritual training will tend to infiltrate the clinical space, paving the way for a subtle and fluid dance between Eastern spiritual and Western psychoanalytic perspectives.

As I have mentioned in previous chapters, Buddhism posits a root source of suffering that stems from our fundamental misperception of reality. The teaching states that when we impute inherent meaning to ourselves, and by extension, to all phenomena, we attribute an inherent character to what is in reality ever changing and therefore lacking in fixed meaning, structure, or form. From a Buddhist perspective, this basic ignorance is the root of suffering. In Tibetan it is called *dak dzin*, which means grasping at self (Sogyal Rinpoche, 1993, p. 121). It comes from within our own minds and can be altered so fundamentally that no circumstance may interfere with our realization of the true and impermanent nature of reality.

It is this basic concept that informs the many teachings on emptiness. While emptiness is easily misunderstood as a kind of annihilation theory, it is meant to help Buddhist practitioners recognize that the absolute separation we feel from others is a fiction we might wish to challenge. We are all, says the doctrine, forever changing in a current of moment-to-moment reality, in dependence upon a constantly changing set of causes, conditions, people, and places that are "empty" of any fixed essence or nature. When we challenge our misperception of fundamental separateness, an authentic interest in others may more readily follow. The teaching suggests that if we are not by our very nature inherently separate but in dependence upon all other beings, who are in their own ways influencing this current of endless causes and conditions that help compose our reality, we might grow more curious about these other beings, who, it turns out, have something to do with us and our own moment-to-moment reality.

In this way Buddhist thought posits a central relationship between emptiness and the birth of authentic compassion. If we recognize our basic interdependence, we will come to realize that every thought, action, and word has real consequences in the relational realm. With this realization comes the possibility that the suffering of others may be assuaged or in some way influenced by our behavior, and even our thoughts and feelings. So, says Sogyal Rinpoche, "We need no-self to really get to the roots of compassion, what it is born from. It does not come from a moral code, but from seeing the nature of reality" (1993, p. 39). Grasping at a solid and inherent ego identity, a fixed sense of "me-ness," is understood to be the primary impediment toward generating a genuine empathy and concern for others. According to the Dalai Lama, we develop this empathy and compassion when we realize that "fulfillment of our aspirations requires dependence upon others" (1995, p. 60).

I believe that Horney was attempting to integrate this Buddhist teaching of emptiness and compassion into her theory of the *idealized image* and its tyranny of the shoulds—how it should fend off potentially dangerous "others" through its own perfected and impenetrable identity structure. Horney recognized running through her analysands' psyches a stream of hatred toward themselves and others that she connected to a steadfast aversion toward the reality of who they were, including their fears, their shortcomings, and their unshakable, imperfect humanness. She discovered that when this (always unconscious) aversion was dominant, there was also a powerful attachment to highly rigidified identities that served a two-fold purpose: to lift oneself up, over, and against others who were perceived as threatening and frightening competitors, and to camouflage one's real, frightened, and suffering self. She found that when people invested meaning in solidified identities that lacked the suppleness necessary for working with the ever-changing life circumstances, feelings, needs, and wishes, an absence of real feeling for others ensued (1950).

Idealization of identity was, for Horney, a refusal of reality. In contrast to Kohut's theory of idealization (see chapter 4), in which idealization of others—including one's parents, analyst, and teachers—facilitates the necessary capacity for ideals, Horney's idealized image was a losing bat-tle with a fantasized self. It involved the process of building a false and rigid identity to hide behind. While in the grips of such idealization, analysands would be unable to make conscious the prior suffering that fueled their idealized self-image. If they were to do so, they would have to face the wrenching schism between their earliest feelings of aliveness and spontaneity, and the false and falsely idealized identity used to nego-tiate a basic feeling of being unsafe.

In the analytic dyad, an analysand locked in a Horneyan idealization would resist the analyst's efforts to address the reality of her early child-hood experience, unable to relinquish the fictive and idealized lens through which she has come to view her life.

For Horney, the antidote to this enervating process of idealizing one's self-image was the willingness to take genuine interest in the reality of one's own suffering. Without a compassionate curiosity for the experience of ongoing vulnerability, interpersonal struggles, and the many ways one may have been hurt, healing was forever elusive. In this way Horney posited an affective dualism in which hostility toward self and others could not coexist alongside an authentic compassion. Engaging with reality ush-ered in the latter, while rigidified identity ensured the former.

Buddhism teaches that relationships suffer when we are gripped by erroneous notions of fixed identity (Thurman, 1998, p. 147). When an absolute and impermeable sense of *I* and *You* dominates our thinking, there is a comparative and evaluative tendency that quickly infiltrates the relational sphere. For if we perceive ourselves to be fundamentally sepa-rate and invested with inherent and unchanging attributes, chances are that one person has to be better than another—thus the need either to camouflage our own sense of inherent inferiority or to actively under-score our clear superiority.

This evaluation of basic worth, when it is predicated on false notions of inherent value or lack thereof, can easily eclipse any real or lasting curiosity about one's self. What, after all, would be the point in investi-gating a self that cannot change? Wouldn't a resigned, quietly defeatist acceptance make more sense? And furthermore, what would be the point in getting curious about and intimate with others who, at bottom, have nothing to do with us, or who by their very nature are so much better that it induces in us nothing but self-attack?

I suspect that this teaching on our conventional misperception of reality as a root cause of suffering influences many Buddhist analysts' perception of psychological and interpersonal suffering. Buddhist psychoanalyst Jeff Shore points out that there is no "root illness" identified in psychoanalytic theory (Shore, 2002, p. 34). There are myriad sources for psychological pain and dysfunction identified in the literature, including detached, erratic, or controlling parenting, early childhood loss, sexual trauma, the impact of war and poverty, and physical abuse. But other than psychiatric diagnoses of mental illness caused by chemical or neurological imbalance, there is no internal root cause of psychological suffering posited in psychoanalytic theory. Shore wonders, as do I, how an analysand can bypass the tendency to continually default to some manifestation of a root illness if it is never identified, addressed, and potentially resolved (ibid., p. 43).

Psychoanalytic theory has tended to propose that we suffer due to external circumstance and/or relationship with primary caretakers, despite Freud's strong wish to locate the source of psychological difficulty in our psychosomatic wiring, which forever feels impinged upon by the external world. There can be no reasonable doubt that this psychoanalytic belief has much truth. When parents or caretakers are unkind, abusive, negligent, or sexually inappropriate with their children, chances are their children will suffer terribly. So too, if we are affected by war, genocide, or acts of terrorism, the psyche will respond with all manner of neurotic and psychotic symptoms. But as I stated above, it is not within the power of psychoanalytic treatment to eliminate these experiences.

As long as people procreate they will act out their own psychic wounds in their parenting. And it seems likely that as long as the human species survives, there will be violence, war, and mind-bending brutality. People will continue to suffer as the result of trauma and loss, and if they are in psychoanalysis, they will continue to bring the after-effects to their treatment. I agree with the sage suggestion that because we come equipped to have experiences that we are little able to tolerate, make sense of, or utilize constructively, the chances of bypassing trauma are close to none (Bobrow, 2003, p. 234). Perhaps this is why Bion's ultimate reality was symbolized by O (so reminiscent of zero), a truth we resist mightily. Our likelihood of escaping some form of devastation we will throughout our lives work hard to forget are close to none.

I believe that what Shore is suggesting is that psychological healing must therefore address how we relate to suffering as a category of human experience, and not merely to the circumstances and content of this suffering. If it fails to do so, then the treatment will fail to help analysands discover the personal meaning in *how* they have uniquely engaged the myriad manifestations of universally unavoidable suffering. It will fail to prepare them for a personal relationship to suffering that will invariably continue as life and death continues. And most importantly, such treatment will fail to underscore what I call the ethics of healing, the ways in which working through our habituated response to suffering and thus awakening to the suffering of others brings about compassion for self and others. In challenging the solipsism of a traditional analysis, where this contrasting approach to the mind is included, a more fundamental space is created for how the analysand may come to recognize and care for others.

Underlying this psychospiritual perspective is the Buddhist foundational teaching of *dependent arising*, which states that every effect has a cause. All phenomena are co-determined by mutually informing conditions. What we think and feel are preceded by certain experiences, and the actions we take are like falling dominos triggered by the winding trail of dominos that precedes them. Our bodies, for example, come into being through the decisions and life experiences of our parents, and our parent's union results from the confluence of cultural, economic, gendered, sexual, and historical factors. In short, we depend upon others for everything, including our own bodies. The Buddha told his students that this simple insight was the very heart of his teaching (Smith & Novak, 2003, p. 10). And while the teaching of cause and effect can indeed seem quite simple, it points to *the* critical, often unconscious issue played out in psychoanalytic treatment: the central analytic task of facilitating a safe and healing experience of dependency.

In the preceding discussion, I have made efforts to reveal how psychoanalysts influenced personally by the Dharma might bring these teachings into relationship with their analysands. I cannot fairly or adequately address the broad spectrum of possibilities for integrating or making use of a Buddhist spiritual perspective in psychoanalytic treatment. I am certain that the ways in which a spiritual belief system might manifest in the professional lives of clinicians are radically divergent. Yet I wish to offer at least a glimpse into a possible approach for the Buddhist clinician, to show how this spacious perspective may hold more of the analysand's experience.

When the analysand can bring into the treatment his shadow side and be greeted by an analyst who empathizes, not because she understands the psychological factors contributing to her client's woundedness, but because she knows that suffering is part of the human condition, I believe that the analytic space becomes a more welcoming environment. In such treatment, shadowy behavior and experience are met with an analytic perspective humbled via the spiritual domain. Certainly for Buddhist analysands like me, the experience of working with a spiritually attuned analyst alleviates the profound burden of having to translate on one's own how a psychoanalytic perspective fits in with a spiritual and religious understanding of the world. In this way, defenses may be softened, allowing the analysand to risk stronger feelings of closeness with and dependency upon the analyst.

Theologian Paul Knitter writes that "the very nature of the divine is nothing other than to exist in and out of relationship; for God, to be is nothing other than to relate" (2009, p. 19). Polly Young-Eisendrath, discussing the great Zen master Dogen, observes that "self and other are ultimately interdependent; the self does not exist prior to, or outside of, the other; we only have the possibility of experiencing self or other through relationship" (2002, p. 75). This is both the heart and the beast of religious belief— that there is "something more" than just myself that I must continuously trust and depend upon in order to be. If I am made through another, if I find myself through relating to another, then I am held in being through relationship to this other. This could be described as dependency par excellence, where we come to be with and depend upon teachers, deities, buddhas, and gods to nourish and sustain our very existence.

This cultivation of dependency opens the door for our ability to transcend the self. It is the very heart of religious practice, and I would add, any interpersonal relationship that has achieved real intimacy and depth. In the West, we typically resist cultivating this capacity to depend on others fully, yet long for what it brings: authentic union with others, and a basic trust that someone or something else has our back.

It is possible that this notion of dependency in the religious experience is more troubling for areligious clinicians when the object of this dependency is God. Freud's religious musings may come to mind, and they may think that surely such a God is little more than the parental projections of people struggling to accept the stark reality of their ongoing vulnerability and mortality. It may be difficult for such clinicians to imagine that this dependency upon God could exist in a mature, integrated fashion, where love of God does not translate into a childlike demand for protection and magical gratification of one's personal needs.

I suspect that the difficulty some areligious clinicians have with the notion of dependence on God—a highly charged symbol that may or may not evoke the clinician's own unresolved father and/or mother issues—might have something to do with the readier acceptance in clinical circles of Buddhist practice, where there is no divine referent, no "father in the sky" imagery that belies a mature psyche and cogent intellect. Clinicians, generally speaking, seem far more comfortable with the Buddhist emphasis on meditation or with a mind of clear seeing as the object of our dependence. In this way, Buddhism is understood as more a psychological system than a religion. But I humbly propose that reducing the whole of Buddhist doctrine to meditation practice is wholly to misinterpret and erroneously excise the foundational importance of dependency that is the very seed of Buddhist thought.

Certainly in the Tibetan tradition, where students discover their buddha nature through the teacher, this dependency is the *only* way to recognize and nourish their wisdom mind. In order to discover this deeply buried wisdom, the student must develop an unshakable trust in the teacher, and in the Buddha as the original teacher who began transmitting the lessons of awakening over 2,500 years ago (Sogyal Rinpoche, 1993). In this tradition, without total dependency on the teacher's wisdom mind—despite her clear fallibility—there is no awakening and thus no recognition of our own buddha nature. This is not an unconscious merger, but a powerfully conscious decision to trust in the teacher's inner wisdom and her capacity to transmit this wisdom to another. Buddhist practice emphasizes renunciation—the process of giving up all that impedes awakening—so that we may come to depend totally on the teacher, the Buddha, Dharma, and Sangha, our sacred referents that are the Buddhist route to psychological and spiritual freedom.

I could not fairly suggest that it is only religious analysts who have adequately wrestled with dependency. I believe that any conscious experience of truly loving another will bring one squarely into this deeply felt dynamic. Yet I propose that dependency is so provocative and typically defended against—particularly within a Western culture where independence is our most revered achievement—that the ego, and the intellect in particular, may find cunning ways of denying or controlling the dependence we may struggle against or feel subtly shamed by. This is so for both members of the analytic dyad, and when the analyst lacks conscious experience with the kind of dependency learned and practiced in the religious domain, he may be vulnerable to this unconscious bypassing of dependency in his clinical work.

In the psychoanalytic realm this profound struggle to acknowledge consciously how we have depended upon others in the past, and how we wish to find and surrender to a safe experience of dependency in our adulthood, is a dominant theme. In my own analysis and in my analytic work with children, I have found that the tendency to deny the wrenching experience of dependency needs that are not met, to deny the ways in which we were unable to garner care, love, guidance, and affirmation from those upon whom we completely relied, is perhaps *the* crucible of clinical work.

Object relations theorist W.R.D. Fairbairn discovered in his psychoanalytic work that because of the utter dependency upon our caretakers in early childhood, the young child cannot tolerate bringing to consciousness the ways in which his caretaker may have failed to adequately care for him. Instead, the child will take his parent's flaws and failures upon himself. Fairbairn called this the *moral defense*, whereby the child feels driven to perceive himself as inadequate, flawed, or defective rather than recognize these attributes in the person upon whom he has depended (1952). Having assumed "the burden of badness," he is left with an idealized version of the parent he depends on for his survival (Fairbairn, 1952, p. 65; see also Jones, 2002, p. 55, for illuminating discussion on object relations theory and religious experience).

The evolution of the moral defense into adulthood can be a pernicious development, whereby even the most severely abused person, whose parents were clearly negligent, violent, and/or mentally ill, will continue to invest these qualities in himself as he unconsciously defends his parent or primary caretaker. This psychological maneuver, while an essential means of survival for the young child, is nonetheless predicated upon a continued and self-destructive denial of how one's dependency needs have not been met. In adulthood, and in the psychoanalytic process, it can take on the additional purpose of denying the reality of how potentially shattering it is to lean on another, only to be dropped, forgotten, or pushed away. Rather than facing the devastating pain that would come from bringing such experiences to consciousness, the analysand may instead take refuge (albeit in a self-flagellating manner) in a fixed sense of a self that is by its very nature flawed and perhaps just not cut out for the relational realm.

If such an analysand were working with a Buddhist clinician, there might be floating through the clinician's consciousness the awareness that the analysand is not yet ready to face the reality of who she is and who her primary caretakers were. And while this perception might also be readily apparent to a clinician who does not practice a religious or spiritual tradition, I suspect and hope that for the Buddhist clinician such perceptions would be fused with a deep and abiding compassion for what the analysand has suffered and continues to suffer. Polly Young-Eisendrath speaks of this as a true moment-to-moment experience of *suffering with* the analysand, in which the compassion cultivated in one's spiritual practice may inform the analytic dyad (2002, p. 77). I think of this as the meeting of wisdom and compassion within the analytic space, where insight does not trump direct feeling and experience, but rather mixes with it in order to model a steadfast and gentle care for oneself alongside the willingness to engage a devastating truth.

I propose that this mixing of wisdom and compassion within the analytic space is another central way of modeling dependency. Any analyst worth his or her salt will emphatically state that bringing buried loss and pain to consciousness is hard, gut-wrenching work. It involves tapping into reserves of trust within the analysand that the work will lead somewhere meaningful, that the analyst is capable of ushering in healing, and that the pain suffered will have been worthwhile in the end. In order to get there, the analyst must tack back and forth between a genuine empathic connection with the analysand and a growing insight into the analysand's history, psyche, and potential for healing. The empathy and the insight need one another in order for the analysand to feel safe, understood, accepted, and known. In this way the analyst models his own dependency on the empathy he feels and the insight he gains as a truly healing partnership.

Yet for the analysand locked in an ongoing moral defense of the people he depended upon in years past, a vicious and largely unconscious self-attack may dominate the treatment, and the readiness to feel any authentic compassion for himself does not easily emerge. Even in a seemingly placid and mature analysand, feelings of self-hatred may manifest in compulsive symptoms and other modes of self-sabotage ranging from enmeshed relationships to inertia or a sluggish approach to professional endeavors. This powerful aversion toward himself suggests the denial of a bigger reality that the analysand has been unable to recognize and accept. From a Buddhist perspective, this could be explored as a form of *self-grasping*, whereby the analysand has invested inherent meaning in a self that is illusory in nature but is mistakenly perceived as real and unchanging.

Through the lens of emptiness, a skillful Buddhist clinician might find subtle and gentle ways of challenging such notions of self. But à la Horney's theory, she would also be aware that until the analysand has a genuine feeling of compassion and concern for his own suffering, it will be difficult to transition from the analysand's vigilant finger-pointing at himself for his many purported character flaws and shortcomings to the Buddha's playful toe-pointing to *this* world in which freedom is immanently possible. So too, such a transition would require the analysand to ultimately relinquish the virulent finger-pointing at a negligent or abusive parent or partner that may arise when working through an entrenched moral defense, in order to move more squarely into the felt experience of having depended upon another who could not honor and meet this dependency.

In such work, a Buddhist perspective may be a real boon to the clinician's efforts to have her own direct experience of what the patient has split off from consciousness, and to forego the temptation to temper this intensity with premature interpretation or with consoling words that keep both members of the analytic dyad locked in a discursive and two-dimensional mode. If the clinician has practiced entering into her own shattered places with the sensitivity Coltart speaks of and has consciously mourned the loss of love or basic connectedness she wished for with central players in her own life, if she has not removed herself from such tender psychic places by the use of a protective intellect and has stayed with what Buddhists call *bodhichitta*, or an awakened heart, then she might bring this heightened affective attunement to her clinical work. The analysand may therefore experience a more palpable sense of having been unconditionally received.

I believe that this capacity to tolerate and model depth of feeling without shackling such feelings with interpretation is greatly enhanced by the clinician's conscious experience of depending on something other than his own critical faculties in the midst of destabilizing pain, confusion, loss, or hopelessness. To depend on something other than oneself, something that cannot be influenced or maneuvered by the adroitness of one's own intellect or capacity for insight, is to practice constantly the experience of not knowing how this dependency will be met. It is practice in tolerating the mystery of how our lives unfold and settling into what we do not and cannot know at a given time. Furthermore, it is practice in the humility that comes with a trace of joyful curiosity about what might be revealed or recognized as a particular treatment unfolds. In this way a conscious religious practice may help the analyst suffer through a difficult treatment with an abiding interest in how healing might take place due to something other than the analyst's own skill and analytic attunement. This could be described as a Buddhist "beginner's mind" in clinical action that has mixed with and depended upon another being's wisdom mind.

―――――――――――――――

As I have suggested above, we cannot know how an individual analyst may integrate or utilize his or her own religious experience in the analytic space. The effects of such conscious experience are surely quite divergent and unique. I suspect, however, that when such an analyst is working with an analysand who has brought into her treatment a religious experience or identity, the religiously attuned analyst will have at his ready a particular lens he is likely to utilize, and a depth of insight into both the healing aspects and psychological pitfalls of religious belief and practice.

I recall in my own analysis many years ago feeling troubled by my efforts to claim a separate sense of self from my colorful family of origin. I was in a stage of development when individuation felt particularly crucial to cultivating a life that was authentic and would reflect my own genuine interests, desires, and dreams. Yet the analytic process of further defining and growing attached to my "self" felt entirely dissonant with my deepening Buddhist practice, in which concerted efforts at loosening the grip on self were ongoing. Wasn't I essentially grasping at a self that didn't exist? It felt somehow spiritually remedial in nature, something a benighted soul might struggle with—surely not the stuff of a bodhisattva!

Having intuited that there was something psychologically necessary about this process of discerning how an authentic "me-ness" might manifest in my life, I continued. But with the backdrop of Buddhist teachings on emptiness and no-self, my own analysis sometimes felt like an ersatz effort at wellness. Wasn't the idea to keep renouncing attachment to self and lean into the groundlessness that was absolute reality? I was working toward enlightenment, not Freud's common unhappiness.

At the time I was fortunate to be working with a therapist conversant in Buddhist teachings, someone I knew to be interested in meditation and Eastern spiritual practice. She did not deny the veracity of the emptiness doctrine, but she had a way of subtly conveying that I could continue to cultivate an authentic sense of who I was, to keep building up my own subjectivity, without this necessarily becoming a fixed identity that would be impervious to the many changing circumstances of my life. She also pointed out that, for me, relinquishing subjectivity had been a primary coping mechanism in a family of big personalities where efforts at visibility were an ongoing challenge. I had learned to let go of self perhaps a bit prematurely in my development.

I found these reminders, which were always respectful of the Buddhist teachings I took to heart, to profoundly affirm that it was indeed possible to pursue a mature and conscious spiritual practice that could harmoniously interface with my own unique mosaic of attributes, needs, and early childhood imprints. In our work together I sensed that I could enter into the tradition of Buddhist practice and explore the meaning and experience of emptiness of self without losing my own personal relationship to such practice. There could be, perhaps, a meaningful and revelatory dance of self and no-self that could reinforce the benefits of knowing one's self, of honoring the need for subjectivity in the conventional world, while still allowing a fluidity of self that seemed just as essential to psychological and spiritual wellness.

As the years progressed, I noticed that this psychological struggle with no-self teachings was not uncommon among American Buddhists. I began to wonder how many had felt an attraction to Buddhism in part due to a wealth of experience with relinquishing their own subjectivity. In addition to being a tradition that encouraged awakening, Buddhism was also, I had begun to notice, a potential place of hiding.

Psychoanalyst Michael Eigen writes of his work with Buddhist analysands that the need for more fullness of feeling is at times defended against through an appropriation of emptiness (Eigen, 1998a). In this way his analysands, some of whom were seasoned practitioners and Buddhist teachers, had unconsciously used the teachings to protect against a genuine direct experience of feelings perhaps too painful to confront and integrate. Eigen discerned a certain "emotional hydroplaning," where the felt recognition of self and other, the potentially shattering impact of relationship with another, were staved off through spiritual practice and refuge in a hidden self masquerading as no-self.

In this way, his patients filled the "pregnant void" of emptiness with their own split-off self-experience. The emptiness of self was more of a Jungian shadow, containing the repressed truth of painful feelings they preferred not to consciously suffer.

As I have suggested above, the teachings on emptiness and no-self are potentially powerful psychological tools that can help sensitize both members of the analytic dyad to projections that protect the analysand from a conscious experience of disowned or split-off feeling. An analyst who recognizes the profound meaning in the emptiness doctrine may offer its psychological value—that all perception must be recognized as evolving from the perceiver and not the perceived (a helpful way to encourage the withdrawal of projections)—while also recognizing how it may be used in the service of psychological splitting or disavowal. In this way the analyst may help the Buddhist analysand come to recognize that emptiness can be applied to all phenomena, including the teaching of emptiness. Even the emptiness doctrine is empty of inherent meaning; it is rather a "womb of awakening" and thus ripe for our projections and potential misappropriations.

This process, however, may be particularly challenging for the analyst to negotiate if the analysand has cultivated a full-throttle "Buddhist Identity" predicated on having transcended any "real" problems by operating in a realm of absolute truth where all "conventional" perceptions are in fact illusory. Analysts who have confronted such treatments will know the difficulty I speak of, where the analysand's insight and intellect add to the insidious ways in which spiritual and religious identity can come to be highly defensive in nature. But the great value of analysts who have personal experience with Buddhism, or with the larger realm of religious belief and practice, is their ability to discern and explore the defensive elements of religious belief without pathologizing, *à la* Freud, the whole of religious experience.

There is a true both/and phenomenon at work in such treatments, whereby the analysand may have experienced tremendous psychological healing within a given religious tradition while simultaneously having successfully hidden the most wounded and undeveloped parts of their psyche (Engler, 2006). They may have developed real skill as spiritual teachers, having attained a genuine insight into arcane theories and religious teachings, while at the same time sustaining jarring psychological splits and interpersonal roadblocks.

A spiritually attuned analyst is in a unique position to bring a combined respect for the ways in which religious practice and identity can both heal and harm the same individual throughout his or her life. Such a clinician may be more inclined to recognize that the problem is not inherent in the religious belief or practice, but rather in the ways it has been utilized by an individual with particular conscious and unconscious needs, wishes, and childhood experience.

For the analysand, or for that matter any Western Buddhist, who has developed a particularly fossilized identity born out of the need to be insightful, self-sufficient, and "in the know," Buddhist practice can lend itself to a somewhat fantastical and highly alluring notion of *enlightenment* as the resolution of all conflicts, difficulties, and problems. This concept fits in nicely with the unconscious interpretation of no-self as a means of relinquishing the interpersonal messiness of subjectivity. As Alan Roland points out, the self who belongs to everyone (by virtue of our interdependence) may unconsciously profit from belonging to no one in particular (1996). When everything is empty—including ourselves and therefore our relationships—there is little to fear, and little to engage with.

If this psychological struggle to sustain a sense of authentic and conscious subjectivity that can relate to others has roots in early childhood experience of having been cared for by narcissistic or abusive parents who could not tolerate or recognize the child's subjectivity, chances are that the wish to relinquish self and therefore be "needless" will cast an ever-present shadow on the analysand's spiritual endeavors. But it is no easy feat to give up a particular relationship to a spiritual system that seems to sanction and even revere such renunciation of self as *the* gateway to a life free from suffering, and ultimately to enlightenment.

Just as I struggled with this process of building up my own subjectivity in combination with a deepening spiritual life, throughout my twenties and into my thirties I imagined that with a deep enough realization of the Dharma surely the chronic struggles of being human, of suffering through the legacy of losses and psychic wounds, would come to a natural end, or at least be radically diminished. It seemed reasonable to expect that being a true spiritual devotee would ultimately translate into a joyful life in which one's perception is so fundamentally altered that no external circumstance could generate the feelings of exasperation and disappointment that seem to define much of secular consciousness. I had tasted such clarity and joy during intensive retreats, or when practicing particular teachings with certain high lamas. The Buddha, after all, taught that when we recognize our true nature, we will experience an abiding freedom in *this* life.

With such an expectation, however, each new experience of pain, frustration, anger, and weepy sorrow brought with it the additional suffering of shame for somehow still operating within a conventional purview. For in the midst of crushing blows, of profound sadness or heated anger, I did not feel inclined to merely "note" my feelings as I had been taught to do in Theravada practice, to touch them and then let them go. I *felt* them— a process that seemed altogether more primordial in nature than the cognitive process of "noting." This experiential relationship to feeling seemed decidedly counter to what my placid teachers in the Theravada tradition encouraged. I wished dearly to know when the hell enlightenment as I understood it would come.

Here again I reaped the benefits of work with a clinician sensitized to the potential psychological complexity of Buddhist practice. When I broached the discomfort of certain feelings, most notably anger, desire, and sorrow, she was inclined to acknowledge that indeed, strong feelings can feel burdensome, particularly when we prefer not to feel them. In essence, when aversion (one of the three poisons) toward the affective realm is operative, feelings may bring with them an additional wave of toxic shame. She was not asking me to act out difficult feelings—to curse out or shoot my eternal frat house neighbors, or to wallow in the muck and mire of historical sorrows. Instead, she was encouraging me to explore with greater depth what it meant to "touch" the feeling realm, and conversely to remain attuned to the ways in which a subtle attachment (another poison) to being free from all difficult feeling might render life a rather tepid experience.

Over the years I began to notice something interesting about my own relationship to fraught affect and challenging life experience: people seemed to feel wholeheartedly affirmed when I spoke openly about feeling as though I "was going nuts," "about to evaporate from exhaustion," or "contemplating homicidal action." In the ready gleam of their eyes, I noticed that strong feeling and back-breaking, soul-sucking difficulties were markers of humanness; they spoke to our very aliveness and shared limitations. People enjoyed hearing an honest acknowledgment of such humanizing and humbling affective experience. I could read the subtext of these conversations: "I guess I'm not the only one who is constantly falling to pieces? Well, hallelujah!"

During this time, my understanding of enlightenment and the ways in which the psyche interfaces with spirituality began to shift. Perhaps a true psychospiritual awakening was recognizing with real courage, clarity, and openness of spirit our undeniable idiosyncrasies, our character flaws, irrational fears, fantastical desires, and ongoing interpersonal difficulties. Perhaps enlightenment meant the willingness to wake up to the unfolding reality of having a complex psyche and personal history shaped and informed by so many others with comparable complexities. Most importantly, I wondered if true enlightenment meant first and foremost relinquishing the shame of our perpetual dance with insight and ignorance.

Psychoanalyst Jack Engler speaks of this altered perception of enlightenment that includes our emotional patterns, our character, and history. He notes the investment that Buddhist practitioners may unknowingly have in achieving a state of mind that is permanently freed from imperfections and character flaws. It is a constant temptation for Buddhists, particularly Western Buddhists, to imagine that with enough spiritual practice we may eradicate lifelong struggles and interpersonal tendencies. He quotes a Zen roshi who responds to a student's question regarding such notions of enlightenment in the following way:

> Before awakening, one can easily ignore or rationalize his shortcomings, but after enlightenment this is no longer possible. One's failings are painfully evident. Yet at the same time a strong determination develops to rid oneself of them...Continuous training after enlightenment is required to purify the emotions so that our behavior accords with our understanding. This vital point must be understood. (Engler, 2006, p. 19)

What I glean from the roshi's helpful teaching is that the experience of *mindfulness*—both the gateway to and defining attribute of enlightenment—does not eliminate the misperceptions that tend to dominate our waking reality; rather it allows us to remain conscious in the throes of such misperceptions. In the Buddhist canon, mindfulness is depicted as a guiding light along the path to enlightenment. In mindfulness—the process of seeing things as they are without attempting to change them—one is freed from uncontrolled reactivity and conventional efforts to conform reality to our many wishes and desires (Bennet-Goleman, 2001, pp. 4–6).

Joseph Goldstein describes mindfulness as a kind of emotional life-vest (2003, p. 142). With mindfulness training, one may feel a broad spectrum of emotions or perceive situations according to such emotions without building and reifying identity predicated upon such feelings and perceptions. Stephen Batchelor speaks of the way mindfulness may "catch" an emotion at its inception, before it becomes a full-blown marker of identity (1997, p. 60). In this way mindfulness may allow us to remain sharply focused on affective experience without telling ourselves fallacious stories about who we are, as in *I am so angry with my partner; I am by nature an angry person* or *I feel sad; I guess I'm just a depressed and depressing person.*

In the Tibetan Book of Living and Dying, Sogyal Rinpoche describes mindfulness as the process of

> ...bringing the scattered mind home, and so bringing the different aspects of our being into focus, (what) is called 'Peace-

fully Remaining' or 'Calm Abiding.' 'Peacefully Remaining' accomplishes three things. First, all the fragmented aspects of ourselves which have been at war settle and dissolve and become friends. In that settling we begin to understand ourselves more, and sometimes even have glimpses of the radiance of our fundamental nature. Second, the practice of mindfulness defuses our negativity, aggression, and turbulent emotions, which may have been gathering power over many lifetimes. Rather than suppressing emotions or indulging them, here it is important to view them, and your thoughts, and whatever arises with an acceptance and generosity that are as open and spacious as possible. Third, this practice unveils and reveals your essential Good Heart, because it dissolves and removes the unkindness or the harm in you. (1993, p. 61)

When I read such descriptions of mindfulness, I am (perhaps somewhat ironically) of two minds. On the one hand, I know the psychospiritual gold in mindfulness of which Sogyal Rinpoche speaks. This ability to enter into one's emotional experience with a true curiosity that does not default to fictive, often divisive, and therefore compelling narratives about ourselves and/or others is a tremendous interpersonal and psychoanalytic asset. On the other hand, mindfulness teachings do not acknowledge the unconscious and the potential reality of unconscious resistance to such mindfulness practice, to the "good heart" of which Sogyal Rinpoche speaks. This sort of resistance is well known within psychoanalytic treatment, where even the analysand's most passionate interest in living joyfully, developing talents, and feeling loved and loving others is continuously and compulsively sabotaged. Freud called this self-sabotage a resistance to wellness that often resulted from the unconscious guilt produced by the analysand's anger toward a caretaker he also loves (1933).

In Sogyal Rinpoche's description of mindfulness, I hear the end results of mindfulness, but I do not hear the many psychological stages involved in reaching such a mindfully lived experience. Michael Eigen speaks of the way his Buddhist analysands adapt life to a mindful persona rather than bring mindfulness to a spontaneous and full life (Eigen, 1998a). When this happens, one's life is carefully maneuvered to bypass experiences (usually interpersonal) or feelings that are not easily managed.

Through such a maneuver, one can sustain one's identity as a mindful person through avoiding any situation that challenges one's notion of mindfulness, e.g. steadfast peace and calm.

Just as interpretations of enlightenment can easily be used to defend against our own split-off humanness, mindfulness can unconsciously be used as a kind of psychic goalie that "catches" emotions before they are fully felt or even made conscious. In this way it can help a practitioner remain defended against the feelings or experiences that can evoke such feelings, potentially wreaking havoc with an identity predicated on unshakable mindfulness.

I believe that this is another critical issue for Buddhist clinicians working with analysands who are in some way ensnared by teachings that interface with their particular psychological need to keep the affective realm carefully contained and at a safe distance. Again, these are tricky scenarios, particularly if the analysand has cultivated a defensive pride in her capacity to live mindfully, when it may seem to the analyst that the analysand's overarching relationship to life has been limited or maneuvered so that she is less likely to come up against experience and ensuing feelings that challenge her capacity for mindfulness.

I propose that if an analyst can utilize her own more integrated relationship to mindfulness in such treatments, she may enter into the analysand's conscious and unconscious experience with an enhanced attunement and tolerance for what cannot yet be changed or healed. So too, it seems possible that if the analyst has brought mindfulness into the analytic space, she may be better able to express her own frustration, anger, sadness, and a host of other challenging feelings within the analysis in ways that are not reactive, inappropriately self-referential, or generally unhelpful to the analysand, but instead model the ability to mix mindfulness with a true depth of feeling in the context of relationship (see Coltart, 1996, for illuminating discussion of the analyst's emotive expression).

In Sogyal Rinpoche's description of mindfulness as the route toward recognizing our most basic goodness there is a helpful reminder to clinicians that buried within each analysand (in addition to unconscious suffering, woundedness, and splitting) is a shared goodness—one's buddha nature. From a Buddhist perspective, the treatment difficulties I speak of above do not and cannot eradicate a deeper psychospiritual reality. Jeff

Shore speaks of his vision of psychoanalysis as the encounter of two buddhas (Shore, 2002, p. 43). He asks a critical question: Who and what do analysts see when looking into the eyes of their analysands? Ideally, mindfulness would help the Buddhist analyst relate to his patient's wisdom mind and to her own capacity to see clearly, whose realization must be dearly wished for, without attachment to when and how it emerges.

Such an analytic perspective speaks to the trust a spiritually inclined analyst would have in his patient's own psychic process. "The analyst does not have to do it all," says Ann Ulanov. "The psyche does it, or something through the psyche does it" (2004, p. 27). If an analyst has practiced depending on something other than his own psychoanalytic acumen, trusting that his analytic skill set is supported by something that also supports his analysand, he may bring both a deeper respect and reverence for the analysand's own wisdom and insight, and an increased tolerance for his own limited ability to help alleviate his patients' suffering as quickly or as skillfully as he would like. Such a perspective introduces another reality that allows both members of the analytic pair to be changed by the treatment through a constant exchange of wisdom, patience, and tolerance for what is not yet known. The boundaries are respected, but this altered perception fundamentally changes the understanding of how healing is ushered in through treatment.

I broach this issue of how multiple dependencies—on theory, on the spiritual realm, and on good counsel—allow the analyst increased humility and conscious awareness of her own limitations because of its implications in treatments that readily move toward healing and those that seem utterly ineffectual or even counterproductive. For the analyst who has come to rely solely upon psychoanalytic theory, her training, or even the wise counsel of colleagues and supervisors, there is a danger of ego inflation when the treatment goes well that can easily give way to anxiety, self-attack, or burn-out when it doesn't. For the analyst who has personal experience with reliance upon a nonmaterial realm there may be an increased capacity to accept the mystery that is at the core of every treatment (Coltart, 1996).

An analyst can and should make every effort to foster healing for her analysand, but when these efforts do not bear fruit, or when they do but in ways not imagined, the spiritually attuned analyst may feel less inclined to take this development upon her own ego as the only engine of change.

Instead, she may approach analysis as a process with increased curiosity about what neither member of the analytic pair can know, as a shared endeavor of "not-knowing" that they must suffer through together, awaiting changes that will result from myriad factors and influences.

Working within an analytic space where such humility and open-minded curiosity is dominant requires a certain strength of spirit. From a Buddhist perspective, such an analyst would be on friendly terms with the impermanence that is one of the three marks of human existence. A "not-knowing" analytic space would make room for how and when the analyst's techniques or personal approach reach their healing limits, for analysands whose life circumstances suddenly and radically change and whose needs change accordingly, or for the analyst whose own perspective is altered by changing life circumstances or the many relational dynamics in the analytic pair.

In the Tibetan tradition such an analyst would be described as a "spiritual warrior." These warriors are said to have remarkable courage and are characterized by a keen mind, gentleness of spirit, and fearlessness. Spiritual warriors may be frightened, but not so much that they are unwilling "to taste suffering, to relate clearly to their fundamental fear, and to draw out without evasion the lessons from difficulties" (Sogyal Rinpoche, 1993, p. 36).

In my own analysis I have been on the receiving end of my analyst's courageous capacity to experience with me the suffering I have shared. In this process I have learned about the willingness to join another person in his own shattered places, and to jointly summon the courage to glean insight from what we have weathered together and defer to what we cannot control.

In my experience on the analyst's side of the analytic pair, I think of a little girl I have been working with for several years. She is, for the most part, nonverbal with adults, presenting herself as a rather emotionally and verbally muted child. Yet in the confines of our small play therapy room she growls when missing a ball I've tossed her way, falls off her chair from laughter when I spontaneously dance to a song she likes, and begs to stay when our sessions have ended, often barricading the door with every moveable object she can find. In short, she is a fantastically alive little girl. But she has also known the wrenching and deadening pain of loving a mother who has flitted in and out of her life, sometimes leaving for months at a time, sometimes showing up looking bedraggled and sickly from a harsh life of severe addiction.

I believe that this little girl has found a way to protect herself from tasting any more suffering than she has already known by reining herself in, making herself small and impervious to the world of unpredictable, self-involved adults. In our work together she is mostly verbal, but not always. At times, sometime for weeks at a stretch, she merely chirps, or shrugs her shoulders in response to my questions. Words come to a halt. Even eye contact is rare. Having seen her aliveness, these retreats can be painful to witness, and also disheartening. I wonder: Am I doing enough? What if she remains so timid and withdrawn in her relationships that others will be unable to see or appreciate her many remarkable gifts—her fantastic sense of humor and sharp intellect, her strength and sweetness? Who will look out for her when she's older but still carrying these hidden wounds?

These are reasonable and relevant questions to ponder. But what allows them to remain questions and not become rigid fears is my own trust that in the process of genuinely sharing her pain and entering into those psychic spaces where she was not held and was left to feel that life is a perpetual free fall, she may come to trust that she's in a world where people will reach out to catch her. And furthermore, that such people will not be endowed with magical powers, but simply and very kindly held by their interdependency in the web of beings of which we are a very small and precious part. They are, as she is, in dependence upon the goodness of people and the spiritual practice that allows us to remain standing when this goodness is absent.

I think too of another little girl I worked with several years ago. Her mother had died tragically when she was eight years old. During one session, she lay on the floor, covering my feet with her back resting against my legs. She seemed utterly deflated by this loss, listless and grief-stricken. In a quiet voice she said, "My life is ruined." I wasn't sure I'd heard her correctly. I asked her if this is what she said. She nodded. When I asked her why she felt this way, she said matter-of-factly, "Because my mom is dead."

I felt her devastation and affirmed that having lost her mother was incredibly sad and upsetting. It was a terrible shock that she never expected. She nodded. At the same time, I felt another reality—that she would not be alone in suffering through this loss, that others would rally around her, keeping her in being. Gently, I told her that I had an idea. She wanted to know what it was. I told her that no one in her life would ever be exactly like her mother. Her mother was a special person, unlike anyone else in the whole world. But I had a feeling that she would continue to meet other girls and women: some would feel like sisters, others like great teachers, perhaps some like angels, and some even like a mother. And they would want to help her. One day, having been cared for by all of these people for so many years, she would be ready to help another little girl who felt the way she did now.

When I finished sharing my vision of interbeing, she sat up and began drawing a picture of herself, with shiny long hair and glowing eyes, surrounded by a sea of other vibrant little girls and "mommies." I sensed that what I had shared merely brought into sharper focus something that she intuited but needed to have affirmed: that suffering can be dreadful and truly deadening, but that it is also a powerfully unifying force, a way to enter into our shared human condition and be held by the compassion and care we are endowed with. She was not alone in having lost a beloved and critical person in her life. I knew something of the pain she felt, and hoped to impart that I too had survived through the kindness of others and through my trust in something other than my own wits to negotiate the pitfalls of grief and despair.

I speak of my interaction with this little girl in order to underscore two last, pivotal differences between analytic work that is informed by a spiritually or religiously oriented analyst and one that is not. In a traditional analytic treatment, in which the agent for change is understood to be the analysand's introjection of the analyst, two defining variables are at play (Ulanov, 2007). First, such a paradigm suggests that the success or failure of the treatment is solely dependent on the analyst, and by extension, that the analyst must be unusually insightful, fully integrated, and consistently attuned to the analysand's needs and complex psychic reality. In short, the analyst is cast in the role of the interpersonal superhero.

As I've said, it has been pointed out to me in my own training that I might want to bypass the tempting assumption that I am necessarily any better than my analysand's parents or primary caretakers. I, alone, am not the exclusive agent for transformation, but rather a facilitator who works to restore the analysand's own connection to his intuitive capacity for trust, wisdom, and an open-hearted willingness to risk dependency. With this understanding, I would operate with the knowledge that healing comes from myriad sources and in ways that may ultimately have little to do with me.

The second critical factor in a more traditional analytic perspective is the almost exclusive emphasis on patients' unmet needs, what they can get, psychologically and otherwise, from others, and how they might be more fulfilled in their romantic and professional endeavors. The treatment is meant to bolster patients' subjectivity, with the analyst making every effort to join them in their perspective and to build up their ego capacity to function and thrive within a given milieu. While these are certainly critical endeavors, I argue that such efforts may ultimately be a losing psychic battle when the reality of how analysands show up in the lives of others—what they give of themselves and how they respond to other people's suffering—is dismissed as only a peripheral focus.

In Buddhist psychology it is said that people are happiest when they wish others to be happy. Shantideva, the great eighth-century Buddhist philosopher, says, "Whatever joy there is in this world, all comes from wanting others to be happy; and whatever suffering there is in this world, all comes from wanting oneself to be happy" (Thurman, 1998, p. 187). Shantideva's suggestion is something different than a messianic drive to save others, to be identified as "The Giver," one who has purged himself of all needs or wishes. Rather, the idea is that when we shift our focus from what we can get to what we can give or help others get, we become less tethered to a chronic and nagging awareness of what we lack.

With this shift in focus, even people with seemingly very little in their lives by way of material wealth or primary love relationships may come to feel a genuine sense of abundance and real agency. Most importantly, they have given up a sure-fire method for generating suffering: the constant, potentially life-wrecking worry and torment over when their own happiness will come.

When analysts fail to integrate this perspective into analytic treatment, even the most gifted, affluent, and well-loved analysand may continue to tread psychic waters, viewing life through a lens of deprivation, unable to recognize how this feeling of lack will invariably influence both his capacity for real joy and his genuine curiosity about the suffering and happiness of others. I would argue that when the primary focus of analytic treatment is the analysand's own unmet needs, the happiness he wishes for can remain a maddening and elusive entity. Conversely, when an analyst has practiced and integrated an understanding of interbeing, our total dependence upon others for every facet of our lives, she may find another way to understand and relate to suffering and unmet needs that more effectively generates a lasting happiness for her analysand.

On a final note in this chapter, I will share a personal experience with this altered perspective on obtaining happiness through the wish for others to be happy that I happened upon through my own analysis. Several years ago, sadness, anguish, and feelings of profound frustration were dominant in my analysis. My analyst seemed to be pushing me into an ongoing mourning process that was about as much fun as a fork in the eye. Yet I continued, with a flood of tears and a chronic distrust that there would ever be enough change, either internally or externally, to allow for a happier and more joyful life. The analysis was mostly painful, and I was distressed by my own remarkable willingness to remain in a maudlin and exclusively self-focused state of mind.

Every week I would leave feeling self-conscious about the blotchy skin and blood-shot eyes that revealed my interminable weeping. Yet I still took notice of an elderly man I saw every week, waiting outside. This was unusual for me, as I am inclined to protect my own privacy and the privacy of others awaiting their analytic sessions. With this man, however, I felt more inclined to take note, to pay attention. He was quite hunched over, with a thick gray beard and gnarled hands, but his eyes were strikingly vibrant and emotive. We smiled and said hello each day, and eventually he looked up from his perpetually stooped position and said, "Funny how we keep meeting like this." I laughed and we began to talk, albeit briefly. He told me he was a painter—I could see the traces of cobalt blue and forest green on his fingers. He was quite ill, he said, but nonetheless in the most creative period of his life.

Week after week I would shift gears in the most radical way, going from angry tears to an almost instantaneous delight in seeing my fellow analysand. I could see that he was suffering through a debilitating illness and quite possibly in the last stages of his life, but also that he had lived a full and open-hearted life. In short, he seemed remarkably alive to me, and so very precious for this aliveness.

One day as he was saying goodbye and making his way down the long hallway to my analyst's office, he stopped, turned around, and said, "You are the kind of person who makes other people happy." Suffice it to say, I had never been happier than I was in that unlikely moment shared by two analysands. I walked away with enormous gratitude for his generosity of spirit and his enlivening presence. And while my intention is not to discount the meaning and importance of what was happening in the hour prior to our weekly meetings—the angry tears, the disbelief at how difficult it was to heal old wounds—I was nevertheless powerfully struck by Shantideva's insight.

The truth was that when I saw my elderly friend, I showed up for him with real curiosity and presence of mind. I was not focused on my early childhood struggles or on how acts of terrorism were reinforcing my fears about living in an unsafe world. I was simply interested in his own efforts to be happy, to continue painting and examining his psyche until the bitter end.

In this way I had made a very small contribution to his happiness, and this made me happier than I had ever been before.

healing goals in buddhism and psychoanalysis
enlightenment and integration

8

A s I begin this last chapter on the end goals of Buddhism and psychoanalysis, I think of my experience and relationships with a Tibetan lama and a Western psychoanalyst for lo these many years. Having come to know them both well, I fully trust that they harbor a similarly deep and long-lasting wish for my happiness, for a life that is filled with creativity, love, and a bolstered ability and desire to love and care for others. I believe that they both experience the world as a place of connectedness, where one person's kindness and strength of spirit may set in motion auspicious happenings even for complete strangers. They are both highly intuitive people, with big hearts and active minds. They are complex and sensitive men who can laugh easily, and who also express an authentic compassion that informs their ability to remain conscious in the midst of pain and loss. I believe that in their own ways they are both solidly on the bodhisattva's path of commitment to helping others find happiness and freedom from suffering to the best of their ability.

Despite these shared attributes, wishes, and lifelong goals, their methodologies, as we have seen, are remarkably divergent. So too, their understanding of what constitutes real happiness and freedom from suffering, while occasionally harmonious, are nevertheless altogether different. In this chapter I will explore the ways in which Buddhist teachers and Western psychoanalysts understand and seek happiness and freedom from suffering. While emphasizing the primary goals of each tradition, I hope to shed light on the contrasting beliefs of each tradition that guide students and analysands toward their shared wish for healing and wellness.

———————————————

It is not uncommon for my lama to call and ask me if I'm enlightened yet. Years back, I used to laugh with discomfort and try to play along, suggesting that maybe next week I would "see the light." Okay, he'd say, unimpressed, following with a quick "Just joking." More recently I've tended to say, "Maybe tonight," or even, "Call back in an hour." Sometimes this gets a bigger chuckle. I've been contemplating saying "yes" the next time he asks, just to hear his reaction, and also to explore whatever feelings and psychological backlash come on the heels of such an outrageous assertion.

I have come to wonder if I offer these humorous deflections because enlightenment strikes me as being an intimidating Buddhist fantasy that doesn't really jibe with my sense of ongoing human complexity and my many unexpected regressive twists and turns even in the midst of great psychic and spiritual growth spurts. As I consider this question, I have found myself pushing more deeply into this notion of achieving enlightenment—freedom from suffering—*in this very life*. The Buddha, after all, felt strongly enough about this possibility that he made the end of suffering his third noble truth and identified a path to this end in the fourth. Why not consider this a possibility? Or at the very least, wrestle with the healing aspects of such a notion?

In Buddhist doctrine, enlightenment is understood as freedom from all mental defilements. Having achieved such a purified mind would place one squarely in the realm of nirvana, which means the extinction of all afflictions (Cleary, 1994, p. 14). Such a purified state would allow one complete and utter freedom to choose how to live and die (Sogyal Rinpoche, 1993, p. 14). The Dalai Lama defines enlightenment as a "state of total freedom from the subtle imprints and the obstructive habitual tendencies created by our misconception of the nature of reality" (1995, p. 11). Contemporary Buddhists have also described it as a state of "perfect wisdom and compassion and freedom from any kind of suffering" (Brown & Engler, 1986, p. 207).

Students of Buddhism, almost regardless of the tradition, are taught that enlightenment is a totally purified state of mind whereby suffering comes to a categorical end, where one lives in a state of joyful attunement and permanent happiness. There are contrasting definitions that suggest enlightenment merely shows up our obstructive tendencies and instills in us a dear wish to overcome them. But these definitions are not particularly prevalent in Buddhist teachings.

Early on in my spiritual practice, it wasn't the notion of joy or happiness that I struggled with so much as the notion that such feelings and insight would necessarily be permanent. Over the years I found myself growing partial to an understanding of enlightenment that combined such depths of happiness with the vagaries of human consciousness and unconsciousness that seemed to me to be the only real constant in my lived experience.

I will explore this sticking point further, but before doing so I wish to express that like most of my fellow sangha members, I was and still am quite drawn to such notions of unshakable good-natured living. In the early stages of my Buddhist studies, just as my ever-critical eye honed in on potential loopholes in enlightenment theory, I also felt enlivened by the possibility that one's internal world was not necessarily dictated by the external world. As I had learned from reading Victor Frankl years before, it seemed logical that if we could not control the vicissitudes of our external environment, it would behoove us to focus on our internal worlds and our responses to such vicissitudes.

With this in mind, I grew more curious about the potential impact of Buddhist practice and its purported end goal. I had read that the Dalai Lama associated suffering with an undisciplined state of mind, and happiness with a disciplined state of mind (1995, p. 16). His emphasis on the determination to achieve an abiding internal place of rest was quite compelling given his own staggering personal losses. As a survivor of cultural genocide, a man who had lost his country and suffered through a terrorist regime, like Frankl, he clearly knows more than his fair share about external circumstances that would seem sufficiently powerful to eradicate his ability to cultivate such internal peace and discipline of mind.

In his teachings of the Buddhist doctrine on dependent origination, the Dalai Lama reminds students that suffering never exists in isolation. When we suffer, it is always in dependence upon causes and conditions.

In Buddhism the emphasis is almost exclusively on one's response to pain as the primary cause for continued suffering. For this reason, psychoanalyst and Zen teacher Joseph Bobrow points out that the third noble truth is not a proclamation of suffering magically extinguished, but rather an end to the habituated ways in which we typically react to commonplace suffering. Students are encouraged to use their spiritual training to end *the causes of suffering*, rather than the suffering itself (2003, p. 244).

In the Mahayana path this process includes the meditation practice so central to the Theravada tradition, and most importantly the work and commitment of the bodhisattva. Through caring deeply for others we begin to recognize the genuine happiness that results when we soften the typically tenacious grip we hold on ourselves at the expense of connection with others. As one's attachment to self dissolves, the psychic ground is readied for enlightenment. Jack Engler writes:

> Enlightenment occurs when all grasping at self and objects, even in their subtlest forms, is relinquished and all reactivity in the mind is exhausted. Only then is identification with...self surrendered and the mind awakened to a way of being not organized around consolidating and protecting a separate self. (Engler, 2003, p. 70)

The bodhisattva's path is said to facilitate the attainment of the six perfections that are necessary preconditions for the good heart and awakened mind of enlightenment: generosity, ethical discipline, patient endurances, joyous effort, concentration, and wisdom (Dalai Lama, 1995, p. 65). The Dalai Lama teaches that it is only through caring deeply for others that we attain such a good heart. In this way he posits relationship as the central vehicle for the realization of wisdom and the attainment of enlightenment.

This relational focus, whereby spiritual development happens only within the realm of interpersonal contact, is pivotal to the Mahayana teachings. According to Mahayana teachings, we cannot realize our wisdom mind by focusing exclusively on our own purification. Such a purified mind comes through one's efforts to care for others, to help them be free from all manner of suffering and achieve the happiness they desire. Through this work we come to recognize the basic interdependence that points to the reality of emptiness—that all phenomena lack inherent and fixed meaning. And through the realization of emptiness, we achieve freedom from all self-centric mind states.

In Tibetan Buddhism there is a decidedly non-Western approach to this process of shedding delusions and purifying our mind. I think it is fair to suggest most Westerners envision achieving great and noteworthy change—either within themselves or for others—through much hard work and unpleasant sacrifice that they hope will be acknowledged and/or rewarded in some discernable way. There is typically the shadow of Western individualism in such pursuits, where one's own concerted efforts at spiritual discipline and necessary sacrifice may serve to reinforce one's ego position. My sense is that, in contrast, the rather down-to-earth and communal culture of Tibet, where people are disinclined to talk at length about their various struggles, sacrifices, and hard work, but rather simply carry on with what they must do, has engendered a very different understanding of mind training and the bodhisattva's path (Fields, 1992).

Sogyal Rinpoche points to this divergent approach to enlightenment, stating that "We don't 'become' a Buddha; we simply slowly cease to be deluded" (1993, p. 53). Described in this way, enlightenment seems considerably less formidable. It is not something one must grasp hold of, with endless expensive retreats and throbbing knees from unrelenting meditation sessions, but something one can simply, and with a quiet discipline, allow to happen: the very natural process of discovering and living into our most basic nature of goodness and freedom from confusion, selfishness, and reactive ill-will toward others. In this way awakening is a shedding of the mind's delusions.

Having become more acquainted with Tibetan culture and with Asian Buddhist society, I suspect that this less ego-based approach to positive mental and spiritual change has something to do with the increased ease with which enlightenment "theory" is taught and practiced. I also imagine that the foundational belief that we are by our very nature good-hearted people free from mental hindrances leads to the belief that enlightenment is not so much an extraordinary achievement as a process of remembering and easing back into our most basic nature.

Even the meditation process, from an Asian Buddhist perspective, is described as the means through which we bring the mind home to rest (Sogyal Rinpoche, 1993, p. 62). It's a gentle process of slowing down, allowing thoughts to come and go without attempting to join them or run from them, and permitting oneself a growing place of respite between thoughts that so easily lead to illusory notions of self and others. It is a disciplined means of relaxing deeply into our true wisdom mind, which is free from all grasping and craving, and in which there is an unobscured sense of being. And as we "work" into this place of rest, where we recognize that our true mind is nongrasping when freed from the comparative illusions of our discursive and ordinary minds—at rest it does not take itself to be a discrete phenomenon but merely is—we more naturally cultivate the qualities of altruism, patience, and loving kindness that help all others who share this basic nature of beingness. In such a process there is an increased sense of expansiveness that is not ours alone, but a true web of interbeing.

It is a gentle, inward-looking but outwardly attuned process that is more a *restoration* than a miraculous achievement of something altogether new. It is a kind of homecoming to the good and pure mind of clear seeing.

As I consider a psychoanalytic response to enlightenment, I imagine my analyst's quizzical expression when in years past I have described a Buddhist concept that doesn't quite resonate with his beliefs and understanding of wellness. Despite his clear respect for and interest in the spiritual realm, as an analyst he is not alone in having some difficulty with the notion of enlightenment as a return to a conflict-free mental zone. In psychoanalytic theory some degree of suffering and conflict is considered inherent to the human condition (Rubin, 1996, p. 84). This is one of the primary differences in these two healing traditions, and it has much to do with their disparate goals.

Freud's instinct theory was one of invariable internal conflict. He posited an ongoing battle between our id-based drives for pleasure and unfettered aggression, our ego's efforts to keep us viable within our external environment, and our internalized (often harsh) morality, which comes through the superego's efforts to keep the id squarely in line. His was a rather pessimistic view of humanity: he wished to help people manage their neurotic symptoms and settle for the "common unhappiness" that comes with the necessary compromise of being part of a human family and society (Freud, 1930). Freud's psychoanalytic goals involved the achievement of mature sexual relationships and work lives that would sublimate the lifelong instinctual conflict zone of the human mind.

Carl Jung had quite a different vision of the psyche, and one more compatible with Buddhist notions of deeply buried wisdom. Jung, like the Buddha, posited a wisdom of the psyche (see Ulanov, 1988). He believed we come fully equipped with a set of compensatory functions that allows us to live meaningful and creative lives. For Jung, the analytic goal involved helping people achieve a steady reliance on this wisdom that facilitated an ongoing conversation between one's own ego and the unifying archetypal energy of the Self—that supreme psychospiritual structure that gathers all our psychic parts into wholeness (Jung, 1951, CW9, para. 1–42). In Jung's theory there is an ever-present sense of tremendous human potential, where our humanness is nurtured both by our own internal wisdom and our conscious contact with the *numinous*—the mysterious realm of the extramundane.

But Jung's theories have not been widely taught or examined in most psychoanalytic circles. Instead, the legacy of Freudian theory has been more dominant, with many salubrious alterations and reconstructions throughout the years. For one such influential Freudian, Melanie Klein, a psychoanalytic goal involved solidly internalizing the good experience of one's primary caretakers in one's early childhood alongside the bad, so that one could move through the paranoid-schizoid stages of early infancy and achieve a more depressed position, coming to feel regret for the anger felt toward a parent that is also loved.

Klein's model is one of integration, but still, depression is an *achievement* in her paradigm. While she masterfully emphasized the importance of working through our earliest experiences of aggression, envy, and fear in order to move toward enjoyment and gratitude, I think it fair to propose that she was ultimately less focused on our human capacity for joyful transformation. Her psychoanalytic goals were still in line with Freud's common unhappiness, despite her focus on integration.

Joyful transformation became more present in Winnicott's vision: he emphasized the important difference between mere health and the creative life that emerges out of one's true self. It was this experience of authentic freedom and a creatively lived life that he sought to bring about through psychoanalytic treatment (1971).

For Winnicott, creativity exists in that precious and lively space between our own subjective experience and the objective world. We discover ourselves and the reality of others through the interaction of our internal worlds and our environment. In order to achieve contact with one's true self, and thus to live into that enlivening space between the "me" and the "not-me" world, one must use one's ruthless ability to love in an all-out, un-self-conscious way and be granted a necessary time where one is relatively unconcerned with the environment (Jones, 1997). Just as critical to Winnicott's theory is the young child's ability to destroy her own projected image of others through destructiveness that is appropriately received, and so to discover who it is who survives her destruction.

A Winnicottian world is an intensely relational one in which the true exchange of unfettered love and aggression allows real contact between one's own subjective reality and the objective reality of others. One could argue that for Winnicott the dualism of a true *I* meeting a true *You* that is something more and other than what I wish you to be is a real psychological achievement and thus a challenge to the nondualism—the interbeing—of Buddhist doctrine. I will explore this in further detail when I consider the overarching goals of these two traditions. But before doing so, I wish to elaborate on some additional key configurations of psychoanalytic end goals.

For Heinz Kohut, the analytic goal involves reestablishing an empathic connection between oneself and others that does not result from perfect mirroring or perfectly idealizable qualities, but rather from being nurtured by and in connection with healthy people throughout one's life. In this way Kohut also emphasizes the necessity of relatedness that continues throughout every life stage. In his treatment efforts he endeavored to help people develop sturdier self-structures, but he felt strongly that even the healthiest self is like a healthy lung that is only as functional as the quality of the air it took in (1984, p. 77). For Kohut, the giving and receiving of empathy was at the core of his treatment and what he most wished to impart to his analysands.

Some contemporary psychoanalysts have taken Kohut to task for being exclusively focused on the empathic needs of the analysand rather than on the ways the analysand may become more available to and empathic toward others (see Benjamin, 1999). I agree that Kohut stopped just short of recognizing an augmented psychoanalytic vision that moved beyond the exclusive ego-orientation of Freudian treatment into a more explicitly bidirectional relational objective that included its benefit to the analysand and the people who populate his or her world. Other psychoanalytic theorists, such as Charles Strozier, suggest that Kohut's psychology was ultimately a theory of connectedness and the recovery process of disrupted union (Strozier, 1997, p. 177), and further, that Kohut directly challenged the solipsism of a Freudian model through his emphasis on empathy as the central psychoanalytic tool and ultimate psychological achievement (ibid., p. 178).

Wilfred Bion, despite his own analysis with Melanie Klein, a true Freudian devotee, took the treatment process into decidedly new and spiritually inclusive territory. With his psychoanalytic blueprint of healing as the movement toward ultimate reality, symbolized by O, through acts of faith unfettered by K, or thought used in the service of shielding oneself from ultimate reality, Bion ushered in a process of healing that utilized a fully conscious thought so that one could withstand and integrate the shattering impact of what Christopher Bollas later called consciousness of the "unthought known" (1987). While his end goal used thinking as a high-octane fuel for the psyche, his psychoanalytic landscape was one of profound affective reality, where the analysand became willing to risk contact with formerly unprocessed experiences of loss, of reaching out for others who could not meet us or met us and then severed the connection.

In Bion's theories one can discern the threads of a Freudian goal, in which unconscious contents are brought to consciousness, and a Kleinian integration of devastating early childhood feeling with maturing cognition. Bion integrates his predecessor's insight into a vision that includes the pain and conflict he too would suggest is part of the human relational journey, but for Bion, pain and conflict point to the possibility of real transformation through conscious interaction with reality. Bion moved beyond Freud's common unhappiness into the realm of electrifying aliveness. In such a realm there is a clear shift in the clinical focus from survival and security 'in one's environment to learning to tolerate the ever-growing intensity of who we are and what we have lived through (Ulanov, 2007, p. 16).

In all of these psychological theories the emphasis is placed on the transformation of personal suffering (Jung remains the exception, although he too emphasized the necessity of fully examining personal content). Here we have another critical difference in the focus and methodologies of Buddhism and psychoanalysis, and in the work of the two healing dyads. In psychoanalysis, the analysand's personal struggles, history, and psychological and emotional patterns are fully explored, with great attention paid to his projections and transference onto the analyst. In Buddhism, it is universal modes of suffering that are recognized and parsed in the doctrine and in the relationship between the Buddhist teacher and student (Young-Eisendrath, 2003, p. 318). As Jack Engler suggests, and I agree, it is assumed that personal content will also be addressed in the work between the religious dyad, but this is often not the case (Engler in Unno, 2006, pp. 23–24; see also chapter 7).

Nevertheless, I propose that a Buddhist point of view in regard to our ultimate human potential can both temper the profoundly self-centric exploration of the analytic process and augment the psychoanalytic vision for healing and wellness. Nina Coltart speaks of the value in her analytic work of bringing into the treatment her own abiding belief in impermanence (1996, p. 128). She suggests that if the analyst really knows in the depths of her being that everything changes, including the most dreadful types of suffering, such a perspective can influence and support both members of the analytic pair. She is promoting neither a childlike optimism nor an inappropriate sharing of the analyst's views within the treatment. Coltart recognizes that sometimes things change for the worse, but she attempts to offer an example of how the analyst's spiritual training may open up new possibilities for clinical treatment (ibid.).

I believe that Coltart is also addressing the importance of imaginatively engaging the notion of life beyond our current modes of suffering. She points to the third noble truth—the end of suffering—as an interesting addition to psychoanalytic perspectives. This noble truth, followed by the eightfold path—the way out of suffering given in the fourth noble truth—emphasizes the ways in which we create our own suffering. It is not a magical philosophy predicated on illusory hopefulness, but rather a teaching on the importance of understanding how we are intimately involved in the causes and conditions that exacerbate our commonplace suffering. It is, in this way, a system of supreme personal accountability that offers a path to enlightenment if we are willing to keep a vigilant focus on our own perceptions, beliefs, and actions rather than on the external world over which we have limited control.

This enlightenment can be envisioned as a true awakening to reality that does not bury us in sadness or a Kleinian depression, but opens new connections to our basic and shared human value. Through such an awakening one might begin to envision a sense of possibility, where the ripple effects of wisdom and goodness that come from within us and from others flow throughout our life. I believe such a perspective is necessary in psychoanalytic treatment, where the awareness of one's personal problems, particularly when trauma is involved, can act as a kind of albatross, leaving the analysand feeling overwrought with the enormity of pain and loss, and only tenuously connected to life beyond this personal legacy. The intense and often painful exploration of the analytic process can also lead to new and/or reinforced addictive behaviors used to soothe oneself in the absence of a spiritual practice that might more effectively contain and potentially heal such overwhelming emotion and insight.

It is here that I would challenge Stephen Batchelor's assertion that beliefs are not central to the Buddhist path, or for that matter any path of healing. I think of a conversation I had with my Buddhist teacher some years ago. I happened to be in the throes of tremendous doubt and fear about the way I imagined my life unfolding. There were whole days when I felt continuously mystified by the many decisions I had made throughout the years that seemed to bring me to an utterly senseless place in life. I moved through life with a chronic and unbeatable feeling of self-imposed entrapment. As one might expect, my analysis during this time was a rather weepy and ponderous process.

In the midst of this chronic doubt and confusion, my teacher and I had driven together to a talk he was scheduled to give. Driving along a New York State highway with a few hours to go, we mostly talked about the Lotto. He told me that I shouldn't expect to hear from him again if he strikes it rich. He would run for the hills (which shall remain nameless) and eat fresh yak meat every day. Then he threw his head back and cackled wildly in his usual manner, and followed with a deadpan "Just joking."

After a moment or two of silence, he proceeded very simply to tell me how good things were for me: I was educated, studying the Dharma, and living in a place where there were many intelligent and curious people who would be interested in my research. I was focused on healing and sharing this with others. These were wonderful circumstances. Then we carried on talking about the Lotto.

When I got home that night, I sat in my kitchen and realized with some bemusement that he was right. The reality he depicted was something I hadn't considered or consciously lived into, and yet it seemed as fair and resonant as the doubt and self-laceration that had become a twenty-four-hour drone. Remaining conscious of the rich and abundant life he described required that I believe in my own basic value and potential for a full, nourishing, and relational life. It required consciousness of and belief in something more than my capacity for survival.

I think too of those moments in my own analysis when I found myself evoking a rather bleak vision of what life had in store for me: ongoing isolation, frustrated opportunities, and personal disappointments. I recall one such session when my analyst looked me in the eyes and asked, "Why is this your vision for yourself?" He continued by offering a radically more joyful scenario that left me wrinkling my brow, wondering who the hell he was talking to. He clearly hadn't been paying attention all the years prior.

During one such session, I said, "You're asking me to believe in something I have never experienced." He nodded with total assurance. "That's right."

It was not enough, however, for me to hear my analyst's more hopeful vision, or to observe *his* trust in the potential impact of belief. I needed another belief system to challenge the Western psychoanalytic view. In Jeremy Safran's *Psychoanalysis and Buddhism*, Jack Engler and psychoanalyst Stephen Mitchell have an interesting conversation that speaks to this point. Stephen Mitchell wonders if the very concept of no-self is as much a construction as the reified self we mistakenly take ourselves to be (see Safran, 2003, p. 85). Mitchell suggests that we cannot know what the self is and would be better off exploring the impact of how we view the self, either as fixed, multiple, or no-self (ibid., p. 87). As a Buddhist, however, Jack Engler suggests that the issue of self and our beliefs about self beg for a greater willingness to pin down which experiences of self generate happiness and which do not. I agree with Engler that it is not a theoretical matter:

If we investigate the consequences of each view of self, just as Mitchell recommends, we will find that some lead to the end of suffering while others only create more suffering…Our well-being depends on our being able to discriminate which is which. (Ibid.)

In my analysis, I was reminded that attachment to the belief in an inherent self left me feeling either fated to a life that lacked the spontaneity and vitality of unexpected discovery, growth, and meaning I wished for, or pressured to fulfill a more desirable destiny as depicted by my analyst. The thought that I was tethered to a future predicated on *who I am* writ large left me feeling ill at ease and somehow destined for subpar efforts at success. It was not just that the nature of the fantasy was problematic, but that the fantasy was perceived as a fixed reality destined to meet up with a fixed self that I must honor and live up to. However, when I focused on the Buddhist teaching of impermanence, emptiness, and noself, and on the constantly changing circumstances of a given life, I began slowly to relax back into life, knowing that neither myself, my bleak view of the future, nor my analyst's sterling fantasy were fixed phenomena. These beliefs, which I had contemplated over many years, helped me to reframe my perception of how life might unfold. I felt better when doing so, less anxious and more attuned to what I could and could not control in regard to my future.

It is reasonable to question whether or not I would have come to this felt awareness through my experience in psychoanalysis alone. I would argue that in addition to the many ethical, moral, and social considerations that are far less likely to be addressed in psychoanalytic treatment than in Buddhist studies and practice, even the seemingly comparable psychological concepts in each tradition—in this case the fluidity of self— will impact the practitioner in very different ways.

In Buddhist practice, ideas and beliefs that are emphasized and integrated into a long-term meditation ritual may find their way into one's unconscious, where they seem to take root, mixing with one's unconscious beliefs almost like a dream that one struggles to remember but which nevertheless casts a shadow that can't be totally ignored. When meditation is used as a means of focusing on certain core teachings, it can facilitate a far less intellectually driven relationship with ideas. The beliefs or concepts are not argued, deconstructed, processed through affective response, or passively accepted. Instead, there is a means of *being with* such ideas/beliefs that is more experiential in nature and offers a greater potential for transformation. It seems possible that I was able to receive my lama's assessment of my particular life circumstance in part due to the many years I spent contemplating impermanence, the preciousness and auspicious circumstances of human life, and our capacity for a genuinely changed perspective in dependence upon the nature of our minds.

And in Buddhist practice, the contemplation of ideas usually predates—often by decades—our conscious realization of such ideas. Emptiness and no-self, for instance, are integrated into meditation practice for many practitioners well before these concepts begin to come alive in their day-to-day interactions. But meditation prepares the mind so that it may one day land with a resounding "Yes, of course!" This is something different from a passive surrender, and more a personal discovery.

I suspect that if I hadn't brought to my own analysis years of training in and meditation on emptiness and no-self, it would have been difficult for me to recognize that when my analyst challenged my vision of life in the future, he was pointing both to the truth of emptiness and to a flexibility of mind that would allow me to imagine myriad ways in which this emptiness might be filled.

In reality, my bleaker vision was a clear fiction, something that I had projected onto a future that did not yet exist. And informing that vision was an unspoken identity, a sense of adventitious self I was still very much attached to but unable to see. Somewhere within my psyche was an unconscious sense of self predicated on a tacit ceiling on happiness that had trumped my belief in buddha nature. In his radically different vision, and in the context of a personal discussion, my analyst had helped me to remember that living from the "pregnant void" of emptiness meant living into endless possibilities. Nothing was everlasting, not even my notion of a fated self. Buddhist philosophy, however, would take this assessment several steps further, suggesting that not only was my fated self an ephemeral entity, but that the only thing that would last once achieved was awakening to my basic goodness, my buddha nature. A permanent peace of mind was possible.

Before I wrestle with this enticing notion of permanent peace, I wish to clarify that I was well served by the sacred space provided in psycho-analysis to admit freely my particular fears and angst, with trust that these troubled mental states would be warmly received without immediate efforts to rectify them. Through this experience, I was beginning to trust that there was room for my humanness in the context of interpersonal relationship. But I also needed the Dharma to challenge these fears so that I could continuously, and through ongoing ritualized practice, come to trust in an essential goodness within myself and in all others that would hold my human struggles with the tenderness of buddha nature. Through this double vision I felt myself moving toward the steadfastly joyful life I most wanted.

Buddhist psychoanalyst Jeffrey Rubin states (perhaps somewhat wryly) that in the Buddhist doctrine everything changes but enlightenment. In this theory of unchanging psychospiritual wellness, "Buddhism attempts to eat its cake of flux and have it too" (Rubin, 1996, p. 90). Rubin challenges a notion of purified mind that is permanently freed from influence by the unconscious (ibid., p. 90). While he too recognizes the value in imagining increased potential for joyful, transformed living in the psychoanalytic domain, he is suspect of theories that suggest any static mind state.

Mark Epstein offers a similar caveat for enlightenment theory, propos-ing that a true awakening does not eliminate the challenges of self-experience, but rather reveals these challenges so that instead of grasping at self without consciousness of doing so, we may be better able con-sciously to witness this process and to integrate what we learn and observe. Epstein goes on to say that we "do not have a fixed self, in either sense of the word" (2007).

While it is tempting for me to make theoretical assertions based on what I have experienced in my spiritual practice and in my relationship to many great teachers in the healing work of Buddhism and psychoanalysis, I remain uncertain about our capacity to achieve a permanently conscious mind of clear seeing. Yet I am sure that wrestling with this possibility is worthwhile, both spiritually and psychologically. On the one hand, the psychoanalytic perspective, which takes into account the nonlinear nature of psychological change and growth, offers a palpable sensitivity and compassion for the experience of unexpected regression in the midst of concerted efforts at healing. Psychoanalysts have a unique opportunity to witness the many twists and turns of the psyche with analysands who may attain exceptional levels of achievement, integration, and maturity in certain areas of their lives only to revert to a place of psychic infantilism in other areas.

I think of children I have worked with. One week they may carry on emotionally sophisticated and dynamic conversations with me, talking about friends, new ideas that they have discovered, and their feelings about teachers or family members. They play with real vigor and ignited imaginations. This can be followed by weeks of cooing, throwing toys, and reverting to a totally nonverbal, body-based developmental stage. The psyche seems to be a highly labile entity, sometimes dominated by remarkable integration of intellectually and emotionally developed states, while at other times appearing to be solely under the influence of one delimiting aspect of being or one dominant life experience.

I think too of the many Buddhist teachers I have known. From afar they have all tended to present as people who transcend the trappings of a conventional perspective: the petty frustration, quickness to anger, and major interpersonal strife are largely absent. And I have admired these teachers for their remarkable insight and equanimity in the face of major difficulties and loss. That said, I am also aware that up close I have at times discerned the presence of pain and complexity that doesn't necessarily seem to heal through their intensive spiritual practice alone. They too have psyches that respond in very personal ways to loss, grieving, and the shared marks of human life.

As my Buddhist analytic predecessors have all addressed, in psychoanalysis there is a greater emphasis on the meaning in personal experience. It is, in part, for this reason that the analyst may be better able to show real compassion to the person suffering from his or her uniquely personal history that has manifested in particular ways. Within the analytic space, there is more room for the analysand to speak of her suffering in ways that are not generalized or made to fit into clear moral, ethical, or philosophical paradigms. So too there may be increased sensitivity and understanding when the growth and healing that is achieved is suddenly reversed or even wiped out by some unforeseen event or the new and surprising emergence of more formerly split-off parts of the self. As Polly Young-Eisendrath points out, there is a true moment-to-moment suffering with the analysand that speaks to a very powerful analytic compassion. And through this compassion, the analysand may come to experi-ence a greater tolerance for the ways in which healing and growth are mixed with sudden regression or unexpected modes of retreat.

I believe this roomy and focused approach to the complexity of the psy-che is a necessary component of any true healing path. At the same time, there is a particularly nourishing quality to imagining a time when psychic retreat and regression might come to an end. I have not yet experienced such a move into steadfast clarity and equanimity, but I have felt the enliven-ing impact of belief in such a mode of consciousness. I think of Jung, who said that we cannot prove the existence of God, but can and must explore the irrefutable belief in God. I think too of another teacher who said many years ago that we cannot know whether or not rebirth or *bardo* states (tran-sitional periods following death) are true, but we can explore whether or not such beliefs and concepts are helpful in our lived experience. Jack Engler was pointing to a similar insight in his dialogue with Mitchell: that we can feel and know which beliefs about the self hurt or help.

As for the goal of enlightenment in Buddhist practice, I cannot know whether or not I will ever live into the evenly placid mental states of the buddhas and bodhisattvas. But I can imagine what such a life might feel like. In this imaginative process, I needn't develop an attachment per se to the possibility of enlightenment, but I can play with and investigate what such a life might look like. What I imagine is an experience of interper-sonal contact in which fear is less dominant; curiosity for self and others is increased; openness of communication is gentle but direct; and hurts, frustrations, and losses are fully felt and are shared openly, but are also fully and genuinely relinquished so that care for and interest in others, alongside one's own continuous full-throttle living, is possible. I like the way this sounds, and I like the way I feel in this imagined experience.

In this description of a life of awakening, I think of my lama. He is not a perfect person—he does not brush his teeth as often as he should, he sometimes falls asleep in the middle of a conversation, and he gets dis-tracted by his cellphone before it even rings. But I have also observed that he has an unusual impact on others. They seem to feel more alive and more seen in his presence, as I often do. So too, they feel called to be as gentle and direct with him as he is with them. But this does not necessar-ily translate into a conflict-free experience. By way of example, I offer one such conflictual encounter.

Last year, while we were driving home from a teaching my lama had given in Vermont, he asked me about my current writing project. He was curious to know more about my research and my goals. In fairly general terms I explained my interest in Western Buddhists and their psychological relationship to the Dharma. I wished to explore the psychological and cultural barriers that interfered with the transmission of the Buddha-dharma. Mid-sentence, he put his finger in the air and said authoritatively, "Do *not* write an exposé!"

I was stunned. First, I considered myself to be very much an insider and thus not inclined to expose anything other than my own psyche and spiritual journey. Second, he was telling me what to do with *my* work, *my* writing, and by extension, *my* life. The irony of this response, with its ver-boten grasping at all things "I, me, or mine," was not lost on me, which only added to my distress. In my anger (yet another decidedly "un-Buddhist" response) I reached for a large bag of potato chips and began crunching madly with growing ire that I hoped to quickly sublimate. He finished me off with, "It should be *charming*."

Charming? He could not have found a more patronizing, unknowingly misogynist adjective for a rigorous process that would be anything but charming. Lugubrious, possibly, dense or thought-proving, yes (I hope). But charming? In the days that followed he called quite a few times. I ignored his messages, until finally I relented, picking up the phone with muted enthusiasm. He asked me if I wanted to have a thousand of the best *momos* (Tibetan dumplings) he could find. No, I said. "Yak butter?" No thanks, I muttered.

"Do you think I'm the nastiest person in the world?"

"Yes," I said. He told me he'd just lost his appetite. Then, after an awkward and fraught moment, he proceeded, asking me, "Should I *always* be nice, or be nice with a meanness that is really just play and jokes, or be truly nasty? You tell me." I sat quietly for a moment and answered: "You should be nice 80 percent of the time, playfully nasty 15 percent of the time, and truly nasty 5 percent of the time."

"Good," he said. "Now I know what to do."

It is said, and I agree, that Buddhism does not utilize dialogue as a methodological tool for healing as it is used in psychoanalysis (Young-Eisendrath, 2003; and see Rubin, 1996). Instead, students typically listen carefully to their teachers and sit quietly with their own minds. If they are having difficulty with any of the practices or teachings, or even personal matters, they may ask for guidance, but usually the response will come in the form of general spiritual counsel, moral guidance, or philosophical insight (Aronson, 2006).

I am grateful to have a teacher who can tolerate this kind of (semi-) open dialogue that acknowledges interpersonal experience. Through such exchanges I have learned about the ways in which our human falli-bility might mix with a mind of clear seeing. Having been influenced by traditional Tibetan culture, my lama was not without his gendered blind spots—thus the command that my work should be "charming." Yet he was just as able to remain in connection when I was inclined to retreat altogether, and furthermore, to admit his own interpersonal cluelessness. Like everyone else, he needed help, a blueprint for how to be human in the relational world, and he seemed unafraid to ask for such help, even from a student. Yet, unlike most people, who have not experienced the impact of long-term spiritual endeavors, my lama, through nearly half a century of intensive Buddhist practice, was quick to return to a genuinely peaceful, humble, and easy-going state of mind. While I was inclined to stew in mounting feelings of frustration, disappointment, and even indig-nation, whatever patriarchal buttons had been pushed in his own psyche were just as easily released back into a less controlling, more connected, happier, and relational mode of being.

In his teachings on happiness, the Dalai Lama speaks of the way Bud-dhist meditation practice reinforces a higher baseline of happiness regard-less of external circumstance (Dalai Lama & Cutler, 1998, 10–11). With extensive exploration of our perception and the ways in which we per-ceive both internal and external variables, the experience of moment-to-moment happiness is cultivated and reinforced. Current research has confirmed that such spiritual training may improve the baseline of hap-piness human beings return to even after traumatic experience (ibid.; Walsh & Shapiro, 2006).

While much of this increased happiness has to do with the reduction of anxiety and agitation and the increased mental clarity that come from the meditative experience in concentration practice, I propose that here again beliefs are paramount. If we believe that our most basic shared nature is one of freedom from conflict and mental defilements, and if we are sensi-tive to the many ways in which this nature may become intermittently camouflaged by layers of trauma, defensive rage, and/or interpersonal difficulties, we will be on the lookout for this buried goodness and wisdom within ourselves and others. In the midst of relational conflict, such a belief might create ready incentives for efforts at humble reconciliation, eased in with the good humor that comes from a generally happy state of mind.

In regard to the interpersonal dynamics and focus of the two healing dyads, the impact of this belief (or lack thereof) in original goodness can be profoundly influential. A Buddhist teacher would seek always to relate to this goodness in his students and to affirm its reality. A classically trained psychoanalyst, in contrast, would be far more attuned to the repressed and dominant conflicts in the unconscious. As a system of Western thought influenced by notions of original sin, psychoanalysis has tended to operate with a pessimistic view of the human psyche.

Given my own analytic training and the personal experience that is resonant with much of this training, I have a deep respect for the power of the unconscious and for the impact of repressed parts of the self we cannot tolerate bringing to consciousness. I could not reasonably argue that conscious beliefs (for instance, in one's basic goodness) alone can influence more deeply buried beliefs and affective experiences housed in the unconscious. But I am reasonably sure that they matter. I agree with Stephen Batchelor's and Paul Knitter's assertion that one must have an experiential and highly personal encounter with religious doctrine in order to practice a spiritual tradition with authenticity. We cannot merely consume beliefs and expect to be positively changed by them. But the focused and disciplined contemplation, practice, and study of Buddhism are something quite different from passive consumerism. As Knitter observes, the Buddhist path is born out of a search for a system that really works (2009).

It is in the spirit of such a search that I have embarked on this exploration of Buddhism and psychoanalysis as highly divergent yet harmonious healing traditions. I have attempted to explore their contrasting theories, methods, and end goals with particular emphasis on the healing dyads because I believe that enlivening human relationship is simultaneously the generator, container, and goal of our awakened being. It is perhaps for this reason that I have been partial to the Mahayana Buddhist path, with its emphasis on achieving enlightenment through caring for others. Most of all, I have been moved to investigate what types of healing most effectively allow us to bring both our human complexity and our buddha nature into the realm of interpersonal relationship, so that relationships may be nourished by both and withstand the wily impact of the unconscious.

Throughout my own healing journey, I have discovered and experienced an ongoing need for both traditions. In psychoanalysis, I have benefited from the attention given to the particularities of my life experience and psyche, and the ways I uniquely move through this complicated world. In this way there has been a deep respect paid to the reality of my subjective experience. This process has also included my personal and psychological relationship to a Buddhist spiritual practice, and to the many provocative challenges of sustaining a cross-cultural relationship with a spiritual teacher. I have felt supported in recognizing the potential places of ensnarement in my spiritual practice so that I might bring a greater consciousness to how the Dharma mixes with my own mind. In this way my analyst has helped me to deepen my Buddhist practice, and has reminded me that like all meaningful and worthwhile gifts, it is not without formidable challenges that touch on personal wounds and wishes.

At the same time, I have benefited from having a larger container provided by my spiritual practice for what I learn and experience within my analytic work. With Buddhist doctrine, spiritual study, and meditation practice as ballast for the highly personal exploration of psychoanalytic treatment, I have felt supported in reorienting my personal insight to the collective human experience of suffering and healing. In my spiritual practice I have learned that suffering and the wish to be happy and fully alive are markers of human life. Ann Ulanov writes that our personal experiences of suffering act as our particular link to the collective (2007). Even the most unusual of circumstances, or suffering that seems to be the stuff of science fiction, need not be mere fodder for pathology: a spiritual practice that affirms our interbeing and shared buddha nature can render such experiences reinforcement for one's sense of unity and connection with the larger human family.

Throughout this exploration I have attempted to discern what each tradition fails to address, not so that the reader would be well versed in the shortcomings of these traditions, but to honor the complexity of an authentic engagement with any healing path. In my own experience, I have struggled with the effort to recognize the particular ways in which each tradition offers powerfully healing, yet for me imperfect, methods for achieving happiness and freedom from suffering depending upon one's cultural heritage and personal history. At the heart of this struggle, I believe, is the ability and willingness to face what cannot be changed within a given tradition, even to mourn the ways in which a beloved method, theory, or teacher cannot meet our many needs, while sustaining a deep commitment to the relationship despite ongoing disappointments and frustrations with imperfect systems and healers (Eigen, 1998a).

This is the nature of transformative relationship as I see it: a willingness to stay even after, especially after, what is lacking in the relationship and in each member—whether it is two people or one person and a healing tradition—becomes readily apparent. This, as Michael Eigen suggests, is how we build character (ibid., p. 222).

Throughout my exploration of psychoanalysis and Buddhism, I have come across many theorists who propose an integration of these two contrasting systems in which the boundaries are collapsed and the methods merged. While I have expressed a profound appreciation for the many ways in which my analytic experience has supported my spiritual practice and vice versa, I have also come to learn that each tradition has evolved out of a unique, complex, and precious history that cannot be altered. They are changing and malleable traditions, with room to learn from and adapt to the experience of their current and diverse practitioners, but they are nevertheless effective only insofar as they remain bound to their origins. We learn from the particularities of our own being, through coming up against the boundaries of religious and psychoanalytic traditions.

I have not called for either Buddhism or psychoanalysis—and by extension, their primary healers—to change into something it is not, but rather for increased friendly curiosity and evenly hovering attention in both traditions so that my fellow contemporary Buddhists, for whom the Western ego and the psyche are pressing realities, may continue to move toward a true psychospiritual awakening. I believe that psychoanalytic theory and treatment would be well served by an increased respect for human potential that transcends the mere "psychopathology of the average, so undramatic and so widely spread that we don't even notice it ordinarily" (Maslow, 1968, p. 16). Having worked with clinicians who bring personal experience with the spiritual and religious domain to the analytic space, I can speak to the immense value of a perspective that holds dear the potential not only to survive pain, suffering, and trauma, but to live into and through our ultimate reality as precious human lives.

Most importantly, I have attempted to explore how Buddhist practice, alongside respect for the complexity of the human psyche, with its conscious and unconscious halves, influences our interpersonal lives. Anyone who has embarked on a long-term spiritual and/or religious path will know well the reality of devout followers and advanced practitioners who are also challenging or in some way unpleasant to deal with interpersonally. We wonder (and let's face it, perhaps unknowingly *we* are the problematic or troubled players within our spiritual communities) how it is possible to work deeply into a religious or spiritual tradition that calls for humility, patience, and compassion, for wisdom and loving kindness, only to turn around and reactively chew out or ignore a neighbor, one's child, or one's partner. Why doesn't spiritual practice necessarily translate into the heightened ability to enter into and sustain human relationship with all the laudable characteristics of the religious persona? How is it we can be focused and placid while sitting on cushions, only to fall apart the moment we open our eyes and see another human being? Where does this striking split come from?

I hope that this work has offered an entry point into these ongoing questions, particularly for Western Buddhists who are also interested in psychoanalytic treatment. This endeavor comes from the recognition that I, alas, am not immune to such splits; but I am ever curious to learn more about how they may be healed and approached with the friendly curiosity and evenly hovering attention the Buddha and Freud both called for in their respective milieus. If relationship, as I have suggested, is indeed the goal of awakening, I hope that this exploration has in some way reassured the reader that relationships—between traditions and between healers and those seeking healing—while forever imperfect, are worth our every effort.

acknowledgments

I T IS WITH HEARTFELT GRATITUDE for my community of friends, family, and mentors that I complete this work. First I wish to thank my dear teacher, the Venerable Khenpo Lama Pema Wangdak, for his steadfast encouragement and uniquely Tibetan sense of humor that buoyed my spirits throughout an ongoing freefall into all sixteen Buddhist hell realms. Finding a true teacher can be an arduous journey, and coming to know Lama Pema has affirmed that the journey is worth every unexpected twist and turn.

My mentor Dr. Ann Belford Ulanov read this draft in its most embryonic stages, and from the beginning offered me her extraordinary gifts of compassion and insight. She is a true psychoanalytic mystic. My thanks also to Jeffrey Rubin, whose wise and patient counsel helped me figure out how and where to train, and whose vision brought me to my doctoral work with Ann Ulanov.

I am indebted to Mark Finn, analytic supervisor extraordinaire, whose marvelous combination of sensitivity and humor has reminded me over and again why I embarked on this path of healing. Through his example, I learn ongoingly why Buddhism and psychoanalysis need each other.

Laura D'Angelo has been a treasured friend, offering me her keen editorial eye and ability to make me laugh about absolutely anything—she is a true bodhisattva. My dear and generous friends Ann Levin and Stan Honda have provided me with endless nourishing meals and held my hand with unrelenting patience. Eva Atsalis has been like a sister, listening to me spin endless tales of neurotic musing with infinite patience and love. Margaret-Anne Smith has been a true friend and ballast, helping me through the toughest parts of the writer's journey with her gentle and supremely kind presence. I also wish to thank my fellow seminarians Kimberlee Auletta, Whachul Oh, and Lizzie Berne DeGear for their amazingly open-hearted support, wisdom, and kindness.

My brother Chris, beloved nieces Samantha, Madeline, and Carley, and sweet sister-in-law Lenna, have encouraged me throughout this journey with unwavering support. Their uplifting words and kind attention have been a balm to the psyche and spirit.

Paul Knitter and Harry Fogarty, two phenomenal scholars and educators at Union Theological Seminary, were both instrumental in my ability to enter into this material with clarity of purpose, offering careful guidance and depth of insight throughout the initial stages of this manuscript. I also wish to thank Bob Pollack who read through early chapters with his wizardly erudition, and the Center for Study of Science and Religion for their inspiring dedication to wellness on a global scale.

Graham Bass has been a gentle and caring witness to my journey into this field, modeling for me how to be a therapist who trusts in the wisdom of his patients. Through our work together, I came to trust that healing is indeed possible. Michele Sakow and the Sakya community have offered warm and enthusiastic encouragement over the course of many years. It is a blessing to be part of such a sweet and caring sangha.

Heartfelt thanks to Jeremy Safran, whose insight and most excellent contribution to this field has been a source of inspiration from my earliest forays into the world of psychology and religion. His confidence in this manuscript was a tremendous gift to me, offered with real generosity of spirit. And for their compassionate counsel, support, and always inspiring approach to clinical work, I thank Michael Eigen and Neil Altman. Through them both I continue to learn how to bring aliveness and integrity to the psychoanalytic journey.

My editor at Wisdom, Josh Bartok, has been terrifically clear-minded, kind, and responsive; I am grateful for his ongoing support. Laura Cunningham and copy editor Eric Shutt have offered their intelligence and skill, ushering me into the final stretch.

I am extremely grateful for my parents, Richard and Regina Jennings, who have been loving witnesses throughout my circuitous journey, cheering me on in their wonderfully colorful way. Through them I learned that a questioning mind keeps us honest and forever discovering more about ourselves and the world we are privileged to be a part of.

Lastly, I am deeply indebted to my patients, particularly the children I have come to know through the Harlem Family Institute. Like all my beloved teachers, they have mixed their precious human lives and open hearts with my own: a life-changing gift I will never forget.

bibliography

Altman, N. 1995. *The Analyst in the Inner City: Race, Class, and Culture through a Psychoanalytic Lens*. Hillsdale, N.J.: The Analytic Press.

Aronson, H. 1998. Review of *Psychotherapy and Buddhism: Toward an Integration*, by Jeffrey Rubin. *Journal of Buddhist Ethics* 5:63–73.

————. 2006. "Buddhist Practice in Relation to Self-Representation: A Cross-Cultural Dialogue," in *Buddhism and Psychotherapy Across Cultures*, ed. Mark Unno. Boston: Wisdom Publications.

Bader, C., Dougherty, K., Froese, P., Johnson, B., Menken, F.C., Park, J.Z. & Stark, R. 2006. *American Piety in the 21st Century*. Baylor Institute for Studies of Religion, Waco, Baylor University.

Batchelor, S. 1997. *Buddhism Without Beliefs*. New York: Riverhead Books.

————. 1994. *The Awakening of the West*. Berkeley, Calif.: Parallax Press.

Bateson, G., Jackson, D., Haley, J. & Weakland, J. 1956. "Toward a Theory of Schizophrenia." *Behavioral Science*, pp. 251–64.

Benjamin, J. 1999. "Recognition and Destruction: An Outline of Intersubjectivity," in *Relational Analysis: The Emergence of a Tradition*, eds. Stephen Mitchell and Lewis Aron. Hillsdale, N.J.: The Analytic Press.

Benjamin, J. 2005. "From Many into One: Attention, Energy, and the Containing of Multitude," in *Psychoanalytic Dialogues* 15 (2):185–201.

Bennett-Goleman, T. 2001. *Emotional Alchemy*. New York: Harmony Books.

Bion, W.R. 1965. *Transformations*. London: Karnac.

————. 1970. *Attention and Interpretation*. New York: A Jason Aronson Book.

Bobrow, J. 1998. "The Fertile Mind," in *The Couch and the Tree*, ed. Anthony Molino. New York: North Point Press.

————. 2003. "Moments of Truth—Truths of Moment," in *Psychoanalysis and Buddhism*, ed. Jeremy Safran. Boston: Wisdom Publications.

Bollas, C. 1987. *The Shadow of the Object: Psychoanalysis of the Unthought Known*. New York: Columbia University Press.

————. 1996. *Forces of Destiny: Psychoanalysis and Human Idiom*. London & New York: Free Association Books.

Boucher, S. 1988. *Turning the Wheel: American Women Creating the New Buddhism*. San Francisco: Harper and Row.

Bromberg, P. 1993. "Shadow and Substance: A Relational Perspective on Clinical Process," in *Relational Psychoanalysis: The Emergence of a Tradition*, eds. Stephen Mitchell & Lewis Aron. Hillsdale, N.J.: The Analytic Press, 1999.

————. 2001. "Standing in the Spaces: The Multiplicity of Self and the Psychoanalytic Relationship," in *Standing in the Spaces*. New York: The Analytic Press.

Brown, D. & Engler, J. 1986. "The Stages of Mindfulness Meditation: A Validation Study; Part II: Discussion," in *Transformation of Consciousness: Conventional and Contemplative Perspective on Human Development*, eds. K. Wilber, J. Engler, and D. Brown, pp. 191–217. Boston: Shambhala Publications.

Burtt, E.A. 1955. *The Teachings of the Compassionate Buddha*. New York: Mentor Books.

Capper, D. 2002. *Guru Devotion and the American Buddhist Experience*. United Kingdom: The Edwin Mellen Press.

Chang, Garma C.C., trans. 1989. *The Hundred Thousand Songs of Milarepa*, vol. 2. Boston: Shambhala Publications.

Chödrön, P. 1997. *When Things Fall Apart*. Boston: Shambhala Classics.

Cleary, T. 1987. *Entry into the Realm of Reality: The Text*. Boston: Shambhala Publications.

————., trans. 1994. *Dhammapada: The Sayings of Buddha*. New York: Bantam Books.

Coleman, J. 2001. *The New Buddhism: The Western Transformation of an Ancient Tradition*. Oxford: University Press.

Coltart, N. 1992. *Slouching Toward Bethlehem*. New York: Other Press.

————. 1996. *The Baby and the Bathwater*. Madison, Conn.: International Universities Press.

Cooper, P. 1998. "The Disavowal of the Spirit: Integration and Wholeness in Buddhism and Psychoanalysis," in *The Couch and the Tree*, ed. Anthony Molino. New York: North Point Press.

Dalai Lama. 1995. *The World of Tibetan Buddhism*. Boston: Wisdom Publications.

Dalai Lama & Cutler, H. 1998. *The Art of Happiness*. London: Coronet Books.

Dayal, Har. 1932. *The Bodhisattva Doctrine in Buddhist Sanskrit Literature*. Delhi: Motilal Banarsidass.

Eigen, M. 1996. *Psychic Deadness*. New York: Jason Aronson.

————. 1998a. "One Reality," in *The Couch and the Tree*, ed. Anthony Molino. New York: North Point Press.

————. 1998b. *The Psychoanalytic Mystic*. London & New York: Free Association Books.

Elder, G. 1998. "Psychological Observations on the Life of Gautama Buddha," in *The Couch and the Tree*, ed. Anthony Molino. New York: North Point Press.

Engler, J. 2003. "Being Somebody and Being Nobody: A Reexamination of the Understanding of Self in Psychoanalysis and Buddhism," in *Psychoanalysis and Buddhism*, ed. J. Safran. Boston: Wisdom Publications.

————. 2006. "Promises and Perils of the Spiritual Path," in *Buddhism and Psychotherapy across Cultures*, ed. Mark Unno. Boston: Wisdom Publications.

Epstein, M. 2001. *Going on Being*. New York: Broadway Books.

————. 2005. *Open to Desire*. New York: Gotham Books.

————. 2007. *Psychotherapy Without the Self*. New Haven & London: Yale University Press.

Fairbairn, W.R.D. 1952. "The Repression and Return of Bad Objects," in *Psychoanalytic Studies of Personality*. London: Tavistock.

Ferenczi, S. 1949. "Confusion of the Tongues Between the Adults and the Child (The Language of Tenderness and of Passion)." *International Journal of Psychoanalysis*, 30:225–230.

Fields, R. 1992. *How the Swans Came to the Lake: A Narrative History of Buddhism in America*. Boston & London: Shambhala Publications.

Finn, M. 1992. "Transitional Space and Tibetan Buddhism: The Object Relations of Meditation," in *Object Relations Theory and Religion*. Westport, C.T.: Preager Publishers.

————. 1998. "Tibetan Buddhism and Comparative Psychoanalysis," in *The Couch and the Tree*, ed. Anthony Molino. New York: North Point Press.

————. 2003. "Tibetan Buddhism and a Mystical Psychoanalysis," in *Psychoanalysis and Buddhism*, ed. J. Safran. Boston: Wisdom Publications.

Finn, M. & Gartner, J. 1992. *Object Relations Theory and Religion*. Westport, C.T.: Preager Publishers.

Frankl, V. 1955. *The Doctor and the Soul*. New York: Vintage Books, 1986.

————. 1959. *Man's Search for Meaning*. New York & London: Washington Square Press.

Freud, S. 1912. "Recommendations to Physicians Practicing Psycho-analysis," in *The Standard Edition of the Complete Psychological Works of Sigmund Freud*, ed. and trans. J. Strachey, vol. 12 (1953–1974). London: Hogarth Press.

———. 1915. "Instincts and their Vicissitudes," in *General Psychological Theory*. New York: Touchstone, 1997.

———. 1916. "On Transience," in *The Standard Edition of the Complete Psychological Works of Sigmund Freud*, ed.and trans. J. Strachey, vol. 14 (1914–1916). London: Hogarth Press.

———. 1917. "A Difficulty in the Path of Psycho-analysis," in *The Standard Edition of the Complete Psychological Works of Sigmund Freud*, ed.and trans. J. Strachey, vol. 17. London: Hogarth Press.

———. 1923. *The Ego and the Id*. New York & London: W.W. Norton & Company, 1960.

———. 1930. *Civilization and Its Discontents*, ed. J. Strachey. New York & London: W.W. Norton & Company, 1961.

———. 1933. *New Introductory Lectures on Psychoanalysis*. New York & London: W.W. Norton & Company, 1965.

Fromm, E. 1960. "Psychoanalysis and Zen Buddhism," in *The Couch and the Tree*, ed. Anthony Molino (1998). New York: North Point Press.

Gabbard, G.O. & Lester, E.P. 1995. *Boundaries and Boundary Violations in Psychoanalysis*. New York: American Psychiatric Publishing.

Gay, P. 1998. *Freud: A Life For Our Time*. New York & London: W.W. Norton & Company.

Geertz, C. 1979. "From the Native's Point of View: On the Nature of Anthropological Understanding," in *Local Knowledge: Further Essays in Interpretive Anthropology*. New York: Basic Books.

Goldenberg, I & H. 1991. *Family Therapy: An Overview*. Pacific Grove, Calif.: Brooks/Cole Publishing Co.

Goldstein, J. 1976. *The Experience of Insight: A Natural Unfolding*. Santa Cruz, CA: Unity Press.

————. 1994. *Transforming the Mind, Healing the World*. New York: Paulist Press.

————. 2003. *One Dharma*. San Francisco: Harper Collins.

Goleman, D. 2003. *Destructive Emotions: A Scientific Dialogue with the Dalai Lama*. New York: Bantam Dell.

Gross, A. 1999. "Unconditionally Steadfast: Amy Gross Interviews Pema Chödrön." *Tricycle: The Buddhist Review*, 43–49 (fall).

Gross, R. 1998. *Soaring and Settling: Buddhist Perspectives on Contemporary Social and Religious Issues*. New York: Continuum.

————. 2008. "Introduction to the Dharma," Lecture at Union Theological Seminary, New York, NY.

Guntrip, H. 1968. *Schizoid Phenomena, Object-Relations, and the Self*. London: Hogarth.

Hanh, T.N. 2001. *Anger: Wisdom for Cooling the Flames*. New York: Riverhead Books.

Hoffer, A. 1985. "Toward a Redefinition of Psychoanalytic Neutrality." *Journal of the American Psychoanalytic Association* 33:771–95.

Horney, K. 1937. *The Neurotic Personality of Our Time*. New York: W.W. Norton & Company.

————. 1939. *New Ways in Psychoanalysis*. New York: W.W. Norton & Company.

————. 1945. *Our Inner Conflicts*. New York: W.W. Norton & Company.

————. 1950. *Neurosis and Human Growth*. New York: W.W. Norton & Company.

————. 1987. *Final Lectures*, ed. D.H. Ingram. New York: W.W. Norton & Company.

Horrobin, D. 2001. *The Madness of Adam and Eve: How Schizophrenia Shaped Humanity*. London & New York: Bantam Press.

Illovsky, M.E. 2003. *Mental Health Professionals, Minorities, and the Poor*. New York: Brunner-Routledge.

Jacobs, J.L. & D. Capps, D. eds. 1997. *Religion, Society, and Psychoanalysis: Readings in Contemporary Theory.* Boulder, Colo.: Westview.

Jones, J.W. 1997. "Playing and Believing: The Uses of D.W. Winnicott in the Psychology of Religion," in *Religion, Society, and Psychoanalysis: Readings in Contemporary Theory*, eds. J.L. Jacobs and D. Capps. Boulder, Colo.: Westview.

—————. 2002. *Terror and Transformation: The Ambiguity of Religion in Psychoanalytic Perspective.* New York: Brunner-Routledge.

Jung, C.G. 1929. "Commentary on the Secret of the Golden Flower," Alchemical Studies, Collected Works 13. Princeton, N.J.: Princeton University Press, 1967.

—————. 1932. "Psychotherapists or the Clergy," in *Psychology and Religion: West and East*, CW11, para. 520, trans. R.F.C. Hull. New York: Pantheon, 1958.

—————. 1938. "The Autonomy of the Unconscious," in *Psychology and Religion: West and East*, CW12, paras. 1–43. New York: Pantheon, 1958.

—————. 1939. "Conscious, Unconscious, and Individuation," CW9:1, pp. 257–289, paras. 489–524. New York: Pantheon, 1959.

—————. 1944. *Psychology and Alchemy*, CW12, para. 11. New York: Pantheon, 1953.

—————. 1948. "A Review of Complex Theory," CW8, pp. 92–104, paras. 194–219. New York: Pantheon.

—————. 1951. "Archetypes of the Collective Unconscious," CW9, paras. 1–42. New York: Pantheon.

—————. 1965. *Memories, Dreams, Reflections.* New York: Vintage Books.

—————. 1971. *Psychology and Religion: West and East*, in *The Portable Jung*. New York: The Viking Press.

Khan, M. 1974. *The Privacy of the Self.* London: Karnac Books.

Klein, M. 1975a. *Love, Guilt and Reparation: And Other Works 1921–1945.* New York: The Free Press.

————. 1975b. *Envy and Gratitude: And Other Works 1946–1963*. New York: The Free Press.

Klinger, R. 1980. "The Tibetan Guru Refuge: A Historical Perspective." *The Tibet Journal* 5:9–19.

Knitter, P. 2009. *Without Buddha I Could Not Be a Christian*. Oxford: Oneworld Publications.

Kohut, H. 1966. "Forms and Transformations of Narcissism," in *The Search for the Self*, ed. P. Ornstein, vol. 1, pp. 427–60. New York: International Universities Press, 1978.

————. 1971. *Analysis of the Self*. New York: International Universities Press.

————. 1977. *The Restoration of the Self*. New York: International Universities Press.

————. 1978. *The Search for the Self*. New York: International Universities Press.

————. 1984. *How Does Analysis Cure*. Chicago: University of Chicago Press.

Kohut, H. & Seitz, P. 1963. "Concepts and Theories of Psychoanalysis," in *The Search for the Self*, ed. P. Ornstein, vol. 1, pp. 337–74. New York: International Universities Press, 1978.

Kornfield, J., Dass, R. & Miyuki, M. 1998. "Psychological Adjustment Is Not Liberation: A Symposium," in *The Couch and the Tree*, ed. Anthony Molino. New York: North Point Press.

LaPlanche, J. & Pontalis, J.-B. 1973. *The Language of Psychoanalysis*. London: Karnarc Books.

Layton, L., Hollander, N. & Gutwill, S., eds. 2006. *Psychoanalysis, Class and Politics: Encounters in the Clinical Settings*. London and New York: Routledge.

Lemle, M., Director. 2002. *Ram Dass: Fierce Grace* [Film]. New York: ZeitgeistFilms.

Loewald, Hans. 1978. *Psychoanalysis and the History of the Individual*. New Haven, Conn.: Yale University Press.

Loy, D. 2003. *The Great Awakening: A Buddhist Social Theory*. Boston: Wisdom Publications.

Maslow, A. 1968. *Toward a Psychology of Being* (2nd ed.). New York: Van Nostrand.

Mason, R.C. 1980. "The Psychology of the Self: Religion and Psychotherapy," in *Advances in Self Psychology*, ed. Arnold Goldberg. New York: International Universities Press.

Miller, J.D., Scott, E.C. & Okamoto, S. 2006. "Public Acceptance of Evolution." *Science, 313*(8):765–66.

Molino, A. 1998. "Slouching Towards Buddhism: A Conversation with Nina Coltart," in *The Couch and the Tree*, ed. Anthony Molino. New York: North Point Press.

Neumann, E. 1969. *Depth Psychology and a New Ethic*. New York & London: Harper Torchbooks.

Ogden, T.H. 1979. "On Projective Identification." *International Journal of Psycho-Analysis* 60:357–373.

—————. 1994. *Matrix of the Mind: Object Relations and the Psychoanalytic Dialogue*. New York: Jason Aronson.

—————. 2004. "The Analytic Third: Implications for Psychoanalytic Theory and Technique." *Psychoanalytic Quarterly*, LXXIII:167–95.

—————. 2005. *This Art of Psychoanalysis*. London & New York: Routledge.

Olendzki, A. 2008. "Outline of Abhidhamma." *Insight Journal* 29:15–17.

Paden, W.E. 1988/1994. *Religious Worlds: The Comparative Study of Religion*. Boston: Beacon Press.

Payne, R.K. 2006. "Individuation and Awakening: Romantic Narrative and the Psychological Interpretation of Buddhism," in *Buddhism and Psychotherapy Across Cultures*, ed. Mark Unno. Boston: Wisdom Publications.

Podgorski, F.R. 1986. "Kalyana Metta: The Buddhist Spiritual Guide." *Journal of Dharma* 11, 1:29–36.

Pruyser, P. 1968. *A Dynamic Psychology of Religion*. New York & London: Harper & Row Publishers.

Ray, R.A. 1994. *Buddhist Saints in India*. New York: Oxford University Press.

Roland, A. 1996. *Cultural Pluralism and Psychoanalysis*. New York & London: Routledge.

Rubin, J. 1992. "Psychoanalytic Treatment with a Buddhist Meditator," in *Object Relations Theory and Religion*, eds. Mark Finn & John Gartner. Westport, Conn.: Praeger.

—————. 1996. *Psychotherapy and Buddhism: Toward an Integration*. New York: Plenum Press.

Safran, J. 2003. *Psychoanalysis and Buddhism*. Boston: Wisdom Publications.

Shantideva. 1979. *A Guide to the Bodhisattva's Way of Life*, trans. S. Batchelor. Library of Tibetan Works and Archives, Dharamsala: Indraprastha Press.

Shore, J. 2002. "A Buddhist Model of the Human Self," in *Awakening and Insight: Zen Buddhism and Psychotherapy*, eds. P. Young-Eisendrath & S. Muramoto. New York: Brunner-Routledge.

Siegal, A.M. 1996. *Heinz Kohut and the Psychology of the Self*. London: Routledge.

Smith, H. & Novak, P. 2003. *Buddhism*. San Francisco: Harper Collins.

Sogyal Rinpoche. 1993. *The Tibetan Book of Living and Dying*. San Francisco: Harper Collins Publishers.

Stolorow, R. & Atwood, G. 1992. *Contexts of Being: The Intersubjective Foundation of Psychological Life*. New Jersey: Analytic Press.

Stolorow, R.D., Brandchaft, B. & Atwood, G.E. 1995. *Psychoanalytic Treatment: An Intersubjective Approach*. New Jersey: The Analytic Press.

Storr, A. 1996. *Feet of Clay*. New York: Free Press Paperbacks.

Storr, A. & Stevens, A. 1989/1994. *Freud & Jung*. New York: Barnes & Noble Books.

Strozier, C. 1997. "Heinz Kohut's Struggles with Religion, Ethnicity, and God," in *Religion, Society, and Psychoanalysis: Readings in Contemporary Theory*, eds. J.L. Jacobs and D. Capps. Boulder, Colo.: Westview Press.

————. 2001. *Heinz Kohut: The Making of a Psychoanalyst*. New York: Other Press.

Sullivan, H.S. 1953. *The Interpersonal Theory of Psychiatry*. New York: The William Alanson White Psychiatric Foundation. Reprinted: New York: W.W. Norton & Co., 1997.

Surya Das, L. 1997. *Awakening the Buddha Within*. New York: Broadway Books.

Symington, J. & N. 1996. *The Clinical Thinking of Wilfred Bion*. London: Routledge.

Symington, N. 2003. "A Contemplative Response," in *Psychoanalysis and Buddhism*, ed. J. Safran. Boston: Wisdom Publications.

Thurman, R. 1998. *Inner Revolution*. New York: Riverhead Books.

————. 2005. *Anger*. New York, New York: Oxford University Press.

Tsomo, Karma Lekshe. 1995. *Buddhism through American Women's Eyes*. Ithaca: Snow Lion.

Ulanov, A. & B. 1991. *The Healing Imagination*. Switzerland: Daimon Verlag.

Ulanov, A. 1986. *Picturing God*. Switzerland: Daimon Verlag, 2002.

————. 1988/2000. *The Wisdom of the Psyche*. Switzerland: Daimon Verlag.

————. 2001. *Finding Space: Winnicott, God, and Psychic Reality*. Louisville: Westminster John Knox Press.

————. 2004. *Spiritual Aspects of Clinical Work*. Switzerland: Daimon Verlag.

————. 2005. *Spirit in Jung*. Switzerland: Daimon Verlag.

———. 2007. *The Unshuttered Heart: Opening Aliveness/Deadness in the Self.* Nashville: Abingdon Press.

Unno, M. 2006. *Buddhism and Psychotherapy Across Cultures.* Boston: Wisdom Publications.

Walsh, R. & Shapiro, S. 2006. "The Meeting of Meditative Disciplines and Western Psychology." *American Psychologist* 61, no. 3:227–239.

Westkott, M. 1997. "Karen Horney's Encounter with Zen," in *Religion, Society, and Psychoanalysis: Readings in Contemporary Theory*, eds. J.L. Jacobs and D. Capps. Boulder, Colo.: Westview Press.

Winnicott, D.W. 1947. "Hate in the Countertransference," in *Through Pediatrics to Psycho-Analysis.* New York: Brunner-Routledge, 1992.

———. 1950 "Aggression in Relation to Emotional Development," in *Through Pediatrics to Psycho-Analysis.* New York: Brunner-Routledge, 1992.

———. 1952. "Anxiety Associated with Insecurity," in *Through Pediatrics to Psycho-Analysis.* New York: Brunner-Routledge, 1992.

———. 1956. "Primary Maternal Preoccupation," in *Through Pediatrics to Psycho-Analysis.* New York: Brunner-Routledge, 1992.

———. 1960a. "Aggression, Guilt and Reparation," in *Home is Where We Start From.* New York: W.W. Norton & Co., 1986.

———. 1960b. "The Theory of the Parent-Infant Relationship," in *The Maturations Processes and the Facilitating Environment.* New York: Karnac, 1990.

———. 1968. "On The Use of an Object," in *Psychoanalytic Explorations.* Cambridge, Mass: Harvard University Press, 1992.

———. 1971. *Playing and Reality.* New York: Brunner-Routledge.

———. 1986. *Home is Where We Start From.* New York: WW. Norton & Co.

———. 1987. *The Child, the Family, and the Outside World.* Cambridge, Mass.: Perseus Publishing.

————. 1988. *Human Nature.* New York: Brunner/Mazel.

————. 1990. *The Maturational Processes and the Facilitating Environment.* New York: Karnac.

————. 1992a. *Psychoanalytic Explorations.* Cambridge, Mass.: Harvard University Press.

————. 1992b. *Through Pediatrics to Psycho-Analysis.* New York: Brunner-Routledge.

Wishnie, H.A. 2005. *Working in the Countertransference: Necessary Entanglements.* New York: Jason Aronson.

Yalom, I.D. 2003. *The Gift of Therapy: An Open Letter to a New Generation of Therapists and Their Patients.* New York: Harper Perennial.

Young-Eisendrath, P. 1996. *The Gifts of Suffering.* Reading, Mass.: Addison-Wesley Publishing Company.

————. 1998. "What Suffering Teaches," in *The Couch and the Tree,* ed. Anthony Molino. New York: North Point Press.

————. 2003. "Transference and Transformation in Buddhism and Psychoanalysis," in *Psychoanalysis and Buddhism,* ed. J. Safran. Boston: Wisdom Publications.

Young-Eisendrath, P. & Muramoto, S. 2002. *Awakening and Insight: Zen Buddhism and Psychotherapy.* New York: Brunner-Routledge.

index

about the author

PILAR JENNINGS is a psychotherapist and psychoanalyst who has focused on the clinical applications of Buddhist meditation practice. She received her Ph.D. in psychiatry and religion from Union Theological Seminary, and has been working with patients and their families through the Harlem Family Institute since 2004. Prior to this training, she earned a masters in medical anthropology from Columbia University, and a bachelors in interdisciplinary writing from Barnard College of Columbia University. Dr. Jennings is a long-term practitioner of Tibetan and Theravada Buddhism. She lives in New York.

JEREMY D. SAFRAN, Ph.D, is Professor of Psychology at the New School for Social Research, where he was Director of Clinical Psychology from 1993–1996, and 2005–2009. He also is a faculty member at the New York University Postdoctoral Program in Psychotherapy and Psychoanalysis and the Stephen A. Mitchell Center for Relational Studies. In addition he is president of the International Association for Relational Psychoanalysis and Psychotherapy. Dr. Safran has published several books including *Psychoanalysis and Buddhism, Emotion in Psychotherapy, Negotiating the Therapeutic Alliance, Interpersonal Process in Cognitive Therapy,* and the forthcoming *Psychoanalytic and Psychodynamic Therapies.*

about wisdom publications

To learn more about Wisdom Publications, a nonprofit publisher, and to browse our other books dedicated to skillful living, visit our website at www.wisdompubs.org.

You may request a copy of our catalog online or by writing to this address:

Wisdom Publications
199 Elm Street
Somerville, Massachusetts 02144 USA
Telephone: 617-776-7416
Fax: 617-776-7841
Email: info@wisdompubs.org
www.wisdompubs.org

Wisdom is a nonprofit, charitable 501(c)(3) organization affiliated with the Foundation for the Preservation of the Mahayana Tradition (FPMT).